LEGION OF THE LOST

LEGION OF THE LOST

The True Experience of an American in the French Foreign Legion

JAIME SALAZAR

A BERKLEY CALIBER BOOK

THE BERKLEY PUBLISHING GROUP
Published by the Penguin Group
Penguin Group (USA) Inc.
375 Hudson Street, New York, New York 10014, USA
Penguin Group (Canada), 90 Eglinton Avenue East, Suite 700, Toronto, Ontario, Canada M4P 2Y3
(a division of Pearson Penguin Canada Inc.)
Penguin Books Ltd., 80 Strand, London WC2R 0RL, England
Penguin Group Ireland, 25 St. Stephen's Green, Dublin 2, Ireland (a division of Penguin Books Ltd.)
Penguin Group (Australia), 250 Camberwell Road, Camberwell, Victoria 3124, Australia
(a division of Pearson Australia Group Pty. Ltd.)
Penguin Books India Pvt. Ltd., 11 Community Centre, Panchsheel Park, New Delhi—110 017, India
Penguin Group (NZ), cnr. Airborne and Rosedale Roads, Albany, Auckland 1310, New Zealand
(a division of Pearson New Zealand Ltd.)
Penguin Books (South Africa) (Pty.) Ltd., 24 Sturdee Avenue, Rosebank, Johannesburg 2196, South Africa

Penguin Books Ltd., Registered Offices: 80 Strand, London WC2R 0RL, England

While the author has made every effort to provide accurate telephone numbers and Internet addresses at the time of publication, neither the publisher nor the author assumes any responsibility for errors, or for changes that occur after publication. Further, publisher does not have any control over and does not assume any responsibility for author or third-party websites or their content.

PRINTING HISTORY
Berkley Caliber hardcover edition / August 2005
Berkley Caliber trade paperback edition / August 2006

Berkley Caliber trade paperback ISBN: 0-425-21015-4

The Library of Congress has catalogued the Berkley Caliber hardcover edition as follows:

Salazar, Jaime, date.
    Legion of the lost : the true experience of an American in the French Foreign Legion
    p. cm.
    ISBN: 0-425-20283-6
    1. Mercenery troops—United States.   2. Mercenery troops—France.   3. France—Description and travel.   I. Title

U768.S25 2005
355.3'59'0944B—dc22   2005048889

PRINTED IN THE UNITED STATES OF AMERICA

10 9 8 7 6 5 4 3 2 1

To the memory of Alan and Pat,
in the tradition of Henry.

PREFACE

This is it, the last chance I'll get! It's dark and we're stopping at a service station store. They probably need cigarettes. I speak through the surveillance grille: "Permission to use the toilets, *sergent*?"

The Tunisian *caporal chef* in the driver's seat twists around. "You'll piss when you're told to piss."

"*Du calme, du calme,*" the *sergeant-chef* mutters. "Could do with a piss myself."

They come around and unlock the rear door. "Don't think of doing anything stupid." The *caporal chef* prods me in the guts with his nightstick. "When this hits bone, I don't know how to stop."

I step out, clear my throat as if about to ask a question, and take off in a desperate sprint. He swings at me and misses. I dodge through lines of parked cars. The paddy wagon roars to life. I shake it off by running up the feeder road against the traffic flow and out onto the *autoroute* shoulder. Headlamps blind me as cars and trucks hurtle past. The *sergeant-chef* coming after me on foot and gaining; he's not running in outsized prison-issue boots. A gap in the traffic. I dart into the roadway. Another rush of headlamps. Klaxons blare, brakes shriek, light beams swivel, metal tears into metal. One explosive *thump* followed by another. I make it to the central divide, vault the barrier, and pound on, twisting round till there's another gap and careen over to the far side.

Great! The *sergeant-chef's* disappeared. Pulped in the pileup, with any luck. I fight through thick scrub up the steep hillside. *Gendarmerie* sirens. I climb three hundred meters and throw myself flat on the edge of a cliff. So far, so good! They'll wait till first light before sending out the dogs and helicopters. I blink the sting of sweat from my eyes and peer down at the ants below. Now it's that pair that's in the shit. Just before our unscheduled stop they were radioing the regimental depot to say we'd be there in thirty minutes. They'll lose their stripes. I raise my forearm and hold out my middle finger. Thank Christ I always took seriously the bit in the *Code d'honneur* about training vigorously and keeping my body in peak physical shape.

I sit up, wrap my arms around my knees, and close my eyes. *Caporal* Diagana's face appears in my head. "Yankee, go home," he sneers, "and don't come back. We never wanted you in the first place."

I just did something I hadn't planned on, like a drunk man waking up to find he's strangled his wife. Perhaps I should have stayed on to prove I can take it?

No! I get to my feet. There can be no turning back this time. A legionnaire who breaks out is supposed to sleep with the fattest woman he can find to smother any nostalgic memories of the Legion and the comrades he has left behind. Once I get off this mountain, former legionnaire 191224 will seek her out.

1.

CHICAGO

The Legion takes every sort of man who may have any reason for joining. A smaller class is drawn from the romantics, born adventurers, the type who form the subject of a poem we learnt in childhood, the soldier of the Legion who sang . . . But I was aye a truant bird and thought my home a cage.

P. C. Wren, *Beau Geste*

How did a well-heeled yuppie like me get into all this? I couldn't blame the Legion. They hadn't asked me to join; they told me it was going to be tough.

After graduation from Purdue University with a degree in mechanical engineering, I could take my pick from a list of Fortune 500 companies looking for recruits. I set my sights on Siemens, the vast German conglomerate that makes everything from streetcars to lightbulbs. At my interview, I took a gamble by telling them that what I hated most was losing. The following day they offered me a job package in Chicago paying more money than I had ever dreamt of.

I and a handful of crème de la crème recruits were signed up for the executive sales program, the fast-track career path to outside sales. We'd be taught in months, we were told, facts and techniques that it took other employees years to learn in the field, but most of us didn't give a shit. We were all armed with bulletproof university degrees, and the American economy was booming. We were invulnerable.

But disenchantment with corporate America set in during the first week. After the introductory handshakes, cliques formed and ring-leaders emerged. When we were given access to expense accounts and fat signing bonuses, we began gossiping about each other—who was bending the rules and how much the others were ripping the company off. Individuals became alienated. I began to see my colleagues less as engineers and more as rats, turning on each other when there was nothing else to gnaw at. On a personal level, it was difficult to find anyone to relate to—I didn't own an SUV and didn't fancy spending my weekends swinging golf clubs and tennis rackets.

In an attempt to conform to the values of my peers, I decided to purchase a car very different from the 1977 Toyota that I'd driven around campus. For the first time in my life, I was buying something big with money I'd earned by my own efforts. I'd grown up with underpaid immigrant parents from Mexico. They worked hard but as a kid I'd gone without hi-tech toys, proper snow boots, and even gloves. I hoped that my BMW 535i would bring me the respect and happiness that I felt I deserved.

The training program itself was both intense and mind-numbingly boring. I started propping my feet on chairs during lectures and occasionally dozing off. During the second training module, our instructor came down on us like a crateload of printed circuit boards. When he declared how disappointed he had been to notice a trainee sleeping in class, I squirmed and avoided the others' eyes, but I wasn't the only wrongdoer. He went on to complain about trainees who were abusing the expense report. There were trainees who had expected the company to pay for an extra night in Atlanta because of a birthday. Others were chronically late; some were making personal use of the car privileges. Then there were those who came in with obvious hangovers. We hung our heads low and whispered to each other about who in particular we suspected did what. I owned up to being a "sleeper" and then joined in on gossiping about who had abused the expense report.

When not attending training sessions, I took refuge in the isolated back office I'd been assigned to. I shared it with a couple of overworked senior sales engineers who left me more or less free to do my own thing. I was able to spend hours daydreaming and reading *The Legion of the Damned* by Bennett J. Doty, which I concealed behind the covers of the personal development workbooks I'd been given on Table Etiquette and Telephone Efficiency.

Whenever I had an opportunity to chat with my officemates, I realized that the executive administrative assistant, a graying woman in her late fifties, was listening to every word from the neighboring office. She made it clear that she disliked me, especially when I got up and closed the interconnecting door.

Corporate hierarchies have eyes and ears. That woman knew more about me than Ronald, the Chicago regional manager. Hardly anybody had seen, much less spoken to him. I often wondered whether he really existed. Perhaps he was simply a mythical creation intended to keep us on our toes.

"Ronald would like to have lunch with you this afternoon," the EAA told me one morning.

I supposed this was his way of getting to know new trainees but when I asked the others when they were having lunch with Roger none of them knew anything about it. I went up to his office. Instead of real lunch, he told me to follow him downstairs "to grab a sandwich." On our return, I braced myself for the kiss of death.

He started by asking how I was getting on in the company. My response was textbook interview babble. I was happy with the daily challenges confronting me, enjoyed working in a team environment, and was eager to contribute. In reality, I was bored off my ass.

"So in what ways do you feel you've contributed up to now?"

"I uhhh . . . "

"There's been word that perhaps you're not as motivated as you could be. I have reports that you've been sleeping in training sessions, that you often arrive late, and that you haven't shown the proper company attitude toward the material presented. What's your take on this?"

I made no excuses and attempted a counterattack. "Well okay, I may be a bit rough around the edges but I'm in this business to sell. I can sell sand to Arabs in the Sahara."

He held up a copy of my Telephone Efficiency test. "In the fifteen years that I've been with this company, nobody has ever failed this before. Just let me ask you, as your regional manager, whether you're really happy working for Siemens?"

"Oh yes, sure thing, very," I lied.

I promised to get my act together but I knew that my honeymoon period with the company had come to an end. From being a star recruit, handpicked for the Chicago office, I was now seen as the one most likely to be "invited" to quit. My world was beginning to fall apart and I was becoming more and more uncertain about where my life was going.

One morning on my way to work, I was sitting in my car, stalled in the early rush-hour traffic. In front of me in a Porche was a man yap-yapping away on his mobile phone. On my right, a career woman adjusting her makeup. To my left, a seemingly hung-over professional in an Italian suit slumped in the driving seat. In the rear-view mirror, a young suburban girl in an economobile, sporting big hairspray hair and probably worrying that she would be fired from her office-temp position for being late again. In the middle of it, I realized, was me, a mixed-up twentysomething who was not only going to be late for work, too, but who didn't give a shit.

"Am I really any better or more useful than the man cleaning the street outside my apartment block?" I asked myself.

Ecclesiastes seemed to have gotten it right: "Vanity of vanities; all is vanity." I realized that if I dedicated my entire lifetime to the company I might eventually end up with a six-figure salary and the title of vice president of some obscure division. I'd become a small tile in the corporate mosaic and then I'd die. My descendents would gobble up their inherited trust fund, and a few years after that, I'd be forgotten. "For there is no remembrance of the wise more than of the fool . . ." I would never be the president of Siemens or General Motors, much less the next Bill Gates. Was an uninspiring, white-collar job in a company of 400,000 employees really what I had been working for all my life? "A living dog is better than a dead lion."

Funnily enough, just as our formal training was winding down, my professional rating began to go up. I had learned to make my superiors feel important and my assertiveness made me stand out as a trainee who was ready to take on any challenge. Ronald's "prodigal son" was even invited to assist in seminars and assign tasks to the other trainees. I went as far as being charming to the EAA. Machiavelli would have understood. At our end-of-training celebration, Ronald drunkenly put his arm around my shoulders and introduced me to the topless strip club waitress. "Meet my star recruit! Jaime Salazar, graduate from Purdue. A young man who's going to go far, very far."

But behind my façade of commitment to the company, I was counting the days until I'd have enough money to quit. I was planning to run to a part of the world I'd gotten to know during summer vacation at the end of my sophomore year; I hadn't a clue what I'd do in Europe but I was prepared for anything—living in a tent, selling burritos on the beaches of Greece, waiting tables in Spain. Anything, just so long as I could feel I was enjoying a real life with real people.

Finally, I went back to see Ronald. "But we've seen such a change in you over the past months," he protested. "It comes to me as a complete surprise to hear that you want to leave us. After all this company has done for you and the opportunities we are offering, I'd have thought we could expect a minimum of loyalty."

Senior management spent the entire afternoon trying to talk me out of it. I replied with standard "broaden my horizons" responses. My family thought I was mad for walking out on a high-paying career. One of my sisters even said I must have been diagnosed as having some terrible disease. The disease, though, was my meaningless existence.

I bought myself a cheap transatlantic flight. The day before I got on the plane, I bumped into an ex-colleague who told me that Ronald had left Siemens for a pay hike with a competitor. What the hell! I was off to places unknown and felt great telling the world to fuck off, blissfully unaware that the world often says fuck off back.

2.

FORT DE NOGENT

The Legion expresses some essential need of the human spirit, the belief that one can break with life and begin again, that salvation is to be found in the quest for danger and suffering.

Liddell Hart

"Oh my god! You threw away your job just like that?"

Katarina was the first person I tracked down after I landed at Paris-Orly. I'd fallen for her in Dresden two summers earlier. When I returned to Purdue, we went our separate ways but stayed in touch by email. She had become a blonde mother-figure for me and was happy to let me sleep in the spare bedroom of the tiny but pricey apartment she was now living in on Rue Marx Dormoy.

"Hah! What is money after all?"

"Well, this is a side of you you never let me see in the old days, when you were dreaming of climbing corporate ladders. Now I'm the one who's busy building a career. So what are you planning to do over here?"

"Don't know."

"I mean, it's not that I mind you staying in my place. Stay as long as you like, but my boyfriend's not keen on it. He was asking a lot of questions this morning."

"I understand. I won't be staying long. I sort of need to keep moving somehow. I don't know what it is. It's like I'm trying to find something without knowing what it is I'm looking for. Does that sound crazy?"

"Sounds like you're frustrated."

"Say, how far is it to Marseille from here? Never been there. Hopefully it's warm enough to sleep out. That'll save me a good fifteen bucks a night for a hostel."

I arrived in the steamy port city of Marseille late one evening, tired and hungry after hitchhiking all the way down. I curled up on the beach and fell asleep to the whispered murmurings of the Mediterranean. In the morning I awoke soaked in sea mist and went off to find something to eat. I was chewing at a rubbery baguette on the *terrasse* of the *Buffet de la Gare St. Charles,* when a lean man in uniform strode past. He was wearing the white *képi blanc* of the *Légion Étrangère.*

The Legion had always fascinated me, so having nothing else to do, I snuck after him onto his train and followed him up the hill when he got off fifteen minutes later at Aubagne. He led me to the headquarters of the Foreign Legion, the *Quartier* Viénot where its senior regiment, the 1er *Régiment Étranger* and its world-famous band, the *Musique Principale,* are based.

My legionnaire had gone into an official-looking building so I followed the signs to the *Musée du Souvenir,* the Legion's museum, where I admired the collection of regimental flags, armaments, and uniforms of various eras—sombreros for the 1860s expedition to Mexico, *képis* with white beau geste neckflaps for the Moroccan campaign in the 1920s. The act creating the *Légion Étrangère* was signed on March 9, 1831, by King Louis-Philippe, with the twofold purpose of mopping up the large numbers of political refugees flooding into France and liberating the educated classes from the obligations of military service so that they could get on with the task of making money. The early Legion was a ragtag lot that included many criminals and other social outcasts. In those days, recruits were shipped straight out to the colonies, where they had to serve for five years before being allowed back to metropolitan France.

The *Salle d'Honneur* contains memorabilia of the 35,000 foreign legionnaires who over the years have laid down their lives for France. For me the most moving exhibits were the Croix de Guerre and Médaille Militaire awarded posthumously to my hero, the poet Alan Seeger, who died fighting in the Great War. Born in New York in 1888, he had studied Italian at Harvard and later moved to Paris to live and write among the American expatriates in the *Quartier Latin*. As the bright sunshine of *la belle époque* became overcast by ominous portents of war, Seeger joined dozens of other American patricians who answered La Republic's call to arms by becoming legionnaires. The Legion was not particularly impressed. He wrote that the NCOs were as heavy-handed with gentlemen volunteers as they were with "refugees from justice and roughs." *Plus ça change plus ça reste la même chose,* I was to discover.

During the battle of the Somme, Seeger's company was ordered to retake the occupied village of Belloy-en-Santerre. As they advanced they were caught in the crossfire of six German machine guns. Seeger was cut down as he waved his comrades on and fell screaming into a bomb crater. Before dying, he cried out for water and his mother. He had written in one of his letters to her: "If it must be, let it come in the heat of action. Why flinch? It is by far the noblest form in which death can come."

Beyond the *Salle d'Honneur* is the Foreign Legion's Holy of Holies, the *Crypte,* off limits even to legionnaires except in the presence of an officer. I leaned in over the velvet rope to read the names inscribed on the wall panels of the 903 officers killed in action. Among them is Lieutenant-Colonel Amilakvari, an exiled prince of Georgia and commander of a Legion unit attached to Britain's Eighth Army in North Africa. Blown away by German shellfire in 1942 during the battle of El Alamein, he is remembered for his words: "We, foreigners, have but one way to prove to France our gratitude for the welcome she has given us: to die for her." Here, too, encased in a glass reliquary, lies the Legion's most sacred relic, the wooden hand of *Capitaine* Danjou killed in 1863 at the legendary battle of Camerone in Mexico. The place reeks of heroic death.

After leaving the museum, I walked along the street to a scruffy Aubagne *bistrot* where I got into conversation with a group of *képis blancs*. One was a Canadian, a disabled paratroop sergeant now serving in the *Musique Principale*. "Thinking of joining, huh? Well, think hard. I know all about you Alan Seeger types. You think you could shoot to kill without having second thoughts? Just never forget, it's the sergeants and corporals who'll be your ultimate moral authority. As a professional soldier, you kill on demand. If all you want is a change of scenery, hell, go back to Purdue and get on with your MBA. France refuses to accept her second-rate military status and goes sticking her nose into all sorts of dirty places like Africa. Ask yourself what you can expect to get out of joining the Legion and weigh that against a whole lot of pain and humiliation."

"Maybe I'm just looking for the next ultimate high."

"Well, okay, that I can go along with. I must admit that nothing I've ever done in my life can hold a candle to my days in the Legion."

"The contract's for five years, right? What do legionnaires do when it comes to an end?"

"Some become freelance mercenaries, some become alcoholics, some commit suicide. The stupidest reenlist. Just remember, kid fellow, nobody will understand your reasons for joining; everyone will suspect your motives. But once you're in, whatever happens after, even if you desert, you'll never be free from the Legion's mystical pull. If you do make it in, you should try to join us gentlemen in the *Musique Principale*. Not that I'll be around here much longer; my contract's up in two months."

"What'll you do then?"

"Return to my Cornell class of '90, private-banker existence. Yep, a humdrum kind of life after five hard years! Anyway, right now, as far as you're concerned, you can forget about your qualifications and you're glossy résumé; they'll impress no one. We don't just take anybody these days. You'll have a lot of tests to go through before you get your contract." He ordered a last *pastis*. "In the Legion you get respect when you spill enough blood to merit it."

From that day on, I couldn't shake the image of the leathery-faced men who undergo the rite of passage into manhood by learning the warrior trade. My Purdue degree was proof enough of my intellectual capabilities but it said nothing about my physical, moral, or spiritual mettle. As a Catholic who fasted during Lent and believed in self-sacrifice, I felt drawn to a life of challenge and discomfort.

As I fell asleep that night on the beach under a star-filled sky, I saw the Legion as a way of redemption for disillusioned men from many lands, and I wanted to be part of it. As a small boy, I had always enjoyed hiding away in my own fantasyland where I was insulated from the outside world and its tribulations. The Foreign Legion was fantasyland for eight thousand overgrown boys of all ages.

Women have always been excellent recruitment officers for the Legion. In 1924, Bennett J. Doty, the Mississippi gentleman who wrote that book I was reading in Chicago, tried to explain his reasons for joining. ". . . Well there it is. Now you know how I ended up in the Legion. Or do you? You see, I forgot to tell you there was also down South a girl I liked a lot. She's married now but not to me."

I met Nadine in a backpackers' hostel in Tours. She was a *Québecoise* and at home with the French language, though Parisians would probably sniff at the way she spoke it. Only nineteen years of age, she was a good few centimeters taller than me with the lean hips and long legs of an Olympic sprinter. She had wavy brown hair, brown eyes, and a rich skin texture. Her features were fine yet strong, her lips full and sensual. But most of all, it was Nadine the person that I fell for.

She invited me along on a trip to the Château de Chambord in the green Loire Valley. She'd read up on the historical background and gave me a running commentary as we walked around. At the end of the visit, we went outside and I pulled a groundsheet from my rucksack. We lay down on the grass next to each other, gazing up at the blue sky and white clouds. It was nice simply to have her body next to mine.

Back at the hostel that evening, I broke out my personal vodka stash, and we began mixing drinks. When I suggested we take a break for a moonlight stroll, she agreed without hesitation. We ended up on a park bench hidden by rhododendron bushes. Back again at the hostel, we joined the others for more drinks and I challenged them to explain how I got the red abrasions on my knees and elbows.

Nadine jabbed me in the ribs. "You baffle me." She giggled softly. "One minute, you act like the corporate engineer personified, the next you're an untamed madman."

Over the next couple of weeks, Nadine restored my lust for life. After the disillusionment I'd felt with my failed relationships and the cardboard people at Siemens, she was an invigorating breath of fresh air. Here at last was someone I really enjoyed being with and who clearly enjoyed being with me. But alas, some things just aren't meant to be. With University of Montreal about to recommence, and a long-term relationship that she was going back to, our paths had to part.

"Nadine," I pleaded, "you've opened my eyes to so much. Life's worth living at last. Who's going to sleep next to me, who's going to listen to me like you do?"

"Oh, don't be so fatalistic. I know you think I'm the one for you, but what you really need is far more than what one person can give you." Her deep, warm eyes sank into mine. "How is it you've managed to make me like you so much in such a short time?"

I trailed after her into the Gare du Nor in Pairs whimpering like an abandoned puppy.

"No," she said firmly. "I got to go and I will."

I said goodbye and walked away down the platform so I wouldn't see her train depart. I'd reached the gate when I simply couldn't bear it any longer. I ran back past the carriage windows to catch a last glimpse of her but the train gathered speed and she was gone.

"So where's Nadine?" Katarina asked as I threw myself onto her sofa.

"On her way back to Montreal but not with me. Will your boyfriend make a fuss if I stay over again?"

"Got rid of him."

"*Bon*. I won't stay long this time. I think I finally understand what it is I have to do."

They say that every would-be legionnaire runs into a priest before joining up. Between the wars, two Englishmen, Tom Cushny and Alfred Perrot-White, had run-ins of that kind. In both cases the priests pleaded with them not to do it. Ironically, the Legion at that time was full of priests, many of whom revealed their religious vocation only when a comrade was lying mortally wounded and no chaplain was available.

In my case, I found myself sitting opposite a hooded Franciscan on the Paris *Métro*. I began chatting with him when the doors closed. "I'm thinking of doing something I may regret." I told him what it was.

"Is the Foreign Legion a step toward something you're searching for?"

"Well, I once considered the religious life myself but I decided I wanted to do something more practical. I look at the world today and see families being killed and tortured in Kosovo, land mines planted decades ago maiming children in Africa. And I ask myself, What am I going to do about it? Why did you decide to become a friar?"

"I used to be an attorney."

"Oh!"

"A lot of people think that being in a religious order is a hard life but it can be the most liberating experience."

"Orwell's notion that freedom is slavery?"

"Something like that. I haven't the same freedoms as most—Jesus Christ binds me. But by following Him, I'm completely free in anything that's important to me."

"What are you off to do now? To meditate?"

"Not quite." He smiled. "I'm out to buy a case of wine."

"Father, I need your blessing for where I'm going."

He placed his hands on the crown of my head and mumbled in

Latin. That blessing stayed with me throughout everything that lay ahead.

Sitting at Katarina's kitchen table that evening, I poured myself another glass of Chardonnay. "Katarina, I'm thinking of taking a break from life." I pointed at my rucksack. "Can I store that in your closet for five years?"

When she had stopped laughing at my decision to join the Foreign Legion, she made a meal and we chatted together quietly before going off to separate bedrooms. The following morning she knocked on my door and presented me with croissants and marmalade. Under my bowl of café au lait I found detailed instructions for getting to Le Fort de Nogent. This is just one of many Legion recruiting posts across France. You can apply to any gendarmere or police station and they'll take you to the nearest Legion post, open twenty-four hours a day, 365 days a year.

I got off the train in a run-down suburb, part of Paris's eastern sprawl, and began the fateful walk that many a man had taken before me. My stomach muscles were tightening with each step. I stopped to ask an elderly man for directions. He shook my hand, croaked, "*Honneur et Fidelité!*" and pointed me on my way. The fort is cold and gray, with the heavy stone walls of a medieval stronghold, a place built to keep people in as well as out. With a sense of impending doom reminiscent of Dante's "All hope abandon, ye who enter here," I passed through the gates and pressed the bell at the side of a massive oak door. A hatch rattled open.

"I want to join the *Légion Étrangère*."

"*Passeport!*" the guard barked.

I slid that precious document with its small-print warning that joining a foreign army is grounds for loss of citizenship through the grille and wondered whether I would ever see it again.

"*Américain?*" said the guard in astonishment. "Ready to give everything up and sign away five years of your life?"

"Yes."

The door swung open and slammed behind me. The guard ushered me into a small, dimly lit room with nothing more in it than a metal table and disappeared. After some minutes he came back and ordered me to empty my pockets, frisked me for "knives, guns, bombs, or gas," and sifted through the items in my sports bag. Because my French was so poor, I didn't respond at once when a *caporal-chef* appeared and ordered me into his office. "Go in now, stupid American!" he shouted in broken English, taking me by the scruff of the neck and shoving me through the doorway. He was a Japanese with body odor. As I was to discover, men from homelands without proper armies are common in the Legion.

Hanging on the wall of the office—and every other Legion bureau I ever found myself in—was the picture of General Rollet, the bearded "Father of the Foreign Legion." I was made to strip to my underpants, and the few dollars I was carrying were stuffed into an envelope. I knew that the chances of seeing my belongings again were slim so I had come provided only with my toiletries, several pairs of underpants and socks, and a few other things I had thought essential. The *caporal chef* dropped into the waste bin the most important items—my Elastoplast stretch tape, my address book, and a novel I was reading, *Quiet Days in Clichy* by Henry Miller.

He hunted around for a sheet of paper for me to print my name on. "You come here because you have crimes in America?"

"No."

"You make girl have baby?"

"No."

"Why you come?"

"Adventure."

"Ha! I hear it all. Great adventure in foreign land. Ha, ha, ha!" He thumbed through English/Japanese and *Japonnais/Français* phrasebooks before sticking in front of me a photocopied sheet with a dozen questions in English and put a finger on the first answer slot. "Work?"

"Mechanical engineer."

"*Mécanicien,*" he muttered, marking me down as a mechanic.

"Region is a five year," he said finally and slid over seven copies of the same form. "Sign contract now!"

The pen trembled in my hand. God alone knew what I was agreeing to and what rights I was signing away. But once I had signed, I felt an indescribable release. I'd finally done it!

I was made to change into a green tracksuit smelling of sweat and vomit with a hole in the crotch, and was thrown into a room with the other new arrivals, a collection of humanity's rejects.

The Legion has always had a bizarre mix passing through its gates, from the legendary gentleman who joined in top hat and tails to men who arrived in tatters and signed with an X. When Americans volunteered for service in the Great War, Legion officers brought their wives to see these strange new recruits, whom they thought were all sons of millionaires. Many, in fact, were. There were also men who sought to live life as a penance, including some masochists who tattooed obscenities onto their palms, so that the first time they saluted an officer they were immediately packed off to the penal battalions.

One after the other, men in the new intake returned from the bureau waving pieces of paper printed with their *nom de guerre*, the new identity under which they were joining the Foreign Legion. Some were guys with a past that they needed to put behind them; some were even French. According to its founding statutes, the Foreign Legion is an army of non-French mercenaries. On paper, apart from the officers, there are no French nationals serving in the ranks. Any Frenchmen are listed as Belgian, Swiss, or French-Canadian. Recruits are given names based on their real initials so that I, as Jaime Salazar, would become Juan Sanchez. Jasper Benson, a black American, was given the name James Bond.

I went through what remained of that day in a state of blank numbness and remember almost nothing about it. Certainly I did not notice at the time that the mattress I finally climbed onto was stained with generations of recruits' body fluids. I must already have been sound asleep when the lights flicked out to start the first of many nights under the Legion's lock and key.

During the two weeks I spent in the Fort de Nogent, one day was very much like another. Our 0500 breakfast was an eggless French affair—coffee in a bowl and a piece of baguette to dunk in it. More interestingly, the Legion is probably the only army in the world where you can help yourself to a breakfast beer from a tap next to the milk and fruit juice dispensers.

Recruits shit *à la turque* into a porcelain hole in the ground. You have to be careful to situate your feet properly on the starting blocks, so as to avoid the sudden swill of water and crap when you pull the chain, or more accurately the string. The smell of that medieval contraption did nothing to relax my bowels. The first time I used it, I made the mistake of dumping directly into the hole, and splashed myself with filth. I had to restrain myself from breaking out of the stall like a wild boar. Wiping while squatting isn't a tidy affair either.

We had to clean our living quarters four times a day. Proper mops don't exist in the Legion; instead we used a wet towel draped over a squeegee. On the first day, I was assigned *corvée* (cleaning duty). This meant missing the midday meal and spending the entire sweaty afternoon working nonstop. While washing the fort's automobiles, I came across an unsightly beaten-up, yellow Renault hatchback with the fort's phone number painted on both sides. Legionnaires drive around Paris in it, hoping to attract new talent. I was surprised that underneath the phone number wasn't written FREE BEER. This isn't the only recruiting technique. There are documented cases of foreigners in France, usually Germans, being arrested on trumped-up charges and given a choice between prison and volunteering for the Legion.

In our room, below the TV was a VCR with a pile of recruitment videocassettes dubbed into various languages. I'll never forget the English version's summing-up: "The Legion will provide little in terms of comfort, but will provide you with uncompromising camaraderie and a life of adventure." It concluded with the words: "The journey begins with you. For the selected few, be strong." This was considerably more realistic than what I'd read in an earlier glossy brochure: "The Legion offers an active outdoors life, sometimes somewhat rough."

Apart from James Bond, the only other Anglophone among us was an Irishman. We naturally gravitated toward each other and got on well. Sean, in his thirties, was a Catholic barman from Belfast. He was a bookish man who kept me from going mad in that virtual prison. But with each passing day I saw him sinking into depression and he began revealing details of his past. "Abandoned me family. Haven't seen them in months."

"Does the *caporal-chef* know about this?"

"That's the first thing he asked. Then wid a stroke o' his pen and me name change, he says: 'Voilà! No more wife and kids!' "

Boredom was the worst thing about our existence in the fort. When a Russian ripped a fart, it opened a genie's bottle that could not easily be corked. Farting sessions broke the monotony. A black Frenchman enjoyed shaking his leg after he had performed, as if dislodging something stuck in his trousers. A Congolese, a replica of rapper Biggie Smalls, ripped farts while attempting difficult breakdance sequences. I matched their wit with a time-honored Yankee tradition by telling the Congolese to pull my finger and, as he did so, letting go a loud one of my own. It seemed amusing at the time.

While I was mopping the floor one evening, a Moroccan shouted at me: "*Mongol* (idiot) *Américain!*" I threw down my squeegee and threatened to beat his ass. Abu, another North African, grabbed my arm and persuaded me that a fight wasn't worth it at such an early stage of selection. He was Algerian but quick to point out that he was of the Berber people, not an Arab. He was a gentleman and a Francophile in spite of the relationship his people had had with the Legion of old. Algeria's military dictatorship, indirectly supported by France, was suffering waves of attacks by Islamic extremists. Entire villages were being butchered weekly and the world was doing nothing about it. Abu had worked in an elite and ultra-dangerous counterterrorist group.

"Ever seen an oven-baked infant?" he asked. "It wasn't an entire baby; the terrorists had eaten most of it. Many of my colleagues were murdered. If I hadn't got out when I did it would have only been a matter of time before I joined them."

Unlike most of the other men in the fort who behaved like unruly children, Abu was a quiet man. His experiences had matured him. He took time to teach me French at nights. I appreciated his friendship but was uncomfortable at the way he often took my hand or ran his fingers down my cheek. At first I thought these were Berber customs but when he stuck his tongue in my ear as we waited in line for the evening meal I decided I'd had enough and told him to cut the shit. That wasn't to be the last encounter I had with him.

The morning after this incident, the Japanese *caporal-chef* announced that we would be departing for the barracks in Aubagne that evening. It had been two weeks since I passed through the gates of the Fort de Nogent. "This is next step," were his parting words. "Whatever done in past now forgiven. Anew, former name and self not exist. You now good men and become regionnaires!"

We were ordered neither to speak to nor even look at anybody in the station or on the train. Was this really something I wanted to get into? While the *caporal-chef* was allowing half the group to buy cigarettes at the Gare de Lyon, I considered making a run for it and was searching out of the corner of my eye for an escape route.

"Don't do it, mate," muttered Sean.

In our reserved car *caporal-chefs* sat in front and back—light security compared to the armed guards used by the Legion in the past when volunteers were ferried across to Algeria. Early the next day we'd be pulling into Marseille. After being awakened by the conductor that night, I noticed that the *caporal-chef* in the back was sound asleep. This provided an opportunity to sneak into the next car and hand my "Dear Family" letter to a civilian. I was running away from home at the age of twenty-five.

3.

AUBAGNE

Here [Morocco] the European is fulfilling his utmost duty as practical educator.
One is shown the city, Volubilis, which the Romans built. In a few centuries, one
will be shown the work of the Foreign Legion inscribed in the rich soil in the shade
of palmeries.

André Maurois

Until the French withdrawal from North Africa in 1962, the Legion's
headquarters base was in northwestern Algeria at Sidi-bel-Abbès,
which was originally built as a regimental depot on drained marsh-
land in 1843. Five years later the metropolitan government decided
to develop it into a fortified township, at first using a workforce
composed exclusively of *képis blancs*. The French Foreign Legion
has always shared the Roman Legions' commitment to infrastructure
improvement as a means of controlling occupied territory. Local
Muslims contemplating the complexities of life in the shade of the
palm trees were astonished to see white European soldiers toiling
away in the heat of the sun to build a gridwork of streets and avenues intersecting at right angles. By the time of independence the
city had a population of more than 100,000.

During the colonization of the Maghreb (Morocco, Algeria,
Tunisia), heat, thirst, and the brutality of the noncommissioned officers (NCOs) often led to violence and suicide. Men were known to
bayonet an officer for no apparent reason, or dash out into the desert
naked to die of thirst. This form of nervous depression became

known as having *le cafard* (cockroach), the French equivalent of Winston Churchill's black dog. It was contagious and could lead to mutiny. The only known remedies were drink, women, and the one thing an isolated commander prayed for—war.

The Legion's archenemy in the 1920s was the nationalist leader Abd el-Krim, who united the Berber tribesmen in the mountains of Morocco against the French and Spanish colonial armies and succeeded in establishing a short-lived independent Republic of The Rif before being overwhelmed by superior firepower. The blue-eyed Berbers have been in North Africa for over three thousand years—long before the arrival of the Arabs and Islamization—and retain many of their pagan traditions and beliefs.

Berber women carried a curved knife to use on any legionnaire they found lying wounded. Captured Christians were seen as gifts from the gods and castration was only a prelude to what followed. They gouged out prisoners' eyes, cut off their ears and noses, and often skinned them alive. Many were buried up to their necks in desert sand and left to await the arrival of jackals and vultures. An additional refinement was to smear their heads with honey to attract ants. Legionnaires always carried a spare round to use on themselves.

Horrors of that kind lent a very real meaning to the Legion slogan of "March or die." In 1924, Englishman Thomas Cushny's unit took an Abd el-Krim village where they found two babbling slaves, nude eunuchs without eyes, ears, or noses. They mistook them for lepers but eventually realized that they were legionnaires, driven mad by torture. Shortly after this discovery, Cushny's unit captured a Berber woman. They were merciful enough to dispatch her by bayonet before cutting off her breasts to make into drawstring tobacco pouches.

In the nineteenth and twentieth centuries, in addition to the endless fighting in the Maghreb, the Legion was in action in sub-Saharan Africa, Indochina, South America, and for a time, even Mexico. The most fruitful source of sorely needed recruits was Germany, despite the efforts of organizations such as the German Protection League

Against the Foreign Legion which portrayed the Legion as an army of drunks, delinquents, and homosexuals. The German contingent was further reinforced after World War II by an influx of former Nazis.

During the Algerian war of independence, the Legion was pitted against the *Armée de Libération Nationale* ALN, a terrorist group responsible for killing tens of thousands of European and Arab civilians. Although French President Charles de Gaulle spoke publicly about keeping Algeria French, he was secretly negotiating complete withdrawal. In 1961 pro–*Algérie française* elements took up arms against the French Republic in the *putsch des généraux,* led by what de Gaulle called *"un quarteron de généraux en retraite"* (a handful of pensioned-off generals). The capital city, Alger, was occupied by the 1er *Régiment Étranger de Parachutistes* and there were rumors of a paratroop drop on Paris. However, national servicemen serving with the French forces in Algeria refused to support the rebels and the uprising was crushed.

Edith Piaf always had immense admiration for the men of the Legion to whom two of her songs are dedicated—*"Mon légionnaire"* and *"Le fanion de la Légion"* ("The Legion Pennant"). The 1er *REP* was ignominiously disbanded for having taken part in the *putsch* but as the former paratroopers were being driven away in trucks, some of them to imprisonment, or execution, they were defiantly singing Piaf's hit song:

> *"Non! Rien de rien . . .*
> *Non! Je ne regrette rien"*

> "No, none, none at all!
> No, my regrets are all gone.
> The fun I've had and the pain,
> I have let it all go.
> No, none, none at all!
> No, my regrets are all gone,
> Washed off, wiped out and away.
> So to hell with the past!"

When the country became independent the following year, the men of the Legion blew up their barracks in Sidi-bel-Abbès and established a new headquarters base at Aubagne, in the south of France, the land that both loved and loathed them.

As soon as we arrived at Aubagne's *Quartier* Viénot, named after a commander of the *lèr Régiment Étranger* who lost his life at the siege of Sebastopol, we were marched off to join recruits from other parts of France for palm prints and photographs. We were ordered to strip naked and a corporal inspected every inch of our anatomy for tattoos, scars, and other distinctive marks, which he systematically photographed to check for any criminal record and for later use in case of desertion. He used up an entire film roll on Sean, who was covered in colorful ink, including a large thigh tattoo reading SKA FOR LIFE.

Now no longer completely raw recruits, we were kitted out with blue polyester tracksuits and addressed as *bleus,* the second lowest form of insect life. On our feet we wore 1970s vintage canvas running shoes, the envy of any Jackson Five memorabilia collector. We were issued small rucksacks containing the bare necessities—T-shirts, socks, underpants, disposable razors, a towel, one bar of unscented soap, and a brick of *Savon de Marseille* for handwashing clothes. Our quarters were in a barracks building facing the parade ground and backed by a recreation compound surrounded by barbed wire where we were corralled in our free time. The toilets in our block were of the Western rather than the Turkish variety, but had neither toilet seats nor paper, which ended up being as valued a jailhouse commodity as cigarettes. All orders were given in French, and regardless of how much we understood, they often terminated with, "*Et que ç saute!*" ("Jump to it!")

Running about amongst the three hundred *bleus* were twenty recruits sporting berets and combat fatigues. They were the *rouges, bleus* who had passed selection and were awaiting departure to basic training with the 4*e Régiment Étranger* in Castelnaudary. While they remained in Aubagne they were exempt from all work details other than supervising the *bleus*. Although they had only a few weeks' seniority, they enjoyed special privileges, such as the right to abuse us and make our lives even more hellish than they would otherwise have been. Nighttime dreams of civilian life and former girlfriends were shattered by the lights snapping on at 0400 or earlier, depending upon how eager the *rouges* were to get us out of bed and start having their jollies.

April afternoons in southern France can be sweltering, but the mornings are chilly and our tracksuits were the only clothing we had. Before breakfast, an air-raid siren sounded for us to stampede to the drill square and stand to attention for inspection. Those who were improperly dressed or shaved were punched and thrown out of line to miss breakfast. After breakfast, the siren sounded again and we commenced *corvée de quartier,* advancing slowly in line across our compound to pick up anything that didn't belong there, from cigarette butts to windblown cherry blossoms.

Bleus are used as a source of free labor for everything from road mending to food preparation. *Ordinaire* (mess-hall) duty was the worst. It meant spending the day washing mountains of pots without abrasive pads or soap, under the orders of a basketball-headed Serbian cook who took particular delight in terrorizing any American or Brit who happened to come his way. The kitchen drains were constantly blocked and the floor covered with an inch of muck. Our hands turned pasty white from constantly being under water. The work finished just before lights out.

During free time, the torrid heat in the compound, coupled with lack of sleep, made staying awake difficult. The *rouges* punched and kicked anyone they caught dozing. The endless stress began to have psychological effects. One afternoon, I suddenly realized that I was squatting by myself in the shade of an oak tree, mindlessly lining up pebbles according to size. At other times, wandering about the compound, watching the jailhouse faces scowling back at me. I wondered how long it would be before I decked somebody. We were all so hyped-up with frustration and resentment that any minor incident could quickly escalate into a brawl. I had already dragged a slumbering African off a table by the seat of his pants and pulled a kitchen knife on a Russian for telling me to fuck my mother.

The *bleus,* like the rest of the Legion, split up into language groups, known as *mafias.* The *mafia Anglaise* was theoretically a group whose mother tongue was English, but because of the shortage of native-English speakers, it was extended to include Germans, Dutch, Afrikaners, and even the few Scandinavians. A tall Englishman from northern England had a scar on his neck from a knifing, and still sported an unsightly mullet haircut. A South African was a bush war veteran from apartheid days. His best mate had fallen out of a helicopter and "was cut to shreds by a gang of niggers." The one Finn had been a lumberjack and an army sergeant, while the Dutchman was a former Hell's Angel.

One *mafia Anglaise* member who didn't stay with us very long was James Bond. He told me that he had robbed a stateside bank before fleeing to Europe.

"Half a million bucks!" I gasped in disbelief.

"Yeah, but I only managed to get over here with thirty grand of it. I'm telling you, electronic theft is as easy as highway robbery in the old days. Homeboy, all it took was a few keystrokes."

"And so now the only thing between you and extradition is seven laps on your running test tomorrow morning."

I chatted with him again at *soupe de midi* the following day.

"I got a few good laps in," he said, "but then I kind of ran out of wind. And shit! They're going to throw me out."

That day's 1400 *rassemblement*—the garbage disposal parade, it was called—was the last I saw of him. Like the other rejects, he was put on the next train bound for the place where he had enlisted or to the French frontier-city nearest to his country of origin.

Everyone disliked the French-speakers because they used and abused the system at the expense of those who didn't understand the language. They were egoists who bossed others into doing things their way. They were also the least disciplined lot and behaved worse than schoolchildren, constantly talking and giggling at *rassemble-*

ment. But, though the *mafia Francophone* was an annoyance, they were paper tigers.

The *mafia Russe,* which included any former Soviet national, was a different matter. Most of them had previous military experience but they were all lazier than sin. Though raised under a communist system that preached "From each according to his means, to each according to his needs," they thought only of themselves. They behaved like animals, cutting in line, pushing and shoving their way as they pleased, yet few of us dared to complain. Although they were quite prepared to steal each other's food, they formed a united front against non-Russians. Anyone who challenged a member of the *mafia Russe* one-on-one soon found himself having to fight five others.

From time to time, during *rassemblement,* a *caporal chef* would order everyone to empty his pockets. When the contents were placed on the tarmac, it was obvious that the Russians were stealing sugar sachets and crackers from the *ordinaire.* Walking along the line of *bleus,* the *caporal chef* would stop in front of a guilty man, give him the order "One pace, forward march!" and deliver a sharp punch to his solar plexus. Those who protested as they doubled up in pain were kneed in the face.

Our tasks included Herculean renovation work at Malmousque in Marseille, the Legion's seaside rest and recreation center for legionnaires on active service or just having completed it. We were ordered to fill in an excavated pit with rocks larger than a man's head, using no tools other than our hands. Each day consisted of bending over, stripped to the waist, to lift and toss boulders into the gaping hole. One morning when I was on my knees, a *cafard*-suffering Portuguese *ancien* (veteran) who went about bellowing: "*Kurwa!* (Polish for bitch, whore) . . . Homosexual! . . . *Mongol!*" grabbed me by the back of my neck and tried to get me to suck him off. Luckily a sergeant appeared and he stopped.

I could see that Sean was becoming increasingly depressed with every passing day. "This ain't an army," he said. "This is Devil's Island."

"Ever read Thoreau, the American writer who went back to nature?" I asked. "I'm really beginning to realize just how feeble we human beings truly are: We need soft beds to sleep in and clean water to drink. We all have a low tolerance for discomfort, and . . . "

"So the Legion is your way of getting back to nature?"

"Exactly. I'm going to learn how to live off the land, sleep rough, and reconnect with my animal origins."

A man I got to know for the first time during our Malmousque stint was Sadlowski, a pleasant Polish giant. As gentleman-soldiers we had much in common. We could have enjoyable conversations together without needing to speak about getting drunk, barroom brawling, or whoring. He had attended the same *Uniwersytet Jagielonski* as another Pole I admired, Karol Wojtyla, Pope John Paul II. Sadlowski had dropped his law studies for a handsome pay raise in the Foreign Legion. He was younger than most of us, barely twenty years of age, but stood two meters tall and had arms like pythons. A thoughtful man and a devout Catholic with a *petite amie* willing to wait five years for him, at the same time he was a hard-contact Kyokoshin martial arts expert.

"You're a thinker," he said to me as he bearhugged a boulder, "and maybe you're a tad too idealistic for the Legion. I can't understand what you wanted to join up for. You had a good life in America. It was totally different for me; the Legion's my lifeline. Things back in Poland are desperate—there's crime and corruption everywhere. The only people making money are the mafia. I liked my studies, but how could I live on three hundred U.S. dollars a month? If I make the cut, I'll join the parachute regiment where I hear you can earn fifteen thousand francs a month and more on missions to Africa! I know a few guys back home who did very well out of it. One saved enough to buy a house and brought back a Djiboutian wife, the only black woman in Poland."

After we'd finished filling in the excavations, three of us were issued one kitchen broom to sweep a parade ground the size of a football field. Then a large squad of us was ordered to clean up a *hangar* that looked like the aftermath of Woodstock. Pots and utensils, some large enough to take a man and caked with grease and the congealed remains of food, were to be sparkling by the time the Portuguese *ancien* returned. Needless to say we were not supplied with soap or any form of scouring pad.

While Sadlowski and I slaved away, the Russians stuffed their faces with scraps of leftovers and washed them down with vinegary dregs from unfinished wine bottles. When they started drunkenly hosing down the caked-on grease with cold water, I realized that we would be there until the following morning unless I took the initiative and found some efficient way of completing our assignment. After experimenting with various techniques, I discovered that the most effective method was rolling the pots and utensils in a mud puddle and scrubbing them with the palm of my hand. In this way we managed to get rid of the caked-on food, but there was still a thick layer of grease that wouldn't budge. I went over to a truck, dipped a bundle of rags into the fuel tank, and handed them out to the others, saying, "We'll clean these pots the Legion way."

After *soupe de midi,* I noticed one of the Russians staring at me. I stiffened and stood up to ask if he had a problem. It was only as I was walking toward him that I realized his glazed eyes were not looking at me but through me. Then the vomiting began. Almost as if they had been waiting for his cue, a dozen more started spewing their ptomaine stomach contents all over their tracksuits.

While all this was going on, unknown to us at the time, just twenty kilometers to the north in Puyloubier pensioned-off legionnaires were happily picking grapes at the *Institution des Invalides de la Légion,* a rehabilitation and retirement home for veterans and the disabled. Puyloubier is part of the comprehensive welfare service that the Legion provides for men who have often broken with their families and countries of origin. For many, *"Legio Patria Nostra"* ("The Legion Is our Fatherland") is more than an empty slogan. The *Institution des Invalides* is also a cash cow. The Puyloubier *anciens* produce the Legion's famous *pinard* (wine), handicrafts that are sold in the *Musée du Souvenir,* and much of what is eaten in the local Legion *ordinaires.* When not carving figuines, tough old wheelchair-bound bastards can be seen scuffling with each other and getting drunk on Kronenbourg or their home-produced Côtes de Provence.

To take my mind off the toil and drudgery of Malmousque, I had three tests to look forward to. The first was a medical examination, so basic that the Hunchback of Notre Dame would have passed it with flying colors. To check my hearing, I was told to face the wall and raise my hand as soon as I heard the examiner whisper.

The following day, we were seated in a classroom for the *test psychotechnique*. Before we started, the *caporal-chef* invigilator explained with a swing of his swagger stick that nobody should be looking anywhere other than straight ahead. For a number of the Yes/No questions I easily saw that both possible answers could be correct—whether I enjoyed physically hurting people, whether I felt aggressive at times, whether I had a history of cruelty toward children or animals. Others were obvious in a different way—whether I heard voices in my head or spoke to myself. As in a crime novel grilling, the same questions were often repeated in slightly different ways to reveal inconsistencies.

The last part of the test was drawing a tree. I drew one with a thick robust trunk, strong branches, and fluffy greenery. Because I finished in only a few minutes, I killed time by sketching in owls on the branches, a running deer, mountains in the background, and a setting sun. I glanced around to see if anybody else had finished as well and had my knuckles slammed by the *caporal-chef*. A number of the *bleus* I took the test with were thrown out at the 14.00 *rassemblement*. Most of them seemed good lads but I hadn't heard how they had answered the question about having sex with animals. Somehow from all this an assessment was made of each candidate's intelligence, aptitude, and psychological stability.

A few days later, we had our running test, the Cooper, in which you run as far as you can in twelve minutes. I was particularly excited about this and set myself a target of 3,200 meters, or about two miles, in spite of having wasted a whole month doing nothing but carrying rocks and washing pots. My adrenaline flow kept up my speed for the first two 400 meter laps, but thereafter I tried to average my lap times to ninety seconds, calculating that otherwise I would be exhausted in the final minutes. Just after the halfway mark, pain invaded my stomach, legs, and lungs but I kept on, telling myself that the agony would pass—at worst it could last only minutes. The sixty-second bell sounded and I made an excruciating attempt to sprint. When the final whistle blew I was three hundred feet short of my target but it was good enough.

After the tests, we were cross-examined by the *Deuxième Bureau,* the military intelligence service known as the Gestapo, which, with the assistance of Lyon-based Interpol, produces in-depth reports on recruits' pasts. I was sent in for interrogation by an *adjudant* (master sergeant), an American Vietnam War veteran. He gave my university diploma, certificates, and updated résumé a cursory glance, before stuffing them back into their manila binder. "Sit down." He slid blank sheets of paper across his desk. "Write down everything you've done in your life up until the moment you're sitting before me now."

While describing graduation from Purdue and embarking on a promising engineering career, I was interrupted and grilled on every minuscule detail of my life. "Siblings? Names and dates of birth? Do they have children? . . . How many people know that you've joined the Foreign Legion? What are their names and addresses? . . . Wait, but you said you were in Stockholm on 27 November 1996, did you not?"

Only at the end of the second day's interrogation did he finally ask me my reasons for wishing to join the Legion.

"I got tired of sitting in Chicago traffic every day, and the Peace Corps is for wimps."

"So how much do you really know about the Legion?"

"I could write a book about the Legion."

"Oh, yeah? You know you'll have to take an oath swearing that you are ready to die for France. How do you feel about that?"

"The last place I want to die is behind a desk."

"Okay, I can see what sort of man you are, but never forget, in the Legion you'll work harder than you've ever worked in your life. I've known men go mad and mutilate themselves with a machete, even take their own lives."

He handed me a document showing exactly how much I owed in student loans, converted to the nearest French franc. The Gestapo had clearly done their homework. "I realize that you've got some debts but you don't need to worry about that. The Legion has already assigned you a *nom de guerre*: SANCHEZ, Juan. Here's what your new identity documents will look like." A month and a day had been taken off my birth date. My parents' names were altered and my place of birth was changed to Kentucky, even though that's an unlikely state for Latinos to be living in. Jaime Salazar would no longer exist.

"Before I dismiss you," he said unfolding a letter, "you should know that the Portuguese *ancien* at Malmousque has recommended your acceptance into the Legion. That's a big point in your favor but you're not on board yet. We still have work to do on your background. You'll find out Friday."

Early that day the *rouges* who had been making our lives a misery departed for Castelnaudary and we all waited anxiously to see who would be selected to take their places. Apart from me, nobody in the *mafia Anglaise* had much to go back to. If they were rejected, one group was thinking of hitchhiking to an Israeli kibbutz, attracted by stories of free wine and free love. The Canadians asked me if they could find jobs in the Texas oil patch without work papers. Sean was considering an application to a millionaire Saudi warlord he'd heard about who was open to recruiting non-Muslims who were willing to convert. "I'm already circumcised," he pointed out.

I strained to hear my name as the twenty new *rouges* were announced. Selection had been a month of seemingly endless labor and bullshit but I realized now that I desperately wanted to wear the coveted *képi blanc*. I held my breath as the *caporal chef* paused dramatically before reading out the twentieth name. It was mine! I was ecstatic to have made *rouge* but the names of Sean and the rest of the *mafia Anglaise* were missing. Of the forty applicants from Fort de Nogent, only Abu, Sadlowski, and I had finally made it. What makes the Foreign Legion such a deadly fighting force is that it can pick and choose its recruits from a pool of highly qualified candidates—men from the British SAS and SBS, Russian Spetznaz, French *Troupes de Marine,* or U.S. SEALs. I was the only Anglophone selected and one of the few civilians.

As we were being marched away to be kitted out, we passed an honor guard drawn up in front of the flagpole. We were halted *au garde-à-vous* while the *Tricolore* was raised and it fully dawned on me for the first time that I was now serving in a foreign army. Our new kit included carefully tailored dress uniforms made of high quality cloth and Bally leather shoes. It felt good to be able to wear the green beret with the Legion's exploding grenade emblem. Legion barbershops, however, don't exist. The *caporal-chef* simply produced a pair of clippers and ordered us to be *boule à zéro* (shaven-headed) by *soupe de midi.*

Now that we were *rouges* our treatment and privileges marginally improved, and the Russians immediately took to abusing *bleus* at every opportunity. The duty *caporal-chef* told us to make sure all *bleus* were in bed at the appointed time, and that none were masturbating in their bunks. Anybody trying to leave the compound was to be beaten with our metal belt buckles.

One night while supervising men in the showers, I heard somebody snicker, *"Mongol Américain."* I spun 'round and shouted for the culprit to identify himself. Raducanu, a short, barrel-chested Romanian stepped forward. He was a former member of Romania's national judo team and one of the most dangerous men in the compound. Nevertheless, he was a hair away from being the person whom I was expecting to deck. Surprised that a pampered American could stand up to such nonsense, he wiped the smile off his face. I decided to make his life just a bit more uncomfortable. In the morning when each *rogue* picked two *bleus* for *corvée,* I went straight for him and another man, a Frenchman I had taken kindly to. Once in-

side our barracks building, I dismissed the Frenchman and had Raducanu mop an entire corridor on his own. When he'd finished, I
walked all over it in muddied *rangers* (French army boots). "Do it
again, *Et que ça saute!*"

"I'll get you one day, you bastard," he hissed.

A highlight of our time in Aubagne was the celebration of Camerone
Day, named after the battle fought by the Legion in Mexico when
France was trying to prop up its puppet Emperor Maximilian of
Hapsburg with a force of forty thousand troops. While the French
army was besieging Puebla, the Legion was given responsibility for
securing the supply route to the coast. On April 29, 1863, the Legion
commander was informed that an important convoy transporting
siege artillery, ammunition, and three million francs in gold, was on
its way up from the port of Vera Cruz. He sent out a company of
three officers and sixty-two men under *Capitaine* Danjou, a Crimean
War veteran with an articulated wooden hand, to provide an escort.
After a night's march, they had halted for coffee at 7 A.M. when they
were attacked by a Mexican force of eight hundred cavalry and
twelve hundred infantry.

Danjou formed his men into a square and made a fighting withdrawal to the deserted Inn of Camerone, which had a courtyard surrounded by walls ten feet high. A Mexican officer bearing a white
flag called upon the legionnaires to surrender. *Capitaine* Danjou
replied by swearing that he would fight until death and ordered his
men to do the same. The battle began at 10 A.M. and the sixty-two
legionnaires and three officers repulsed repeated attacks by the two
thousand Mexicans for eight hours.

In the course of the day, *Capitaine* Danjou and most of the rest
of the company were killed. By six in the evening, the inn was ablaze
and the final assault was launched. *Sous-lieutenant* Maudet and five
men were left fighting with their backs to the courtyard wall. They
discharged their rifles point-blank into the wave of attackers and
charged with bayonets fixed. Maudet and two legionnaires were

shot down before a Mexican officer ordered his men to cease fire and called upon *Caporal* Maine and the remaining two to surrender.

"*Rendez-vous!*"

"Only if you agree to tend to our wounded and allow us to keep our arms."

"To men like you, we can refuse nothing," said the Mexican.

Two years later *Capitaine* Danjou's wooden hand was found by a Mexican peasant and taken back to the Legion's base in Sidi-bel-Abbès. In 1892, a monument was built outside the ruins of the bombarded inn with the inscription:

> *La vie plutôt que le courage*
> *Abandonna ces soldates français*
> *Le 30 avril 1863*

> Soldiers of France
> Deserted by life before bravery
> April 30, 1863

Today, whenever Mexican soldiers pass the memorial, they are ordered to present arms. The story of Camerone encapsulates the Legion tradition of no surrender, even in the face of certain annihilation. Every year on April 30, the battle is celebrated in Legion bases and outposts throughout the world. Although only *rouges,* we were given a section in the stand overlooking *la Voie Sacré,* the Sacred Way, and the massive *Monument aux Morts* (Cenotaph), brought back from Sidi-bel-Abbès.

The ceremonies began with a reenactment of the combat, complete with firefight and explosions. Then, accompanied by the *Musique Principale* playing the Legion's official slow march, *Le Boudin,* a detachment of pioneers in buffalo-skin work-aprons, with regulation beards and axes on their shoulders in a tradition going back to Napoleon's *Grande Armée* paraded past, escorted the bearer of *Capitaine* Danjou's wooden hand in its glass reliquary.

Englishman Jim Worden wrote, "I first heard the account of the

Battle of Camerone while presenting arms on the Legion parade ground at Sidi-bel-Abbès. As I watched a veteran *adjudant* bearing the wooden hand of *Capitaine* Danjou, I could not help noticing that despite the black patch over an empty socket where an eye had once been, tears were running down his cheeks." As the hand passed in front of me, I felt ready to die for the Legion. This was followed by a wide-screen presentation with stereophonic sound of the Legion's campaigns during its more than one-hundred-and-fifty-year history.

Camerone is a special day when legionnaires can escape for once from the tyrannical discipline. Officers and enlisted men mingle and little notice is taken of rank. It is also a celebration for the thousands of *anciens,* who travel to Aubagne for the ceremonies. When the official program has ended, they see their families off to their hotels and join in a joyful free-for-all of drunkenness and fistfighting, to which the officers turn a benevolent blind eye.

The instructors who would be accompanying us to Castelnaudary were *Sergent* Galeski, a brutal Pole with a deceptively gentle face and 666 tattooed across his left bicep, and *Caporal* Qandil, a Libyan martial arts champion with rippling muscles and racehorse stamina. When he asked if any of us had musical aptitude, I marched one pace forward to say that I was a beginner but willing to learn. He waited until I had finished speaking before giving me a punch in the solar plexus for not first calling out my name. But for me it was magical to think that we had been promoted from *bleus* to *rouges.* Though not yet full-fledged legionnaires, we were now *engagés volontaires* (enlisted volunteers).

"Sleep well tonight," said *Caporal* Qandil on our last day in Aubagne. "You'll need it." He was right. It was to be some time before I enjoyed another night of uninterrupted sleep.

4.

THE FARM

Sulley is an absolute shithouse where we will live for the next six weeks. It is a farm situated ten miles from Sidi-bel-Abbès. The dormitories are enormous barns, the lavabo is a horse trough in the open yard. There are no lavatories, but a trench three hundred yards from the barracks; we share it with the flies.

Simon Murray

A small convoy of trucks dating from the 1950s war in Algeria was growling up into the foothills of the Pyrenees. We were on our way from our new base in Castelnaudary to The Farm for the first four weeks of our sixteen-week basic training. Aubagne had been purgatory. The Farm turned out to be a five-star hell where the Legion hammers mindless hoodlums into efficient killing machines.

At first everything seemed to be pleasant enough. On arrival we were marched into a lecture hall for an address from our Platoon Commander, Lieutenant LeFang. This was followed by a beer bash accompanied by plentiful supplies of red wine and pâté. After weeks of spartan living, I concentrated on getting drunk. Amongst the grinning faces I became aware of the cold stare of Raducanu, the mouthy Romanian I'd had a run-in with. I reached over in a comradely way to hand him a bottle of Kronenbourg, which he accepted and raised at me with an antagonistic leer.

That evening *Caporal* Qandil came back from town piss drunk. With the other NCOs looking on, he paraded us and began with what he called *les tests abdominaux*, giving each man a violent punch in the solar plexus. He then inspected us. Improperly polished insteps or any other infractions were punished with lead-weight fists to bellies and heads. When he was satisfied, he called for a *pelle US* (folding trench tool) and went down the line gonging our foreheads with the flat of the blade. The worst part of the anticipation of it.

He ended by having Kapelski lie on the floor for a demonstration of one-stroke decapitation. Was he drunk enough to do it or not? He cocked the shovel above his shoulder with the blade open and came down full swing, to stop centimeters from Kapelski's Adam's apple. The other NCOs let out a hoot of guffaws.

We were then told to bed down on the canvas lawn chairs provided in the *hangar* (farmhouse barn) that was to be our living quarters. We had barely time to close our eyes when we were woken again by *Caporal* Qandil yelling that he was about to be promoted to *général* and that we were going to play helicopter. He had us jump up and down, flailing our arms and making whirlybird noises. Anyone who failed to show sufficient enthusiasm was battered with a broomstick.

To help us get back to sleep, we were introduced to the *piton,* a hill outside the farmhouse providing a two hundred meter run up a forty-five-degree grade. After the fifty meters, we were levering ourselves up by grabbing at tree trunks and clawing at roots. Coming back down was even worse. With the corporals screaming *"Action!"* controlled descent was impossible. I could feel the leather of my *rangers* prising off my toenails. When we finally made it to the bottom, we were turned around and sent up to do it again.

Next morning, having missed our evening meal, we were starving. We filed in *tenue de sport* into the *ordinaire,* hoping for a good thick baguette with butter and jam. Breakfast consisted of nothing more than one half *quart* (quarter-liter canteen cup) of watery instant coffee. Legion thinking is that the quickest way to learn how to soldier without food or water is to soldier without food or water.

"Today we are going to start with an introductory exercise to get you and your feet accustomed to the marching traditions of the Legion," Lieutenant LeFang announced.

The first half hour was brisk and invigorating. The view was splendid, my rucksack sat firmly on my shoulders, and I was looking forward to five more bracing years in the Legion. Then the pace began to get painfully fast. Lieutenant LeFang stormed ahead across rough terrain and up the steepest grades. My thighs screamed in protest. Each step was producing blisters on different parts of my heels, soles, and toes, and my rucksack was gnawing into my shoulders. During our ten-minute break I lay sprawled on the dirt, willing my feet to heal. The only comfort I had was my ration of dark, bitter Belgian chocolate, which I nibbled at every fifteen minutes.

Many were less fit than myself. Kekes, a Hungarian paratrooper, had been marching on a broken ankle. *"Ta foutue d'imagination!"* *Caporal* Qandil yelled. "Nobody fails the introductory march. First aid's for civilians." Next morning a recycled lumberjack from Bosnia was wheeled away paralyzed from the chest down, and Kekes was admitted to the *infirmerie*. His foot had turned gray and the toenails black. You're not considered to merit the *képi blanc* unless you've filled your boots with blood at least once.

Caporal Qandil had recently returned from service with the 3ᵉ *Régiment Étranger d'Infanterie* in French Guyana and proudly sported the badge of the Jungle Warfare School. Rumor had it that his mother had been involved in the drug business in North Africa and was murdered by a rival gang. He had hunted down the two triggermen, buried them in sand up to their necks and, so the story went, pissed, shat and ejaculated on them before bashing their faces in with a shovel.

Sergent Gagné, another of our instructors, was a Paris ghetto *apache* (hoodlum) who'd lost his sanity in the Persian Gulf. Like most legionnaires he sported tattoos—a Harley-Davidson drilled into his left bicep and a bent-over nude on his right who raised her ass when he flexed his muscle. *Caporal* Helmut, a short, thickset West German, was his sidekick.

"Nationalité?" Helmut asked when he heard my accent.

"*Américain.*"

"Splendid," he replied in fluent English, "we don't get many Yanks."

"And I thought I'd find a lot more of you Germans."

"*Ja,* I'm one of the few these days. West Germans, that is. The *Ossies* are as worthless as the Slavs. Let me know if you need any assistance." *Caporal* helm was an unofficial member of the *mafia Anglaise* and had an unusual soft spot for Americans.

Harasim, a Hungarian who blew a knee on the march, was wandering about on crutches as if he hadn't a care in the world.

"Watch it," I said to him. "Crutches won't protect you when the corporals start kicking and punching."

"No problem," he replied. "A kickboxer like me can handle them, even with only one good leg."

Shortly afterwards, Helm and another corporal heard Harazin smarting off about *Caporal* Qandil. They swarmed around him like killer bees and beat him senseless. He was dragged to his feet and ordered to stand *garde-à-vous*. Out of the corner of my eye I saw his crutches fall to the ground; his body followed after like a sack of apples. It was sickening to see a grown man cry.

Most Legion officers are Frenchmen on *secondment* from the *Armée de Terre*. They tend to be from well-established, right-wing families with names often prefixed with an aristocratic *de* or *du*. They do not have the honorific title of legionnaire and do not wear the *képi blanc*—their *képis* are black—but even short-term *secondments* can be career-boosters. Anyone capable of commanding men like the legionnaires is considered to be of outstanding officer quality. Most of them I liked but they were so few and so cut off from our daily routine that they made little difference to what we had to suffer from the NCOs.

Our Lieutenant LeFang was a recent St-Cyr graduate. Whenever spoken to by him, I like the others had to come stiffly to attention and present myself:

"*Engagé volontaire Sanchez. Trois mois de service.*

"*Troisième Compagnie d'engagés volontaires. Section du lieutenant LeFang.*

"*À vos ordres—mon lieutenant!*"

"Enlisted Volunteer Sanchez. Three months' service.

"Third Company Enlisted Volunteers. Lieutenant LeFang's Platoon.

"At your orders—Sir!"

"Ah, one of our Americans, I hear. We don't run into many of your kind. Now, what is it you would like to do for the Legion?"

"I'm a mechanical engineer. Thought of becoming a combat medic but would prefer to be a musician."

"Engineer, *vraiment?* Could be useful! My air conditioner has been giving out lately. But just do not forget, *mon enfant,* you're in the Legion to fight, not to practice your scales."

Several of the *engagés volontaires* made excellent soldiers and some were becoming personal friends. Calderon was a paunchy pit-bull from Nicaragua. He was tidy, well-organized, and very *correct* with his fellow *engagés* but disliked the Russians for their neglect of personal hygiene. He had volunteered for the Legion to get away from fistfights on the streets of Managua. During free time, I often saw him studying a Catholic prayer book. "The Good Lord is giving me the patience not to start pummeling those filthy Russians but it's too easy to get into a brawl here. I wanted to put all that behind me."

I learned a lot from him. I had begun by turning the other cheek to the bullies in the vain hope of stopping their asshole behavior. Calderon was different. Despite his determination to reform himself, nobody in our platoon had a shorter fuse. Whenever anyone cut in line, or stole his food or boot polish, he responded with a quick blow to the chops. He was a small man like me but he commanded respect.

Michaud was a *pied noir,* a descendant from one of the families of European or Sephardic Jewish origin that had settled in North Africa. They had French citizenship but when most of them emigrated after independence to metropolitan France they found they were about as welcome as Mexican illegals in South Texas. Michaud was a man without a real homeland. I got on well with him. He spoke English and translated the barked-out orders for me. We shared similar interests in music, film, and pub culture. He had bummed around Europe for years and picked up five foreign languages before joining the Legion. I discovered that when he was working as a waiter in London we had both lived at the same rundown, drug-infested hostel in the backpackers' borough of Earl's Court. We were pals but as with all Legion friendships, I several times came within an inch of beating him senseless.

Bobby was The Farm's dog, a scruffy old black mutt who had a far more comfortable life than his human roommates. Like all Legion mascots, he spent his time sleeping, wandering about the compound, and snuffling his snout up the insides of our legs during *rassemblement.* Sometimes he got to hump the bitch from another far-off Legion farm.

The Foreign Legion, the stepdaughter of the *Armée de Terre,* is sent off on perilous missions with substandard equipment. During basic training we were kitted out with equipment originally destined for the Dumpster but thought quite good enough for an army of throwaway misfits. We were still wearing heavy steel helmets when other western armies used Kevlar. Our water bottles leaked, our sleeping bags were Algerian war rejects. Camouflage denims were considered unnecessary flamboyance; our combat fatigues were straight olive drab.

The Legion is an army that still awakens to the bugle call and shouts of *"Debout là-dedans!"* (On your feet in there!) We had exactly twenty minutes to wash, dress, tidy up our quarters, and be outside standing to attention for the morning parade. The corporals formed us up before the *Tricolore* and fell in on our right while we were inspected by the lieutenant and the duty sergeant. After *Sergent* Gagné kicked me in the nuts, I never forgot to make sure my *rangers* were mirror-bright. The *sergent chef* called out the numbers of *engagés volontaires* present or absent.

Then came: *"Attention pour les couleurs! . . . Envoyez!"*

Lieutenant LeFang about-faced the *Tricolore* and saluted while two *engagés* standing at *garde-à-vous* slowly raised the flag.

After morning parade, the day began with *pompes* and *pitons.* Push-ups in the Legion aren't just a matter of twenty here and twenty there. The corporals kept us at it until they decided we'd had enough. They made sure they had plenty of time to smoke a Marlboro and go inside for a shot of *pastis,* before coming out again to tell us to stop. After push-ups on the second morning, we were sent to chase away a flock of sheep and lambs that had got into the grounds. It wasn't the last time we saw them.

Theoretically, the emphasis was on self-sufficiency and communal living. We cooked our own meals, washed our own garments, tended to our own orchad garden, and kept the barn and other buildings spotless. The platoon was split up, according to level of fitness, into three *groupes de combat,* which also acted as *groupes de sport.* Each *groupe* was allocated a section of the *hangar.* There were no cupboards so all personal kit had to be kept neatly folded atop a shelf running along the wall. I could see that was going to lead to trouble—communal living works for hippies and monks but not for hardened rogues like us.

I was in the *premier groupe* and *Sergent* Galeski, the most physically fit sergeant, was in charge of us. I soon learned how athletic he was when he gave us our first gut-busting *"petit footing"* (little jog). After running two kilometers to The Farm entrance, we continued along narrow deserted roads and onto dirt trails. I began to lag behind the others in the ascents and had to make desperate attempts to catch up going down. With each successive hill I was praying for us to stop. What kept me going was the shame of giving up; in the Legion, that is unpardonable. This was training for war, not trotting around Central Park to lose the love handles.

"This is what The Farm's all about," said *Caporal* Helmut, drawing the figure of a soldier on the blackboard. "Here's you faggots with no muscles, fat bellies, and little dicks. And here you are again after all the food you're going to get, with big muscles and rock-hard abdominals . . . but still with little dicks."

After the runs we got to stretch out on the grass but even this had to be done "the Legion way." *Sergent* Galeski threatened to kick me in the nuts when I crossed my right leg over my left rather than vice versa. If he'd ordered us to run off and rape a goat, we'd have done just that with no questions asked.

We were then allowed a swift shower. Forty nude skinheads fumbling about with soap in their eyes as they tried to get under one of the three operational showerheads was a homosexual's dream. During those few minutes, I rushed about to handwash my shorts, tank tops, and socks for the following day. There are no laundry facilities for *engagés volontaires*, simply the sinks and a horse trough we used on Sundays for washing our *tenues de combat*.

We spent most of the day fantasizing about eating or nodding off for a nap. *La soupe de midi*, the so-called midday meal, was never at a set time. If we had it late, there was usually nothing to eat in the evening. Before each *soupe* we were treated to one of *Caporal* Helm's *"apértifs"*—*pitons*, sit-ups, push-ups, or *la cord* (rope climbing), depending on how he felt. Then we lined up outside the *ordinaire* for one scoop of ravioli and a pear, washed down with a *quart* from the water cauldron.

When we'd got our rations, we stood at attention behind our metal stools, salivating at the thought of the tiny portions of food before us and waiting for the signal to commence singing the Legion's anthem, *"Le Boudin."* Then the sergeant barked out *"Bon appétit!"* and we replied with a deafening salvo of *"Merci, Sergent!"* Everything was gobbled down in a few seconds.

*   *   *

"Le Boudin," the first of the many songs we had to learn, was composed in 1863 when the Legion was about to embark for the campaign in Mexico. The king of Belgium had intervened to dissuade his subjects from enlisting and Monsieur Wilhelm, the Legion's *Chef de Musique,* expressed the general disgust at what was seen as Belgian cowardice by composing *"Le Boudin,"* which has become the Legion's official marching song. Literally it means "Blood Sausage," military slang for the bedroll for departing legionnaires carried atop their knapsacks.

> *"Tiens, voilà du boudin,*
> *Pour les Alsaciens, les Suisses et les Lorrains."*

"For Alsatians, the Swiss and Lorrainers
Blood sausage, blood sausage, blood sausage.
But for cowards and Belgian complainers,
Boiled sprouts, green boiled sprouts from gray Brussels."

Les chants are given special importance in the Legion. They tell of death, hardship, suffering, and leaving a homeland hoping to return after five years. Some are old Wehrmacht songs like *"Oh, du schöner Westerwald."* Many are for sweethearts left behind—*"Eugénie," "Monica," "Veronica,"* and *"Adieu! ma Charmante Blonde."* The subliminal message is that a glorious death is a passport to eternal life and happiness, not unlike the seventy-two virgins waiting in paradise for the fundamentalist Muslims who die in jihad.

Singing lessons lasted well into the night, with *Sergent* Gagné as our music critic. Not only did we have to sing in tune, we also had to memorize the words. When I failed to satisfactorily recite the song we were working on, I was ordered to run *pitons* and sing out the words as soon as I reached the summit. Those who were untalented musically were made to sing solo and anybody caught snickering soon found himself, like me, demonstrating how much better he could do it by caroling from the hilltops. After weeks of trying, several musically-challenged Russians were banned from singing altogether and ordered to lip-synch.

Any time the platoon marched, even if it was simply from the *hangar* to the drill square, we sang in lockstep, making each pace coincide with the chosen chant's syllables or intonations—no easy task on rough, uneven ground. When our singing was good, we had a rich, affecting resonance. For a Corsican boxer who had abandoned his wife and young son, one of our chants was unbearably poignant—"Who are you? Don't I know you?" a young recruit asks. "I'm your father," an older legionnaire replies. That evening the boxer was found weeping. He deserted during the night.

During classroom instruction at The Farm, once ass hit seat, it took a superhuman effort to stay awake. After nodding off, I was spared the *piton* but my *boule à zéro* head was palmed like a baseball and dunked in a bucket of ice-cold water.

The lieutenant gave us the odd half-hour lesson in French, explaining what a spoon and a fork were and how to use them. When I asked grammatical specifics, he would answer, "Well, our French language is really quite complicated, you know." I tried to keep ahead of the rest in learning French and was annoyed at how the Romanians, Raducanu included, got by quite well without studying at all because theirs, too, is a Latin-based language. I was determined to do better than anyone else and memorized all the key expressions such as *hit, punch, kick, throw,* and *pissed off.* With my steadily increasing vocabulary, I began catching the barked-out orders and working out what was being demanded of me.

The sergeants had a clever way of teaching the names of foods. At *soupe, Sergent* Gagné strolled around asking *engagés volontaires* what various items on their plates were. Anything that they could not name in French, he ate.

An important part of our classroom curriculum was memorizing *Le Code d'Honneur:*

Legionnaire,

1. You are a volunteer serving France faithfully and with honor.
2. Every legionnaire is your brother-in-arms, irrespective of his nationality, race, or creed. You will prove this by according him the unwavering loyalty that should always bind members of the same family.
3. Respectful of the Legion's traditions and honoring your superiors, discipline and comradeship are your strength, courage and loyalty your virtues.
4. Proud of your status as a legionnaire, you will display this pride in your turnout, ever impeccable in your behavior, ever worthy and modest, and in your living quarters, ever tidy.
5. As an elite soldier, you will train vigorously. You will maintain your body at a peak of physical fitness and your weapon as if it were your most precious possession.
6. A mission, once given to you, becomes sacred. You will accomplish it whatever the cost.
7. In combat, you will act dispassionately and without anger. You will respect the vanquished enemy. You will never abandon your dead, your wounded, or your arms.

Much of this is little more than pious aspiration:

Article 1: The Legion's motto, *Legio Patria Nostra,* "The Legion Is Our Fatherland," was more meaningful to us than laying down our lives for a country that most of us knew little about.

Article 2: Respecting our brothers-in-arms regardless of race or religion was laughable. Though it claims to accept men from throughout the world, the Legion is still largely a European, Christian army. There are a few from the Far East but the one or two blacks or Muslims who are accepted are either French Nationals or, like Abu, have a family history of loyalty to France. Even so, *les Africains* are looked on with suspicion and rarely make any significant rank higher than *caporal-chef*. With traditions inherited from former Nazis, the treatment of people of other races or creeds has often been appalling.

Article 7: Having respect for the vanquished enemy is equally un-realistic. The Legion rarely takes prisoners and has a history of mal-treating those it does. As for never abandoning your dead, it must be said that when the lives of living soldiers are at risk, the Legion and no matter what other elite unit leaves the dead to bury the dead.

We were told the organization of the present-day Legion is made up of roughly 8,000 men. Thirty thousand strong during the war in Indochina, it was reduced to a fifth of its original size after the Al-gerian putsch. Today's Legion consists of four infantry regiments, two regiments of engineers, one armored cavalry regiment, the *Demi-Brigade de la Légion Étrangère* (DBLE) half brigade, and the *Détachement de Légion Étrangère de Mayotte* (DLEM), a small unit stationed in the Comoros Islands in the Indian Ocean.

The 13e DBLE, a combined arms unit consisting of one infantry company, one engineering company, and one armored squadron, is based in Djibouti in the Horn of Africa. It exists to guarantee the de-fense of a nation that has no business existing in the first place. But its strategic location provides the region's only deep-sea port and en-ables France to maintain a certain degree of control over the Red Sea and the Suez Canal. It was the only unit where there was much money to be made. Paid upwards of eighteen thousand francs per month, legionnaires in Djibouti stashed away thousands francs a week since they had little to spend it on—whores there are as cheap as Kronenbourg. On top of that, they got a bounty of twenty thou-sand francs at the end of their tour.

The *3e Régiment Étranger d'Infanterie,* the only Legion regiment in the New World, is based in French Guyana to provide security for the Kourou Space Center, the launch pad for Europe's space rocket, *Ariane*. It is a posting for legionnaires who enjoy snakes, reptiles, and insects.

The *5e Régiment Étranger,* disbanded June 30, 2000, was based in Mururoa, Tahiti, and promoted as a vacation home for senior corporals who could spend the long afternoons with Polynesian girls in the shade of the coconut trees. Its responsibility for protecting France's controversial nuclear test center was played down.

In the eighties when President Mitterrand restarted the testing program, the protests of Greenpeace were led by the organization's flagship *Rainbow Warrior*. As the ship lay docked in Auckland Harbor, New Zealand, it was blown up on the night of July 10, 1985, and sunk by agents of the *Direction Générale de la Sécurité Extérieure* (DGSE), France's Secret Service. *Caporal* Helmut claimed that they had received backup support from the *5ᵉ RE*.

A new regiment that few knew about was the *2ᵉ Régiment Étranger de Génie,* a combat engineering regiment specializing in mine laying and sabotage. Based in Grenoble, it forms part of France's *27ᵉ Brigade d'Infanterie de Montagne*. The subtle distinction between *Régiment de Génie* and *Régiment du Génie* emphasizes that the *Régiment de Génie* is a unit not of the French *Armée de Terre* but of the Legion. *Sergent* Galeski explained that because the *2ᵉ REG* was undermanned many of us would be posted there. He tried to dress it up by saying that the *2ᵉ REG* was the Legion's future.

Another important subject on our program at The Farm was the 5.56 mm Famas F1, *Fusil Automatique, Manufacture d'Armes de St. Etienne,* often referred to as *le clairon,* the bugle, because of its stumpy shape. A relatively long barrel (488 mm) for what must be one of the world's shortest assault rifles (760 mm overall) makes it extremely accurate. It is designed to withstand water, mud, sand, dust, and temperatures from -40°C to +51°C, and retains its accuracy for up to 15,000 rounds. Its trigger guard can be pulled away from the rear retaining pin and rotated through 180 degrees for firing with gloves in arctic conditions. Perfectly balanced around its pistol grip, it can fire single rounds, three-round bursts, or in full automatic mode 1,100 rounds per minute. The universal sling enables it to be carried with both hands free while maintaining it on firing stand-by. It can be easily modified to allow for right- or left-hand ejection, for firing from either shoulder. But for all its admirable features, it has a disconcerting tendency to jam.

Memorizing the Famas parts in our own language was difficult enough. Trying to remember thirty different part names we didn't understand was mental torture but with time and enough kicks and punches from *Sergent* Gagné even the slowest learners had mastered terms like *le levier amplificateur d'inertie* (the delayed blowback lever, which reduces recoil). At target practice, he would make us run a 20-meter string from our sights to the center of a poster of a spread-legged woman.

A flip-up grenade-sight/gas-valve called the *alidade* converts the rifle into a grenade launcher projecting as required smoke, tear-gas, anti-tank, anti-personnel, or anti-personnel/anti-vehicle grenades. When pivoted to the vertical position the *alidade* closes the gas vent so that when fired the discharge gases propel the grenade.

I had difficulty understanding and remembering the shouted in-structions about the various actions necessary for the conversion. The first time I had to use the launcher, I was sprawling on the ground behind my Famas propped up on his flick-down bipod, try-ing to align the notch sight with the nose of the grenade and the tar-get. I could sense *Sergent* Gagné at my feet watching me like a hawk and I expected any moment to feel his fist on the back of my head. When it came it was a sharp kick between my ribs and hip bone that popped the vertebrae in my spine as if I was at the chiropractor. Fir-ing grenades in the standing position was nerve-racking. I failed to properly brace the Famas with my left arm and lock the butt firmly against my shoulder. What felt like a stick of dynamite went off in my face and the recoil knocked me tits over toe.

After an afternoon spent firing into a field dotted with thorn bushes, we were ordered to go out and recover all the practice grenades we had been using. When finally we got back to the *hangar,* we had to start cleaning our weapons. Instead of explaining how this should be done, we were simply told to have them spotless if we val-ued our sleep. *Sergents* Galeski and Gagné were experts at finding nooks and crannies that harbored soot. When they returned two hours later to inspect our Famas, they yelled that they were filthy and gave us another two hours of standing up, rubbing, and polishing.

Rifle cleaning was always a circus, with the sergeants strutting around handing out punches for barrels that hadn't been well enough pulled through. Sometimes they decided to entertain us by ordering the Russians who had been banned from singing to sing for us. A lot of the dumber *engagés* seemed to enjoy it all and forgot about the sleep time we were obviously wasting.

The next day ended with bivouac field-craft. *Sergent* Galeski gave us twenty minutes flat to tie a cord between two trees, drape a plastic tarp over it, and carve branches into tent pegs. I realized that I was one of the slower ones and prone to clumsiness when under pressure. *Sergent* Galeski wasn't impressed and the more he shouted the clumsier I got. Sadlowski would have helped me but I was too ashamed to ask.

When we got finished, we had the traditional singsong around the campfire, belting out all the legion songs we had learned, before turning in to sleep in our underpants and T-shirt alongside a chilly Famas tucked into the sleeping bag. *"Ta femme,"* said *Sergent* Galeski, *"c'est ton Famas."* Just as I was drifting into blissful sleep, I had to get up and grope around in the dark for my *rangers* and *tenue de combat* to do my one-hour spell on sentry duty. As I crept out into the night air, I got some satisfaction from mashing a cigar-sized slug with my fist.

A few days later our lessons in tactical field-craft began with a night march in single file up and down ravines. A corporal was sent deep into the woods to demonstrate what we mustn't do on night operations by lighting a Marlboro. Not having been issued individual infrared scopes, we had to take turns looking at him through the lieutenant's.

When we got to a wider valley we were given one hour to dig trenches in the heavy clay soil of the hillside. This was traditional "Legion work" that left us streaming with sweat and blistered hands. We were again given twenty minutes to set up our bivouac. It set to trying to untangle knotted-up cord and tarp with my Famas strapped across my chest and a red-lens flashlight wedged under my chin. As it began to rain, *Sergent* Galeski bellowed at me. He wanted to know why I was still fiddling around when he had already finished.

Calderon and I laboriously camouflaged our position and waited for the expected night attack. We would be going on counterattack before sunrise. We had four hours' sleep to divide between the two of us. In the second hour I heard a Peugeot P4 Cabrio jeep engine racing and whining as if stuck in the mud, and intermittent three-round bursts from a Famas. Ten minutes later the P4 lurched into view, opened fire on us, stalled, restarted, and opened fire again. *Sergent* Gagné was behind the wheel, dead drunk and laughing like a madman. He thought he had caught us by surprise but in reality he'd have been blown to kingdom come.

We were issued blank ammunition and *Sergent* Galeski led us off to counterattack the other *groupe de combat*. After an hour's march in total darkness, he held up his closed fist, signaling us to stop. *"Chouffe bien,"* he whispered and handed me the infrared scope. As clear as day, I saw Dupont smoking a cigarette. I was told to shoot him. Firing at him with my Famas gave the sort of primal high that Neanderthals must have got sticking their spears in mammoths.

Dupont was a harmless Korean, adopted as an infant by Belgian parents. He was a glutton for punishment. After finishing as a *rouge,* he'd commandeered a P4 and crashed it. When he got out of the hospital, he was given ten days in the Legion lockup. Before that, he had spent time inside for farting in the presence of an officer. While we were shaving after the night exercise, *Caporal* Helm gave him *"une séance d'assouplissement des membres supérieurs"* (stretching exercises for the upper limbs). He was made to strip to his underpants and perform push-ups while Helmut administered punches and open-palm slaps to his bare back and sides. As a civilian, he had worked as a cook and consequently prepared all of our meals—his cooking ability was rumored to have been his ticket into the Legion. He'd spent most of his time in Aubagne working in the kitchens of the officers' mess.

Though the *test psychotechnique* in Aubagne was pretty elementary, we couldn't understand how he had managed to pass. During
classroom instruction one day, he claimed that ten times twenty
equaled to one hundred. *Sergent* Galeski undertook to rectify
Dupont's *"problème mineur"* by slapping him around until he understood. *Sergent* Gagné referred to him as *"le Chinetoque"* (Chin-
kee) and was constantly punishing him for knuckleheaded behavior.

After cleaning out old junk from the *hangar* one day, Dupont returned with a chair missing its rear legs. Because he was so busy
sounding off to the other Francophones, he tried to sit down on it
and spent the remainder of the day massaging his ass. He provided
the platoon's entertainment and the corporals adored tormenting
him. He could never keep himself from nodding off whenever we
went into the classroom and spent most of his time running up and
down the *piton*. When the hazing became unbearable his way of getting his own back was by refusing to cook for the instructors.

One steamy summer afternoon, while we were learning how to
use NBC Nuclear, Biological, and Chemical (NBC) warfare suits, we
were told about the four degrees of protection available depending
on the risk involved. Degrees 1 to 4 varied from wearing normal
tenue de combat to wearing the full NBC suit with gloves, helmet,
and gas mask. When asked which degree of protection was best
suited for an immediate gas attack, Dupont answered Degree 1
(without gas mask) so that he would be able to warn the others. *Sergent* Gagné strapped him into the heavy, triple-layered suit, placed
the helmet and gas mask over his face, then sent him off up the *piton*.
Although his punishment was mortally dangerous on that torrid day,
we couldn't help laughing as we watched what looked like Bigfoot
slowly waddle his way to the top. When he finally made it back
down, he was drenched in sweat, his skin purple.

Every third day, the *premier groupe de combat* had night sentry duty.
That meant losing two precious hours of sleep. Many a time, my
dreams of frolicking with former lovers were shattered by an imper-

sonal tap on the shoulder. On sentry duty, we had to fight sleep and the mountain chill. I passed the time hungrily scouring the ground for a plum or cherry that had fallen from the trees. Looking through the lieutenant's window, I saw him sitting in a well-heated room, typing on his laptop. It made me think back to the days when I, too, was an important person, and here I was now just another expendable *engagé volontaire*. During those long chilly hours I looked up into the sky and thought of Nadine in Montreal.

Deprived of sleep, food, warmth, and contact with the outside world, there was nobody who didn't consider deserting while on night sentry duty. At first I fantasized about silently mounting my last *piton* in the moonlight and cutting off toward the Spanish border but it wasn't long before I realized just how difficult deserting from The Farm would be. In the middle of work one afternoon, Abu dozed off behind a tree and was left behind by the work party. As soon as the instructors noticed he was missing, military police arrived out of nowhere, armed with nightsticks.

As I had foreseen, communal living led to friction. One evening before lights-out, I went outside to fetch the T-shirt I'd washed after morning *sport* but it wasn't there. Luckily I'd sewn a nametag on it and I spotted it lying on Raducanu's bed. Cursing in French was not easy for me yet, but I made myself understood to him. He claimed that the sergeants had ordered him to take down all garments hanging on the line. I wasn't prepared to argue. I grabbed my shirt and snarled at him in English, "Don't fuck with my shit."

Next morning I was missing one of my only three pairs of sport socks. The worst about trying to find lost items was that you had to search every *engagé volontaire's* stuff, whether he was willing to let you or not. I didn't bother asking. I waited until our room was empty, then went about rummaging through the others' belongings. While I was searching, Raducanu came in and began shouting. I shouted back. He landed a punch in my guts and I replied with a swift sidekick to his chest. The others rushed in to break up the fight.

While on sentry duty that night, I found myself thinking of attacking Raducanu in his sleep. Next day, staring at him as we rode in the open truck, I caught myself planning to throw him off the moving vehicle. I realized how lack of sleep, lack of food, thirst, and mindless violence had a way of turning even the most Christian men into animals. The Legion was teaching me to nurse my rage till I found the right moment for revenge. I was an example of *un type correct* getting fed up with those who were not.

Professionalism was nonexistent in an environment where it was every man for himself and where property belonged to anyone willing to steal it. I was in a platoon of children in their twenties who had yet to grow out of their playground bully phase. Fighting is a time honored way of correcting immaturity but most of the men were too dumb to realize that fights in the Legion are rarely honorable. Legion brawls result in unsightly scars or disfigurement but no one had a pretty face to lose, so they didn't give a fuck. If I'd punched everyone who pushed or cut in front of me, I'd have been bleeding before every *soupe* and walking around toothless.

In contrast to the well-fed members of the U.S. Armed Forces, legionnaires are largely scrawny, wiry men with tattoos who would win the gold medal in any Barroom Brawl Olympics. Howard R. Simpson in his *French Foreign Legion* mentions that just after World War II, American commanders warned the GIs in France to beware of the men in the "funny white hats," for they were just as deadly in the *bistrot* as they were on the battlefield. Some GIs learned their lesson the hard way.

The instructors ate in elegance in the Farmhouse dining room. We had to set their places for every *soupe,* wait on tables, and serve them liter after liter of wine. Their dishes, stemware, and silverware had to be hand-dried to remove any water stains. *Engagés volontaires* with cooking experience were responsible for preparing all meals. It was odd to see burly men with heavy-duty *rangers* on their feet wearing aprons and fussing over which spices made the food tastier.

When the Russians were on duty they smuggled out what they could and shared it, but only amongst themselves.

Kapelski had an insatiable appetite. Despite his ravenous eating habits he was thin, and everybody believed he had tapeworms. When he was caught stealing overripe bananas from the garbage, *Sergent* Gagné brought him a cookhouse trashcan full of rotting food and ordered him to eat from it. He never had much in the way of social graces but I abstained from joining the others in taunting him. He was cleverer than they thought. It wasn't overripe bananas he'd been stealing at all. He hid proper food in the trashcans when on *ordinaire* duty and ate it later when he was on night sentry duty.

One time when I was working in the *ordinaire* myself I got into an argument with Mikhailov, the former Russian Spetsnaz, about who should be doing the washing up. He threw down the trays he was carrying and raised his fists. Knowing better than to fight him, I backed down and went on rinsing dishes. Only minutes later *Capporal* Helmut strolled in and said how pleased he was to see the former Cold War enemies working together in peaceful harmony.

"Don't mess with Russians," Sadlowski said to me. "They're not like me or you. They're different. They're worse than animals. A bullet in the head's about all they can understand."

One evening, *Sergent* Gagné deliberately left the instructors' storage cooler unlocked so that somebody would help himself to something. Next morning he stormed around screaming that one of his croissants had been stolen. "Who did it?" Nobody wanted to play young George Washington and the cherry tree, so with all of us standing *au garde-à-vous, Sergent* Gagné took the time to smoke his Marlboro down to the filter before flicking it away. *"Le piton, bande de tarlouzes!"* he bellowed. *"SVDC!"* ("The Hill, you bunch of faggots! *Sortez-Vous les Doigts du Cul*—Get your fingers out of your asses!")

After several ascents, he ordered those who'd been on sentry duty the previous night to lie on the grass and relax. By the time the rest of us had done another *piton,* they had their hands clasped under their heads and blades of grass in their mouths. *"Merci, les ca-*

marades!" we were ordered to shout. Then we were brought to the *garde-à-vous* again and the corporals went around us individually, sticking their noses into our faces. *"Le croissant du Sergent Gagné, pourquoi tu l'as graillé?"*—"Why did you eat *Sergent* Gagné's croissant?"

When that produced no result, we had to shake out our rucksacks so they could be searched for telltale crumbs. Forgetting that we'd been issued flashlights, *Sergent* Gagné checked to see whether any of the field candles we used for bivouac fire lighting had recently been lit.

"I'm giving you one last chance to turn yourself in," he howled. "Who ate my croissant?"

No answer.

The platoon set up a kangaroo court to find the culprit and Kapelski, the eating machine, nearly wet his pants thinking he would be the one convicted. However the croissant incident was soon forgotten in all the later excitement over another cherry tree every bit as important as the one belonging to George Washington's father.

Morning *sport* was gradually turning us into two-speed running/marching machines. The running was meant to strengthen us for the slow-burn torture of our long marches. The days when we ran with the lieutenant were the worst. He was a lanky man of about my age with nothing very intimidating about him, but he ran like a gazelle. The runs he took us on were along back roads and through forgotten villages. Occasionally we got to see local girls drive past in open convertibles, their hair blowing in the wind, but they never smiled or waved. They probably saw us as a bunch of foreign skinheads in shorts and tank tops messing up the scenery. In other circumstances I would have feasted my eyes also on the spectacular countryside but the pain every one of us was enduring took away any sense of enjoyment. Appreciating beautiful landscapes during Legion runs is like trying to read *Le Monde* while pedaling a bike in the *Tour de France*.

Sergent Galeski was fond of telling us that *le sport* is "a pleasure if you just switch off the pain." The runs kept getting longer and more arduous. The *premier groupe de sport* didn't go out on twenty-minute jogs; we ran for an entire hour, upwards of fifteen kilometers, at a lung-busting pace. In the first minutes, running shoulder to shoulder with my shaven-headed comrades, I really felt the buddy-bonding *cohésion* of the legion but we soon stopped chatting to focus all our attention on our pounding feet.

The aching began in the legs as glucose drained away and muscles began searching desperately for an energy source. My throat was like sandpaper; my lungs were ripping apart. I just wanted to stop and throw up. I felt I was being dragged along, chained to a P4 jeep, to see just how far I could go. During every march and run, I had to talk to my body, explaining that it was in for a long, hard workout and ordering it to marshal all its resources. To make matters worse, we never knew how long the runs would be and had to run like zombies till told to stop. The only thing that kept me from giving up was fear of becoming a run-drop and getting moved down to one of the less prestigious *groupes de sport*. But in the final minutes when the Farmhouse reappeared on the horizon and a lot of the others started drifting behind, I shadowed the lieutenant, for no good reason other than to be able to say that I finished the run with the leaders.

The *premier groupe de sport* was becoming smaller by the day, with some men dropping into the *deuxième groupe*, or like Harasim, becoming decommissioned altogether by injuries. Premiere group included all the Poles but none of the Russians. Though we rolled with the punches, it was at a terrible cost. Knee problems were the most common, and Sadlowski, who ran well, suffered ligament damage to the point where his left knee went purple and yellow. When he brought it to the attention of the instructors, *Sergent* Galeski responded by asking him whether he wanted to do The Farm over again after it healed. Needless to say, he continued on the agonizing runs. Next on the daily program after the runs was *La corde,* rope climbing. Although I considered myself fitter than most, lack of food was wreaking havoc on my body. I soon developed pains and tears in places I never knew about before. My knees were fine, but my elbows and biceps suffered from tendonitis. Activities such as the *corde* resulted in stabs of pain so bad that I had to buckle over to wait for them to go away. *Sergent* Galeski assured me that drinking more water would help. It was *Caporal* Helm who told me exactly what my ailment was, and, as I imagined, that the only cure was not using my arms.

Unlike other armies, the Legion didn't allow us to clamp the rope between our legs. Climbing up a synthetic rope after others' hands had wet it was far from easy. Though I had no problems with pull-ups, my fine hands were too small to grasp *la corde* properly. I knew my body weight had to be countered by my hands' gripping force, multiplied by the nylon rope's friction coefficient, so I tried using a motorbike kick-start technique and found I was often one of the quickest to the top. Taller men had a lot of difficulty, and there were three, Michaud amongst them, who couldn't master *la corde* at all. Getting halfway up and losing your grip usually meant an awkward fall. For those who failed, the humiliation of being jeered at by the *sous-officiers* was punishment enough.

La corde horizontale was less exhausting but more technical. A heavy rope was fastened from a truck to a tree across The Farm's specially deepened pond. We traversed it or got soaked. The technique was simple enough—drape one leg over the rope and use the arms and other leg to inch forward. The most difficult bit was recovering from flipping tits-over-toe. This involved the near impossible task of kicking the hanging leg hard and fast enough to flip upright . . . often only to flop back over the other side. Halfway across, Michaud lost his nerve, and ended up dangling from both hands. After ten minutes' struggling to right himself, *Sergent* Galeski shouted at him in disgust: *"Dégage-toi, mongol!"* and he splashed into the pond.

It always amazed me how just a bit of engineering theory went a long way in soldiering. I knew that in order to stay upright, my center of gravity needed to remain below the rope, so I kept my limbs and head below or as close to it as possible. After I had made it halfway over, *Sergent* Gagné decided to simulate hurricane conditions, and ordered the others to swing the *corde* from side to side. I managed to hang on for several swings but then it got to the point where the forces were just too great. The jeers of the others were suddenly drowned out as I hit the murky water. I couldn't swim properly in *rangers* so I had to dog-paddle to the slimy shore.

One afternoon after *la corde,* we were set to manicuring the entire landscape under a broiling sun, while the lieutenant and *sergent-chef* sat lazily fishing in the pond. I noticed the Russians pointing at the ripe cherry trees surrounding it and foresaw trouble. Sure enough, we were awakened the following morning by the corporals screaming at us to turn out on the parade ground wearing helmet, webbing, and rucksack, "*Imméd!*" Every *engagé volontaire* was punched and slapped on his way out. No recognizing me at first, *Corporal* Helm raised his fist, then simply pushed me aside. The last ones to exit got a kick in the ass in addition to the punches. In the mad rush, I'd grabbed Sadlowski's enormous helmet by mistake, leaving him mine. He ran out wearing a helmet that perched on top of his head like a bellhop's hat, and was punished for my sins.

We were ordered to do *pompes* for a half hour, though after only minutes we were slumping under the weight of our rucksacks. Then *Sergent* Gagné, with Marlboro clamped between his teeth, ordered us up the *piton* at incredible speed, with *Caporal* Helm punching and kicking the slower ones. Even those scheduled for the *infirmerie* had to run up with their bloody, infected feet in shower sandals. Doing the *piton* in *tenu de sport* was grueling enough, but in full-gear and helmet it was hell. After the *pitons,* we were marched sweating and panting over to the pond and shown a cherry tree with a broken branch.

Only once did *Sergent* Gagné ask who had done it; then we were forced up the *piton* again because nobody had confessed. He stood at the bottom ordering us up and down and bawling for someone to say who had broken the branch. When we were ordered to stop and do knuckle *pompes* on the tarmac, I thought the *piton* was finished but the break was just to allow our lungs to recuperate. Crawling up for the seventh time, grabbing at roots, I could simply go no faster and I prayed that the son of a bitch making us suffer would own up.

Mikhailov began suggesting that it was the wind that had broken the cherry tree. Eventually *Sergent* Gagné managed to drag out of him a clear confession. I'd have crucified the bastard, but because he was a *mafia Russe* member, all we could do was grumble. That evening he claimed to have said he was the culprit to spare the platoon more punishment. Such altruism on his part was highly unlikely but then a fishhook was found firmly impaled in the branch. It was just possible that the *sergent-chef* had got his line entangled in the cherry tree and saw that as a perfect excuse to punish us.

It didn't take a genius to work out that the Legion, or at least the instructors, were ripping us off. Every week we were charged for various items that we needed, ranging from pieces of rope at thirteen francs to Adidas running shoes at twice the price we'd have paid in classy Parisian boutiques. Sadlowski pointed out that everything, save for our signatures, was written down in pencil.

The *sergent chef* came up with a clever idea for making himself even more money. Before marches he opened a store counter in the armory, selling items in high demand such as chocolate at ten francs a bar, which we could get in Castelnaudary for five, and Marlboros. The counter was never open, however, when the lieutenant was around.

The first day, I bought twenty bars of chocolate and a pack of Marlboros for Michaud. The rich, smooth chocolate was pure ecstasy. I sat down in a quiet corner away from everyone else to savor it. I wouldn't have traded it for sex with Nadine. The *sergent chef,* however, had underestimated the demand and ran out of supplies before all his customers were satisfied.

Sukhoi, a former sailor in the Ukrainian navy, came across to me. "All the chocolate is sold out and I didn't get any. You know all about that fishes and loaves stuff, *n'est-ce pas*? Give me some of yours." He was known to be dangerous.

"Okay, since you haven't got any at all," I said, holding out a few bars to him.

He grunted gratefully and walked away.

"Hey dumb-ass, you gave him five bars of chocolate?" laughed Calderon. "I already gave that bum four of mine!"

"The bastard! He's not going to make a fool out of me! . . . Hey, Sukhoi!" I shouted. "Why did you tell me you didn't have any chocolate? You lying bastard! If I were like you, I'd take those bars back, but I'm not even going to mess with it. Just don't ever ask me for anything again."

"This is how business is done," he replied.

"Business? So that's how Ukrainians like you do business! Fine, who wants to make a fool out of me again?" I yelled, holding up a bar of chocolate. "I'll show you business . . . Anyone who wants this chocolate pays me twenty francs!"

Kapelski refused but an eternally hungry Hungarian bought it.

"You see," I said to Sukhoi, "I also can conduct business."

Taking that as an insult, he stuck his face into mine. "I see how you fucking Americans work," he said, prodding me in the chest.

"So this is how you pay me back for giving you my chocolate? You ungrateful prick!"

Regardless of how generous I'd been with him, he was determined to teach me a lesson. "If you want twenty francs, you can have it." He raised a fist. "Ten francs for each black eye."

I felt myself trembling with the flow of adrenaline, but something told me, Not this time. Not with this man.

"So it's like that, huh?" I said and slowly walked away.

Sadlowski caught me by the arm. "*Putain,* shit, I told you before. Don't mess with Russians, especially not with Sukhoi. Believe me, you were wise to walk away. Reasoning is way beyond those Russians."

"I suppose you're right."

"My grandfather warned me about them. They invaded our homeland. They were so poor and ignorant that when they captured our lorries, they spread their bread with axle grease. They're not humans. Watch your back; they're grumbling about you, the *Amerikanski*. They all hate you, not just Sukhoi."

"It'll pass."

"I'm not so sure."

"Can you imagine going to war with these scumbags?" I sighed. "*Sergent* Gagné and the Russian bunch would all end up with a bullet in their backs."

"Twenty francs for chocolate!" *Sergent* Gagné snarled that afternoon. "If I ever hear about that sort of thing again, you'll wish I didn't."

It was clear that the Russians had a cozy relationship with him. They were the same kind as he was—hard men who delighted in intimidating anyone weaker than themselves. Like Germany in World War II, I would now be fighting on two fronts—against my peers, and against the instructors.

The following morning we had group warm-ups, grappling with each other and playing English schoolboy piggyback games. It was clear from the way I was groped that we had homosexuals in our midst and I stayed well clear of Abu. We then formed up in two lines facing inwards and clasped hands with out opposite number to throw a man high in the air and catch him again. When my turn came, I taunted the Russians by calling out: "Twenty francs for my ass!"

Sergent Gagné later singled me out during his Famas lesson. "Johnny from Kentucky, I understand that you're familiar with computers, and that you're a professional. Splendid faggot work! I'll show you just how useful your *bureau* skills are when I send your ass to Guyane with nothing but a heavy rucksack."

"*Reçu, Sergent,*" was all I could reply.

"Twenty francs . . ." snickered Raducanu.

"Hey, fuck you!" I said in English.

"What did you say to me?" yelled *Sergent* Gagné. "Did I hear you say, 'Fuck you, *sergent?*' "

I buckled over from a punch in the solar plexus.

A group from the *Amicale des anciens de la Légion,* the Legion Veterans' Society, was scheduled to visit us for an afternoon and stay on for an evening meal. This meant one full week's preparation and I was given the task of clearing the lightly paved, kilometers-long approach road of crabgrass.

Les anciens are treated with reverence. Not only have they completed their five-year contracts, many are survivors of bloody battles such as Bir Hakeim and Dien Bien Phu. They are the respected custodians of Legion tradition. Like alumni at an old American university, they also provide a source of funding and consequently have considerable clout in policy matters. It was a pleasure to eat and chat with them and, since our singing was now up to scratch, we sang. *"Trois . . . quatre!"* preceded our blasting into *"En Afrique."*

The instructors were on their best behavior that night, with *Sergent* Gagné making a superhuman effort to be cordial and behave like a gentleman, painfully sipping rather than gulping his drinks. "Pardon me, *mon lieutenant,*" he said, reaching for the wine. "I haven't replenished your glass."

Knowing that I knew how to behave politely, *Sergent* Galeski sat me next to the more important guests. His phoniness disgusted me when he introduced me as one of his finest *engagés volontaires.*

Most of the *anciens* were kindly, grandfatherly Germans who had no doubt been genuine bastards forty years earlier. With them were a number of elderly Legion widows eager to show us their faded black-and-white photographs.

"I see you have an Arab here," a Spanish *ancien* said to me. "Heed my warning—never trust them! I've served with these people; they're not like us. They'll knife you in the back, if they can. They can be all nice and friendly to your face, but watch their shifty eyes.

And if *they* don't knife you, a *pied noir* will— they lived long enough with the Arabs to become just like them."

Sergent Galeski noticed that I hadn't eaten my undercooked steak. "How do you expect to finish the marches if you don't eat your meat? I know all about you Americans and your *McDo* fast-food culture. Proper food is what you need. Here, eat this." He placed another piece of bleeding cow flesh on my plate and made me eat while he watched. I gagged trying to wash down unchewed chunks with Kronenbourg, while *Sergent* Gagné scowled at me across the table for having the manners to place my napkin over my lap.

As the *anciens* were making their way out, *Sergent* Galeski formed us up single file. We expected to be ordered to clean up the huge *bordel* we'd created. Instead he ordered us to about-face. "*Objectif* Kronenbourg kegs and wine. *Attaque!*" With Captain Yudelevich looking on, we were allowed to let off steam and enjoy a well-deserved drink.

I was opening an umpteenth bottle of Kro' when the lieutenant reminded me it was the Fourth of July. He ordered me to stand *garde-à-vous* and sing "The Star-Spangled Banner." I sang drunkenly and completely forgot the words halfway through. Everyone burst out laughing when I had to hum the rest of it.

During the commotion, a baby rabbit hopped in on the festivities. *Sergent* Galeski's eyes lit up like a child gazing at an unopened Christmas present. He gently gathered the rabbit in his hands and walked out into the night to do God knows what to the unfortunate animal. By the look on his face, we guessed he'd probably devour it alive.

"I want to get back at these godless *cochons*," Calderon said to the *mafia Polonaise* as he backed his buttocks toward the Russians. "I'm tired of their smells; now I'm going to give them one of mine." Within seconds, the space around us was invaded by the rotting stench of whatever he ate. He and Michaud soon collapsed on to chairs vomiting down their shirtfronts while other drunken skinheads started lumbering around together, dancing to the latest Europop on the radio.

At evening *appel,* we noticed that Kapelski and Dupont were absent. Shortly later, they came hobbling out of the unlit washroom, bruised and battered, with *Sergent* Galeski following behind. Kapelski was in running shoes and tank top, without any trousers. When Michaud burst out laughing, Kapelski broke his nose.

The Foreign Legion's basic battle plan has always been to march somewhere, build a fortification, and hold out in it until everyone is killed. We would soon be learning the first part of this strategy. "Your time at The Farm will end with the two-day march tomorrow," *Sergent* Galeski announced and gave us a brief description of the 80 kilometer route over rough terrain. "After the first of four months' basic training, you'll have earned the right to wear the *képi blanc.*"

In preparation for the march, we were given various inoculations—of what and against what, nobody dared ask. One made me particularly ill, giving me chills, hot flashes, and unbearable aches, but I knew that the *infirmerie* was a place to be avoided at all cost. Trainee medics used *engagés volontaires* as guinea pigs and when you got back you had to face the wrath of the corporals who thought you had no business going there in the first place. I was coughing up phlegm but I was determined to go ahead with the march. I wanted to prove that I was as strong as anyone else. The fat slab of semicooked iron-rich liver that we had for evening *soupe* was a sure sign of what was ahead. Though my body was crying out for nutrients, I couldn't keep any of it down and kept spewing it up.

Caporal Helmut secretly handed me a roll of Elastoplast, which did much to protect my feet from blisters. Seeing me carefully cut it into pieces for each toe, Mikhailov insisted that I give him "just a bit." I well knew that with the Russians there was no such thing as "just a bit"—it was all or nothing. In broken French, he told me that I'd have problems with my face if I didn't surrender any. When I returned from evening *corvée,* I had to shoulder him away from my bed where I found him rummaging through my belongings.

Before turning in I felt I had to do something about my *rangers.* Girlfriends tell me I have the hands of a brain surgeon, and my feet are small and soft. The buckle-and-lace-up design of the boots is like something out of a Mad Max film about the Legion's Moroccan campaign in the 1920s. They have no sole padding, so we marched on two centimeters of rock-hard leather—a bit like the Roman legionnaires in their sandals.

"*Action,* you bastards!" was *Sergent* Gagné's wake-up call in the morning.

I could barely stand to pull on my *rangers.* A lot of other men had feet that were already bleeding from previous marches and I wondered how many were going to finish until *Caporal* Helm made it absolutely clear that everyone made the march. "There are no fucking *infirmeries* anywhere the Legion is likely to find itself in combat."

We struggled into our loaded rucksacks and started off by forcing our way through thick undergrowth. I quickly realized that *Sergent* Galeski was pretending to be lost, and we found ourselves climbing up and down ravines and progressing at a snail's pace until we hit ploughed fields. After trudging kilometers to find a gate in a farmer's fence, *Sergent* Galeski ordered us to get over the two-meter-high barbed wire. The others chucked their rucksacks across and scrambled up, ripping trousers and skin. I blew my back trying to save time by keeping my gear on and jumping down.

The next fencing we came to was electric. We held down the lower strands with the weight of our rucksacks and gingerly stepped through. This was easier to manage but gave *Sergent* Galeski the satisfaction of seeing more than one man dancing around with electrocuted testicles. We slogged on, enraging the local farmers who had to watch soldiers with assault rifles shouting at each other in a babble of foreign languages and making a *bordel* of their fields. Dogs howl when the Legion marches.

"As we go marching and the band begins to play," we sang, passing through a medieval village,

"You can hear the people shout: Lock the doors and shut the shop, the Legion's here today!"

". . . and hide your daughters!" Sadlowski roared.

Whenever *Sergent* Galeski stopped to orientate himself, we bent over, palms on knees to alleviate the pain in our lower backs. The straps of my rucksack were biting into the muscles at the base of my neck and the incessant pounding seemed to be dislocating my shoulders. My back had long since gone numb from the constant friction, likewise my toes. Our feet were swelling and one body area after another began to fail. My knees gave out as the lubricating cartilage slowly ground away. Moving across country in that state was like running an automobile without oil until the engine grinds to a halt.

Within hours, the soles of my feet were blistered and raw. We traversed creeks by stepping carefully from rock to rock. Tempting though it was to give our feet a cooling soak, we knew by now that marching in wet *rangers* only exacerbates the agony.

The breaks were few and we relished each precious second. Whenever *Sergent* Galeski barked: *"Dix minutes de pause!"* we threw ourselves on the ground. Then inevitably would come the dreaded shout: "Rucksacks on your backs, *debout*!" Getting up again on raw feet that had ten minutes to swell was even worse than marching. Mercifully after a few kilometers they became numb again. I fantasized about throwing myself into a roadside ditch and watching the others carry on without me. The only thing that kept me moving was the punishment that would be waiting should I drop out. At one point I began hallucinating and blubbering.

"Fatigué?"

"Never, *Caporal*."

As a punishment for not picking up French fast enough, Sukhoi was ordered to march alone with the lieutenant, carrying the infamous 10-kilogram PP13, an archaic Algerian-era field radio, in addition to his already heavy rucksack and Famas. After the first hour rivers of sweat were rolling down his cheeks and his face was gray.

"*Engagé volontaire* Sukhoi, *à vos ordres mon lieutenant*—permission to hand over PP13?"

"*Non, mon enfant!*"

"Permission to change . . ."

"*Non!*"

"*Mon lieutenant . . .*"

"*Non!*"

With rests every three hours, the forced march lasted till dusk. Just when every man was approaching *cafard, Sergent* Galeski finally called out: "Bivouac!"

The *sergent-chef* was on hand with a truckoad of chocolate and Marlboros. Given the amount of energy we used up on marches, I could always eat enough chocolate to make any civilian sick. I had no problem finishing off seven bars although I knew that high doses of cacao could wreak havoc in my bowels.

After the chocolate, we tore into cold *Rations de Combat Individuelle Réchauffable* (RCIRs—field rations, heatable). Though the tin of pâté always included was good marching fuel, I gave it to Sadlowski. "I don't eat ground lips and assholes."

Sergent Gagné couldn't resist butting in. "Kentucky, I've been picking up on your language. Fuck you, dickhead! How's that?"

I had to laugh, hearing a grown man showing off the naughty words he knew.

We bivouacked in thick forest beside a reservoir where a party of tourists had stopped for a breather. Like a father with his sons, the *sergent-chef* took us up the embankment for a swim. The cold water almost boiled when I immersed my smoldering feet. The *chef* was the first to strip down to his underpants. The tourists were amused to see half-naked, tattoo-covered skinheads tiptoeing into the water. Luckily it didn't unstick the Elastoplast on my toes. I wanted that for the following day. The grueling march was bad enough for a conditioned man like myself but Kapelski especially must have been suffering agony. Having spent much of The Farm in the hospital, he had been thrown straight into the *Képi Blanc* march just after he got out.

We set off again at dawn and the occasional rest periods became progressively shorter, scarcely long enough to chew a piece of candy. When we passed through villages, we often stopped for a visit to the traditional well in the local graveyard where we could refill our *bidons*.

I thought back to the poor devils before me, on forced marches across the burning wastelands of the Sahara. The spirit of Alan Seeger pushed me on. The second day was even more hellish than the first. I started laughing and mumbling to myself again. We were marching in a single file, with me at the end like a wagon in a freight train, blindly following in the footsteps of the man ahead. I kept falling behind and was subjected to a constant stream of Slavic, Germanic, and Latino curses as I trotted to catch up. I panicked when my rucksack straps loosened, resulting in a lopsided load. There was no time for kit adjustments while we were marching, so for hours I would have to suffer the pain of my spine gradually being twisted out of alignment. As we were climbing up a steep gully and I was beginning to feel blood trickling into my *rangers,* Kapelski, who had been limping since the start passed out. His blissful lapse into unconsciousness was short-lived.

"Lift that fucking cadaver!"

The lieutenant glanced back approvingly at *Sergent* Galeski's howl. *Marche ou crève,* March or Die. We jumped to it and got Kapelski going again. The Russians were surprisingly ready to carry his rifle and heavy pack, and took turns at pushing. It was tough for Kapelski but when he finished the march he wouldn't have wanted it any other way.

The last stretch was a precipitous and seemingly endless ascent. I cursed the day I was born but, at the same time, I knew that the next day I would, for the first glorious time, be wearing the Legion's *képi blanc*. After climbing hundreds of meters up the mist-clad mountainside, we broke through the cloud to see the awe-inspiring ruins of the *Château de Quéribus,* "Vertigo Fortress," perched on a crag above us, its tower pointing stubbornly like a stone finger at the sky.

"Fix your eyes on the horizon, all of you," *Sergent* Galeski ordered. "Now blink! Keep your eyes closed and remember what you saw. That's one more shot for your vacation scrapbook—the march is over."

I've never forgotten that image. We sat on rocks, shivering in the mountain air, to rip open our *RCIR*s. My first reaction was to sob from primal fatigue. If I ever return to my homeland alive and reenter corporate America, I thought, I'll set up my own Farm to provide confidence-building weekends for high-flying professionals who think there is nothing in life they can't accomplish.

The next afternoon, tables were set up with lavish quantities of food, beer, and ruby-red. I took a can of Kronenbourg over to Michaud, who'd been barbecuing an entire lamb all morning. "All that for us?" I asked.

"No, for the instructors."

"Where in the hell did it come from anyway?"

"Remember the herd of sheep we ran out a month ago?"

The celebration was a very formal affair with printed menus, reserved seats, stemware, and a parchment composite that included the name and nationality of every *engagé volontaire*. We were all ragged and sickly looking. I'd gone so thin that from my scrawny neck up I looked like a PEZ dispenser. My hands were cracked and raw, my feet leathery hard and infected by fungus. The muscle I'd worked so hard to build as a civilian had long since melted away, cannibalized for energy. But even though we looked as if we had just been released from the gulags, we were machines capable of superhuman feats. The Farm had taught me to run like a hare, march like a mule, and climb rope like a squirrel on crack. No longer was I a mere *engagé volontaire,* I was about to become a legionnaire!

When the time came for the oath of loyalty, we stood *au garde-à-vous* holding our *képis blancs* down the side of our right legs by the peak. "*Nous promettons de servir la patrie, la France, avec honneur et fidélité,*" we roared in one voice. The company captain gave the order: "Don *képis!*" Our hands swept up together to our heads and snapped back down to our sides. Then the lieutenant and captain went about congratulating us individually and decorating us with the badge of the 4e RE and our company pin.

For me, this was the finest hour in my life. The following day we left The Farm to return to Castelnaudary. Those of us at the back of the truck leaned out to give Bobby a wave of *adieu*, which he acknowledged by raising his leg.

5.

CASTELNAUDARY

The rose-tinted Beau Geste vision overrides the truth that life in the Army of Strangers is no picnic.

John Parker

Castelnaudary, "world capital of cassoulet," is a small town, 100 km north of the Spanish border, between Toulouse, headquarters for the European Space Agency and Carcassonne, home to the 3ᵉ *Régiment de Parachutistes d'Infanterie de Marine*. Located in the lovely Lauragais region, *le pays de Cocagne,* with rolling foothills and a pleasant climate, it is the regimental depot for the Legion's training regiment, the 4ᵉ *Régiment Étranger*. Mountain warfare exercises are carried out in the nearby Pyrenees; amphibious training in the Mediterranean; and commando training from the fortress town of Mont-Louis at an altitude of 1600m on the high plain of *Cerdagne* in the Roussillon.

Back under a solid roof again in the 4ᵉ *RE's Quartier Capitaine Danjou,* I was delighted to have a real bed to sleep in. Every morning we stripped our beds and draped them with a red cover. Our blankets were placed at the foot of the bed, folded into a square, with our sheets tightly rolled into sticks and laid in a saltire cross on top. When *Caporal* Qandil made his first bed inspection, he gave me a rabbit punch for having my blanket folds the wrong way round.

Though better fed than at The Farm, we still didn't get enough to eat. Permanent hunger was something we eventually became accustomed to. In the *ordinaire* the *caporaux* were served first, while the rest of us queued behind. As soon as they'd finished eating, the *section* had to stand, trays in hand, and follow them out. Often the last men to collect their food were left with little more than a minute to gobble something down.

As new legionnaires, we were to be paid five thousand francs a month to carry a rifle and kill on demand—not much but enough to bring in a flood of Eastern Europeans. Pay Parade in the Legion is a ritual that serves to reinforce the role of the officers as father figures. The payroll officer lays out one month's salary on the table in front of him. The legionnaire about to be paid stands *au garde-à-vous* and formally presents himself, with name, rank, and service history, scoops the cash into his *képi,* salutes palm front, and about-faces. As we waited the first time to be paid, we were all excited about what we were going to be doing with our thousands in a town like Castel, until we realized how much was to be deducted for our "new" equipment.

I quickly understood why the Legion was in such a hurry after one month at The Farm to have us wear the *képi blanc*—now we could be assigned work restricted to legionnaires. The day after our return to Castelnaudary, the platoon was split into groups for Guard, EIT, *Equipe d'Intervention à Temps*—Rapid Reaction Squad, officers' mess, and *ordinaire* duties, or simply *TIG, Travaux d'Intérêt Général*—sweeping, cleaning, polishing.

Guard duty is performed in *tenue de parade*—a smart parade uniform with gray trousers and a light green shirt. The epaulettes are dark green with red fronds—the official colors of the Legion since 1868. The tightly wrapped, blue wool cummerbund, 4.20m long and 40cm wide, was originally worn under the shirt as a protection against intestinal troubles during overseas postings. Worn over it is the combat belt with bayonet frog. The trousers are bloused over the *rangers* with elastic bands, so that they are perfectly taut up to the waist. *Tenue de parade* varies with the seasons—open-neck shirt with sleeves folded above the elbows in summer, full-length sleeves and green tie in autumn, fitted jacket in winter. The crowning glory of a legionnaire's uniform is, of course, the *képi blanc*. This developed from the khaki *képi* cover with neck flap worn by Legion regiments during the Morocco campaign, which became white as a result of repeated washings and bleaching by the sun.

Pressing *tenue de parade* shirts is a complex task, requiring over an hour's work and another's help. A 2.5 by 3.5cm matchbox is used as a guide for the fifteen regulation creases—two across and three down the back, two in parallel down the outside of each sleeve, and three above the two breast pockets. The horizontal and vertical creases on the back must make a precise T-intersection. Each crease had to be ironed in with scientific precision in order to satisfy *Sergent* Gagné, who verified them with a ruler.

The guard duty itself was a nightmare, with *Sergent* Gagné terrorizing us every fifteen minutes with his inspections. Every article had to be flawless—immaculately bleached *képi*, shirt and trousers without the faintest hairline rumple. The morning began at 04.30, when the six legionnaires on duty scrambled about carefully fitting themselves into *tenue de parade* and giving their *rangers* one last polish. One morning when the guard was called out, I was still being assisted into my cummerbund. I ran out into the corridor five seconds late and *Sergent* Gagné punched me in the eye, twice.

The changing of the guard took place at 06.00. Both guards present arms and the duty NCOs greet each other with a vigorous handshake. After the old guard marches away to the armory, the new guard takes up position. Guard-duty is a twenty-four-hour ordeal. Two legionnaires at a time rotate onto every third two-hour shift. One legionnaire is posted at the gate, while the other stands at ease, Famas with fixed bayonet strapped across his chest. Both must come to the *garde-à-vous* for passing NCOs and present arms to officers. Otherwise, we stood motionless under the broiling sun, with the weight of the Famas hanging from our necks. We tried to ease our aching feet by invisibly shifting our bodyweight every five minutes from one foot to the other. There was nothing to do during those

endless hours except count away the minutes. When we were relieved, we could hardly bend our knees.

Because he had the power to do whatever he liked with us, *Sergent* Gagné ordered me to stand unmoving in the sun for an extra
two-hour shift while he joked with the corporals and taunted me.
Sadlowski was the only other legionnaire who seemed to share my
feelings of injustice. Looking out at me from inside the guardhouse,
he shook his head in disgust. Later he took me aside and told me that
my sacrifices for the Legion were just not worth it. "Get out while
you can."

To make guard duty even more hellish, *Sergent* Gagné forbade us
to sit down, so that we remained on our feet for over twelve hours
straight. I was eating, standing up, carefully making sure I did not
drop anything on my *tenue,* when *Sergent* Gagné saw me pour
ketchup on my *pomme frites* and pop a couple of them into my
mouth with my fingers. He called me over to his table.

"In France, we eat with a knife and a fork, unlike the niggers in
Afrique et l'Amérique who eat with their fingers and drown everything in tomato sauce. Put your tray down here and watch me
closely, Johnny. I'll demonstrate to you how cutlery is used." He
took up my knife and fork and shoveled everything I hadn't eaten
into his mouth.

Next morning after we were relieved, *Sergent* Gagné began
shouting because we had taken the liberty of going back to our
chambres without his explicit authorization. He called us out to
stand in line at attention in the corridor. When he raised his open
palm at me, I held my breath in anticipation of the blow. His hand
came crashing into my chest, completely winding me. "Stop quiver-
ing!" he yelled. "You're supposed to be standing *au garde-à-vous*.
Move again and I'll break your ribs." Sadlowski later explained to
me the martial arts technique of evacuating all air from the lungs just
before impact.

That night after lights-out, a group of Hungarians who'd been
suffering the consequences of *Caporal* Helmut's hatred for Eastern
Europeans woke me up with the noise they were making. I assumed

they were drunk and went back to sleep. An hour later, the corporals screamed at us to get out of bed for roll-call. Nobody knew what was going on until the morning, when we discovered that the Hungarians had deserted. Two days later an American from a neighboring platoon, a former Ranger, also deserted. He'd blown his belly button with an umbilical hernia but the *infirmerie* did nothing more than wrap sport tape around his waist. "If I stay here," he'd said, "the Legion will kill me."

Platoon commanders were held responsible for anybody who didn't finish basic training; consequently, men were often retained long after they were of no use to the Legion—a way of fudging the statistics and keeping reputations intact. Harasim, who was still walking with crutches, waited months for discharge papers that never came. The platoon was convinced that he was faking his injuries. When he finally made a run for it, he left his crutches neatly crossed on his bed.

Zing was a tiny Chinese *engagé volontaire* who was also held in Legion limbo well after being found *inapte au service*. His French was very rudimentary. When he had been spoken to by the lieutenant, he made a valiant effort to present himself by shouting out a high-pitched approximation of what he thought the *présentation* sounded like. The *caporal chef* wasn't amused and slapped him across the ear so hard that he ruptured Zhang's eardrum.

EIT duty was also a twenty-four-hour affair but unlike ceremonial guard duty, it was deadly serious. After only one month's training at The Farm, we were ordered to provide security protection with loaded rifles. Patrols, led by a sergeant, were posted at a dozen strategic points around the barracks. After dark, using a night scope, we kept watch for deserters or intruders. Calderon won praise for bringing down an Arab drug dealer with a commando tackle and shoving him handcuffed into the P4. The Hungarians got away undetected because they'd been tipped off about EIT patrol movements.

During EIT Duty *Sergent* Gagné would sit paging through cheap French porno magazines in the guard room, while those of us not already out on patrol were sent around the barracks to do various TIG duties, all in the name of keeping us busy. One of the things that pissed me off about the Legion was its ability to conjure up work to be done whenever it was known that there were men around to do it.

Mess duty was demanding but less strenuous. The officers and senior NCOs ate in their own mess halls, some distance away from the barracks, in a luxurious nineteenth-century château decorated with souvenirs of every major Foreign Legion campaign, including the baggy black Arab trousers and sandals worn in Morocco. The officers' mess was comparable to any five-star Parisian restaurant, with civilian chefs and place settings including three sets of cutlery and two wineglasses. The Senior NCOs dined in only slightly less elegant surroundings but had to make do with drinking the Legion's *pinard rouge*.

Outside the château, there was an area fenced off as an open-air zoo where the officers could watch exotic peacocks and ostriches while they enjoyed their meals. One day, a Pole on punishment TIG was collecting bird droppings with his *pelle US* and a small bucket when one of the ostriches started pestering him. He kept pushing it away but it wouldn't stop trying to peck at him. Finally his temper gave way and he threw a right cross à la Mike Tyson, striking the ostrich above its eye. The great bird stood for a moment wagging its head from side to side, then suddenly collapsed to the ground. The Pole desperately tried to revive it and eventually it staggered back to its feet. Days later, it died from causes unknown.

During mess duty one day, I was ironing a particularly fine cotton tablecloth worth several thousand francs for an officer's wedding that weekend. One of the Russians got to speaking with me and by the time I'd finished listening to his bullshit, I found I'd made a large burn mark on the white cloth. Minutes later, the *caporal chef* came around to check up on my work.

"*Ces conards de civils*, the dry cleaners didn't get this stain out," I said.

"Well, go get a new one." The *caporal chef* was a personable

Serb who spoke very informally without pulling rank. We started chatting and he told me that he was about to retire after fifteen years of service.

"Fifteen years in the Legion?" I exclaimed. "After fifteen days, *j'en avais déjà plein les couilles*." (My balls were already bursting. I was completely pissed off.)

"Yes, but the Legion's changed a lot since I came in. Those socialists were always doing whatever they could to bring it in line with the *Armée de Terre*. The French have gotten too diplomatic for the Legion's good; they don't have real wars any more. So, soon I'll be off to South Africa to work as a hired gun for Executive Outcomes, a private company that rents out people like me to the highest bidder."

"I'm beginning to feel I'm wasting my time here. The à la legionnaire way of doing things that they keep drumming into our heads is just washing dishes without soap, scrubbing latrines with no disinfectant, and sweeping floors without a broom. I'm beginning to understand why thinking is strictly forbidden."

"Many can't hack it, even if they don't desert. Those who do manage to switch on usually end up on the streets after a decade of service, alcoholic shells of what they used to be. A lot of the *sans domicile fixe* (SDFs, homeless) you see in Avignon used to wear this *tenue*."

He went on to tell me of his adventure vacation riding with America's Hell's Angels, in a leather jacket emblazoned with the words FOREIGN LEGION on the back. "They're a good bunch. I only had to put one man in his place. When he starting running down the Legion as a bunch of pansies, I broke his leg with a baseball bat. Never had trouble with any of them after that."

Now that we were legionnaires, we spent much more time on the shooting ranges. The marching, running, and climbing we learned at The Farm are important to any elite force but marksmanship is essential. Even though I'm of the same nationality as John Wayne and from a homeland where teenagers spray classrooms with automatic firearms on a monthly basis, I was the only legionnaire who'd never fired anything more serious than an air gun. This, however, was an advantage because the Legion teaches everything from scratch and I had no preconceived notions about how to do it. The basic instructions were simple enough—loosen combat belt, lie flat, cock right knee along the ground for better stability, aim, insert magazine, aim once again, steady sights, fire.

There are however additional factors to be considered—breathing, relaxing, aiming, and trigger pressure. Many held their breath during automatic fire or three-shot bursts, so starving their brains of oxygen. To clear my mind and vision, I inhaled and exhaled at regular ten-second intervals. The optimal time to fire was at the last moment when the Famas steadied itself. I even began monitoring my pulse beat, which had a minimal effect on my aim but could produce nearly a hand's breadth difference at two hundred meters.

Relaxing into a natural point of aim meant adopting a position where the rifle is supported by the bones of the arms, not the muscles. To check that my Famas was acting as a natural extension of my body, I took aim with the butt firmly against my shoulder, relaxed, closed my eyes, then opened them again to see whether the sights were still on target. In the lying position with right knee bent, we adjusted the foot farthest from the target to modify the natural point of aim, the closer one operating as the pivot point. By moving the right foot forward or back, the muzzle nudged left or right accordingly. Vertical aim was controlled by lung pressure.

Aiming involved more than aligning the rear sight with the front and the target because the eye cannot focus on two objects at different distances at the same time. I began aiming by leaning my cheek against the butt to make sure the distance from my rear sight and eye remained the same. The front sight pin was then brought up and centered in the rear sight aperture. I went as far as imagining my own crosshairs. Closing my left eye put a strain on the right, causing the eyelid to twitch, so I fired with both eyes open.

Since the target consisted of black concentric circles, we couldn't make out the bull's-eye. Focusing on the target resulted in blurred sights, whereas focusing on the sights resulted in a blurred target. Because of this, our Famas sights were adjusted for us to hit the target center with our sights just on the six o'clock position. This gave us a defined aiming point, allowing us to focus on the front sight rather than the target itself.

It was important to apply trigger pressure slowly and steadily so as not to disturb the delicate aim. The only part of finger that touched the trigger was the middle of the top joint. Using any other part made it impossible to pull the trigger straight to the rear and canted it to one side, taking the front sight with it. Though the finger was laid lightly on the trigger, the rest of the hand clasped the pistol grip like a firm handshake—gripping too strongly made the Famas shake; too loosely prevented proper control.

If the sights drifted off target, I stopped squeezing but maintained pressure until they returned to my point of aim. If anything else went wrong, the trigger was instantly released. The instructors often placed a coin atop the muzzle to test the stability of our aim. In the split second between firing and hitting the target, I guided my round to its destination down an imaginary wire.

As well as firing prone, we were also trained in the standing and kneeling positions. In addition the Legion taught us the firing-over-the-sights technique, which was developed in bush warfare. In guerrilla style, the legionnaire crouches holding the Famas butt in his abdomen. It can be very rapid and highly accurate up to twenty-five meters but technically it is difficult to master because the aiming lines runs not from the eye, but from the nuts, like in precision urinating.

It amazed me how our marksmanship improved with the instructors' shouting and punching. Marching and running were one thing but I couldn't understand how a skill as fine as marksmanship would get any better with the threat of violence—somehow it did. Fear can motivate a man to do incredible things.

Though they hated to admit it, the instructors had to accept that their *homme d'affaires Américain* had an eye for firing true. At first they teased and harassed me for having beginner's luck but successive accurate scores made them think again. *Sergent* Galeski praised the Kalashnikov AK-47 marksman Mikhailov for managing to land all his rounds in a Marlboro pack. The following range morning, I managed not only to do the same, but actually put two out of three rounds directly through the same hole. *Sergent* Galeski said nothing and cleared the electronic screen.

Though everyone enjoyed the mornings on the range, we dreaded the cleaning that inevitably followed. When *Sergent* Gagné found carbon in places where no one else would dream of looking, he didn't simply use his fist. Often he brought down the forearm-length steel legs of the Famas on a legionnaire's head. Sometimes he used the entire stripped-down body. Everyone hoarded bits and pieces to help with the cleaning, such as Zippo lighter fluid for carbon deposits. When we were served shish kebabs at *la soupe du soir,* I pocketed the metal skewer for getting at the hard-to-reach areas of my Famas.

We were given two hours to clean our rifles with drunken sergeants wandering in and out as they pleased. The first men to finish were rewarded by being given the instructors' rifles to clean as well. When we had finished, the whole of the rest of the day was devoted to washing and ironing our *tenues.* If I'd just been left alone to get on with it, I could have done it all in half the time.

All this was part of the unending *sketch* (bullshit), which demonstrated how incredibly inefficient the Legion is at accomplishing the most menial tasks. My greatest mistake before joining had been to work in private industry and see how much could be achieved when there was something more to be made than right-angled shirt creases—money. Serving in the Legion was like going back to childhood. Orders were to be obeyed without question. It was an existence that brought on cravings for simple things like chocolate or time for a leisurely shit. Whenever I could after *la soupe de midi,* I'd stand at the window of my room and watch the sleek Toulouse-bound TGV high-speed train pass by, carrying with it memories of my past freedom and the modern outside world.

*   *   *

As a reward for our efforts at The Farm, we were given an afternoon's leave in Castelnaudary. We were warned that anyone whose *tenue de sortie* did not pass inspection after that day's *soupe de midi* would be confined to barracks, but there wasn't a single man who complained about wasting most of the morning ironing his shirt.

The first thing I did in Castel was to buy myself a slab of chocolate. Given more time, I'd have enjoyed strolling around the medieval town but, while the others went off drinking and whoring, I headed straight for the nearest Internet café. I checked my Hotmail account, hoping that at least somebody out there wanted to communicate with me. Several headhunters were offering small fortunes and cushy careers. I replied that I'd already found a position within the French Ministry of Defence.

Sitting in a comfortable chair in front of a computer screen, it was as if I was awakening from a bad dream. I got into the Legion's public forum website, which I had used for research before joining and announced to everyone that I had made it. Leaving that public message under my real name, I later learned, was a mistake.

Then I decided to make a telephone call to my parents and imagined Father telling me how proud he was that I had grown up into a real man. I thought Mother would be happy that the Legion was finally teaching her *enfant terrible* the virtues of hard physical work. . . . But it wasn't like that.

"Well, everything here is much the same as when you left," Father said. "Mail came in for you, and DaimlerChrysler called about a job offer in Detroit that sounds pretty good. How about it?"

"But I'm over here in the Legion now."

"When are you finished?"

"In five years, didn't you read my letter?"

"Several guys on the shop floor here heard about the Legion. They said it was for criminals, or something."

"Do you think I'm crazy coming here?"

"No, but nobody can understand why you quit a good job to join the army."

"But it's not just an army, it's like a family. We've got a few bad apples in the mix, but these are my brothers. I'd give my life for them. For the first time, I feel like I belong. This is the first day we've been allowed out in our dress uniforms. We look great in our bleached *képis* . . . Life is hard here, very hard, but the honor of having served in the Legion will last a lifetime."

My phone card was about to expire.

"Dad, I'll be back home in a few years with a chest full of medals!"

Later, Calderon and I were sitting at a *bistrot* table concentrating on replacing the liters of sweat we'd lost at The Farm with an equal amount of Kronenbourg. It was a pleasure to be away from the corporals for once, with our feet stretched out and a glass in our hands, but it didn't last long. A drunken Raducanu reared his ugly head to piss on my parade.

"*Achtung,*" he said, "I didn't forget that I got to teach you a lesson."

"You really are a bastard," I said. "I offered you my hand at The Farm, as a man and gentleman. If you were still pissed off with me, we could have settled this back then."

He kicked over a chair and came at me with his fists clenched but the townsfolk of Castel were spared a public slugfest by the arrival of *Sergent* Gagné screeching to a halt outside in a beat-up, soot-belching excuse for a truck.

"Why, our chauffeur just arrived," I said and helped the others carry out our legless brethren.

"One of these days I'm going to have to take on Raducanu," I said to Calderon en route home.

"Stay calm, Sanchez. That kind of trouble now will only damage your passing-out ranking. Without a good placement, you'll have little choice about which regiment you get to be posted to; you could end up in the 2^e *REG*. Relax and play it cool."

"Maybe you're right, but he's wearing out my patience," I said, just as a half-eaten apple hit Calderon on the shoulder.

He leapt to his feet holding on to a roof strut with one hand and holding the apple in the other. "Who threw this?" he shouted furiously.

Raducanu was laughing. Calderon shot the apple at him, hitting him full in the face. Raducanu was silenced but Calderon wasn't.

After lights-out, he pounced on him and inflicted considerable damage in a matter of seconds. When I stepped outside in my underpants, I saw Raducanu with a mouth full of blood. *Sergent* Galeski arrived and put an end to the drunken madness by sending the pair back to bed.

Raducanu sought his revenge later that night. Calderon had handily kept him at bay with his fists in the preceding scuffle, so Raducanu came at him swinging a metal stool. When the others wrestled it away, he broke a broomstick over Calderon's head. Hearing the commotion, the EIT stormed in with loaded rifles and Calderon was rushed to the *infirmerie*. The EIT reported the incident and both men were given seven days in the lock-up, with Rex, the regiment's three-legged dog, who enjoyed biting new inmates.

After the fight, Michaud and the Russians settled back to smoking the hashish they'd bought in town. One of the Poles got up to piss and while he was relieving himself, he heard a grunting noise behind him and turned to see Dupont, completely nude, grasping his erect penis with one hand and fondling his nuts with the other. Laughing like a madman, Dupont bolted off down the corridor. Once his alcohol settled, he tried to crawl into bed with a legionnaire from a different platoon.

As an additional bonus for our hard work at The Farm, the instructors announced a weeklong vacation in the Pyrenees mountain village of Formiguères. We boarded our 1960s trucks, still painted in Desert Storm camouflage, and drove off toward Spain, hoping we were going to be able to catch up on lost sleep. As we approached the snow-capped mountains, the temperature fell to near freezing point. We were still wearing summer *tenue de combat* so the lieutenant allowed us to roll down our sleeves. We drew up at the chalet run by the 4^e RE for mountain warfare training and as a rest and recreation center for officers, senior NCOs, and their families. We were confined to a small corridor and strictly forbidden to look at, much less speak to, the daughters of the Legion brass.

It soon became clear that things were not going to be very different here. On the first day I was put on *ordinaire* duty, not that I cared—it was a blessing to get away from the instructors' shouting and there was a CD player with the Texas single "Black-Eyed Boy." I did regret missing that morning's run on the mountain though, not because I fancied the pain, but because I didn't like the idea of the others getting fitter without me.

Mikhailov was on the same duty. He knew I disliked the Russians but he acted in a friendly sort of way, like a lion sniffing curiously at an injured park ranger. The Poles had told me that he was wanted by the police. An extortion attempt had gone wrong and after a high-speed chase, he'd made Swiss cheese of a carload of mafia but shot down a female passerby in the process.

"You don't belong here," he said as we were setting the tables. "There isn't a single man who wouldn't desert today if he had an American passport."

"Yeah, but I'm different. I volunteered for the Legion because I wanted to make a difference in this world. Living in America, I came to the conclusion that a life rich with experience is more valuable than a life rich with riches. It's just too bad that it's taken me so long to realize that the Legion takes away a man's soul, his sanity, his blood and sweat, and gives him nothing in return."

"Well, well, well," he said, not knowing what to say at hearing me speak in such a thoughtful manner. He was a battle-hardened Spetsnaz—a small, quiet man with furtive eyes, who moved swiftly and silently. Pricked into one of his biceps was a panther with a cane and top hat. Sadlowski had warned me that if I ever fought him, I'd have to kill him. Men like him are never crossed twice.

Others told me he'd had treatment in an army psychiatric hospital after his time in Chechnya. The Muslims had horrific ways of dealing with Christian infidels. In one firefight, a comrade was separated from the platoon and captured. The Chechens had drugged him and skinned him alive. When the Russians found him next day, he was hanging from meat hooks with his skin around his neck and still breathing.

*   *   *

Le sport was becoming more difficult for me at Formiguères. I found I was struggling to keep up with the *premier groupe* and I realized that I was less acclimated to the altitude than the others. The most excruciating march of my time in the Legion was getting to the summit of *Pic Peric*. What we were told was to be a recreational march turned out to be a fully loaded two-day expedition up the 2,810 meter mountain.

We started off at the lower station of a ski lift following the *pistes* in a long zigzag ascent. After two sweltering hours, I looked down the precipice and was astonished to see that we'd climbed a mere couple of hundred meters or so. Tourists and families were strolling about in shorts and sandals, snapping photographs of the sweaty, cursing legionnaires toiling up the mountainside. Once we got above the tree line, we paused for a midday snack. I gulped down nourishment in the desperate hope that my body would recover enough strength for the remaining march. We were supposed to make it to the top and back down before nightfall, when the sheer descent would become even more dangerous.

Before long, I found myself straggling ten meters behind the others and panting throughout every five-minute break. Hoisting my body and rucksack up in half meter steps felt more demanding than performing heavy squats in the *salle de musculation*. Altitude training was just too much for my body to adjust to. Mikhailov slowed and pushed me up as much as he could. Luckily, the *chef* who'd decided that the march would be a good workout, was having similar problems. *Sergent* Galeski ordered the workhorse *Caporal* Qandil to stay behind with us. An hour from the summit, we were using hands, knees, and elbows to lever ourselves up the rockface.

My thighs began to knot. Cramps in the calves can be painful but having both quadriceps simultaneously contract is torture. I had to pummel them with my fists to alleviate the agony. *Caporal* Qandil took away my rucksack, draped it over his own, and scrambled ahead of me like Spiderman up the rocks to the summit. I was becoming severely light-headed and I'd have split my head on the rocks below if the *chef* behind hadn't caught me. When at last I made it to the top, I was greeted by ironic cheers.

After a break to eat, we were ordered to begin the descent before the icy winds picked up. *Sergent* Galeski was annoyed by my performance. Once the lieutenant was out of sight, he hurled a large stone at me, aiming for the knee. I managed to block it with one of my *rangers* but even so I was left with a painful bruise that further impaired my marching. *Sergent* Galeski led us down by one of his "shortcuts"—a sheep slope awash with treacherous scree. We descended in single file and those above were constantly showering us with sudden rushes of dislodged debris, which threatened to sweep us off the mountainside. Michaud saved his life by lying perfectly flat when he found himself beginning to slide away uncontrollably. The Legion had promised that I would live dangerously, and it was certainly keeping its word.

We bivouacked on the lower slopes and enjoyed the last rays of the mountain sun. After eating we were told to wash up and fill our canteens in an icy stream. The instructors pitched tents for themselves but *Sergent* Galeski ordered us to sleep without cover in our cotton sleeping bags wearing nothing more than underpants and T-shirts. That night, I experienced the dramatic difference between day and night temperatures in the mountains. When I was awakened for sentry-duty at midnight, my sleeping bag was covered with frost. Suddenly a freezing gale swept down from the peaks and flattened *Sergent* Gagné's tent. I was ordered to scrabble about in the howling wind and pitch darkness, to search with frozen fingers for rope and wooden stakes to put it up again.

When I was relieved and could get back for some sleep, I kept on my *tenue de combat* and dug around in my rucksack for my rubber poncho, which I wrapped myself in before struggling into my sleeping bag. As the sun rose, I crawled out again and joined the others to shave painfully with the frigid water of the stream. I wanted to get moving as soon as possible but as we marched I felt like I was suffering from a splitting hangover. Michaud didn't look too good either. "They've reduced me to this," he muttered. "All I can think of is somewhere warm to sleep, and something to fill my stomach."

In a scuffle that morning, Sukhoi slammed the barrel of his Famas into the side of Sadlowski's face, leaving an ugly 5.56mm weal on his cheek. He was lucky that the barrel didn't go straight through and knock out his teeth. All that *Sergent* Gagné did about it was to place a weighty rock in Sukhoi's rucksack. When we finally got back down to the chalet we had to clean our rifles. *Sergent* Galeski punched me because I didn't look awake enough.

Next day, the *chef* decided to organize his own tourist excursion in the mountains and asked for volunteers. Noticing that I didn't raise my hand, *Sergent* Galeski volunteered me. Anger and resentment kept me awake much of the night. The *chef's* scenic route took us around crystal-clear lakes and across treeless meadows. I chatted with Szabo, who was systematically victimized for being the only Hungarian in the platoon not to have deserted. He was a quiet, thoughtful type I'd never really before taken time to get to know.

"I understand how you feel," he said as we were lying on a hillside during a break. "The *sergents* hate you for some reason."

"Well there's not much point in worrying about it now," I said. "Basic training should be over soon."

"Here, you've no bread left; have some of my baguette."

Szabo was everything I'd thought a true legionnaire was supposed to be—respectful, hard-working, loyal, never saying No to his *camarades*. Later, we had long talks about our plans after the Legion and the lovers we'd left behind.

Next morning riding back to Castelnaudary in open trucks, Sadlowski admitted to me that joining the Legion had been a mistake. He'd been given an old photograph of the venerably bearded *Général* Rollet, *Le Père de la Légion*, which he always kept above his bed. One night in Formiguères he tore it up in a fit of rage. When we had asked him what had happened to it, he told us that the Legion's father himself had deserted.

"Look, I know the Legion can be hell," I said to him, "but let's not forget why we came—it's tough but it's easy. We eat when they tell us to; we shit when they tell us; we sleep when they tell us; we wake when they tell us. Here, we don't have telephones ringing off the hook, laptops, messages to be dealt with, or closed-door performance appraisals with the boss. I no longer exist. No one in the world knows where to find Jamie Salazar. That, *mon camarade*, gives us a different view on things and a fresh start to our lives."

When we got back to Castel, we busied ourselves preparing for combat exercises in the surrounding hills. We marched smartly out of *Le Quartier Capitaine Danjou* and took the entire afternoon to reach our destination. With Famas rifles strapped across our chests, and the *fanion du régiment* going on before, we were off to conduct war. After kilometers of commando marching, my arms turned purple from my overly tight rucksack straps but there was no way I could stop the column.

As we approached our objective, shots rang out. I was at the front of the *groupe de combat* when we scattered for cover into the roadside ditches. I jumped to the left and the rest to the right so I had to crawl across the tarmac and bloody my elbows to join up with them. We were wearing infrared sensors that indicated a near-miss, bullet wound, or kill. Nobody had been hit and *Sergent* Galeski ordered us up to advance along the roadway. Moving forward in a column, we were sitting ducks for *Sergent* Gagné's ambush. Then I was killed. Even though it was only an exercise, it gave me a queer feeling to be shot dead before I'd even had time to fix my bayonet.

We reformed for another advance. Excited by the thrill of the hunt, we all scrambled and fought to get as many rounds from the *chef* as we could. Because we set off away from the road in extended line formation maintaining equal intervals between each man, we had to push through thorn bushes shredding our arms, necks and faces. Shot rang out again and we strained to see where they were coming from. Though he was well camouflaged, I spotted Sukhoi in the bushes, but the foliage he was hiding behind blocked my laser. Taking cover behind a tree, I shouted fire instructions to the others.

The smell of cordite as we shot to kill was exhilarating. I was changing magazines when Sukhoi broke cover, firing as he ran. The final score: Russian solider—1, *Homme d'affaires Américain*—0.

Sergent Gagné strongly disapproved of anyone getting himself killed more than once but luckily for me he had recently found a new whipping boy. One of the Hungarians who deserted the month before had for some unaccountable reason turned himself in. When the officers in Aubagne asked why he had deserted, he made the error of citing brutality, pointing fingers, and dropping names. *Sergent* Gagné quickly made his life liquid hell. While standing atop of a wall explaining hand-grenade technique, he stamped his boot on the Hungarian's head. As he cowered in pain, *Sergent* Gagné went on to warn him that his face would be black and blue upon the slightest fuck-up.

Before turning in for the night, we learned *"Eugénie,"* another of the buddy-bonding chants that the Legion sings around evening campfires.

> *Eugénie, les larmes aux yeux,*
> *Nous venons te dire adieu;*
>
> With tears in our eyes, Eugenie,
> We bid thee fond Goodbye.
> We sail with the dawn, Eugenie,
> For Mexique's torrid sky.
>
> CHORUS:
> O Heavenly Winds blow swiftly
> To Montezuma's shore,
> And Glory return us soon to
> The Empress we adore.

It was another chant written as the Legion embarked for its expedition to Mexico. Eugénie was a very popular girl's name in France at the time so many legionnaires would not necessarily have been thinking of Napoleon III's beautiful imperial consort.

As we sang, storm clouds were gathering. I was already in my sleeping bag when the chill, wind-driven rain came lashing down and I felt the first trickles begin to seep through. Soon I was lying in a puddle of ice-cold water. I wriggled into my *tenue de combat,* hoping that additional layers of clothing, however wet, would maintain an envelope of lukewarm water around my skin. I finally managed to sleep in fifteen minute snatches.

Le premier groupe de combat awoke feeling exhausted and fell in for the morning roll-call. *Caporal* Qandil, after a night's drinking, staggered along the ranks handing out random punches. When he started swinging a *pelle US,* the relatively less intoxicated *Sergent* Galeski sent him away to sober up and marched us off at a merciless *pas gymnastique* to impress the other instructors with our stamina.

Approaching *Le Quartier Capitaine Danjou,* Legion tradition required us to halt *pour se faire beau*—polish mud-caked *rangers,* scrub camouflage paint from faces, and remove soil from *tenue de combat.* After a day of combat training, a sleepless night and the morning's hazing, being ordered to look bright-eyed and bushy-tailed was just another bit of mindless Legion bullshit. Once the *chef* had rammed the staff of the *fanion du régiment* into the muzzle of his Famas, we marched in through the gates of the 4e *RE* and the sentries presented arms. Before being given anything to drink or eat, we were ordered to clean our rifles.

Every regiment, even every company in the Legion has its own bar. The 4e *RE*'s bar-club was open all day. After a hard week, on one of the few occasions we were allowed in, we were drinking Kronenbourg and watching the German music channel VIVA. Everyone roared and hollered at Britney Spears's lyrics, ". . . Baby One More Time"—an appropriate theme tune for the basic training. The video "Say What You Want" featured the lovely lead singer of Texas, Sharleen Spiteri, in a summer dress, frolicking under a tree and running barefoot across the grass. It was a masterpiece of soft imagery reminding me of the gentleness of a loving woman's touch. I sat in silence, in a different world, trying to forget that I was in the Legion and being transformed into a mindless brute.

On the days we had *club,* asshole behavior always led to violence. When Sadlowski went to buy me a Kronenbourg, I kept his seat from him but half of the platoon were without a chair and I sensed trouble would come my way. Abu sidled over, and sat down right in Sadlowski's chair. I stood up shouting but he just laughed. Not wanting the others to think that anyone could get away with crossing me, I grabbed the chair and literally picked it up with him in it. In no time, the *caporal-chef* threw us out.

"Abu, I need to teach you some Western manners," I said. "Come with me behind the Dumpsters."

He started taunting me and before we got there, I struck him in the face with a flying back-fist. Waiting for him to hit back was my big mistake—always follow through and finish what you start. His first swing missed; then I came in with a sidekick to the chest. It can't have fazed him, for I suddenly felt overcome by a pleasant dreamlike calm, as if I had floated out of my body and was far away from the Legion. But, no I wasn't, I was looking up at him from the tarmac. I realized that he'd knocked me out with one blow, the first time I'd ever lost consciousness. Feeling the pain in my jaw, I made the split-second decision to throw in the towel. I got up and tried to shake hands with him but he turned away, grunting to himself. At least he accepted that the fight was over.

That evening, Raducanu lurched drunkenly into me, looking for trouble yet again.

"So what are you going to need to help you this time, a metal stool or a broomstick?"

We stood eyeball to eyeball, breathing heavily. He was shorter than me and very unsteady on his feet. I toyed with the idea of a swift kick to his face. Couldn't be simpler! A well-aimed *ranger* would shatter his jaw. Instead of waiting around as I had with Abu, I would attack and follow through instantly with my fists. That's what I should have done but I walked away from it. Two fights in one day were just too much for me to handle.

"Please, Michaud," I said when I got back to my room, "a chunk of hashish or a downer. Something, anything to keep me from going crazy in this fucking madhouse."

We lit up joints and lay back on our beds. He was feeling fed up with the Legion, too. We began talking about hitchhiking and came up with a plan. We'd both desert and buy a van together to tour around the Mediterranean. Over more hashish and Kronenbourg, we brainstormed the idea even further into a surefire way of making money as well. We'd set up an escape network for the Legion. We'd hang around Castelnaudary bars to contact would-be deserters and, for a modest fee of ten thousands francs, offer to smuggle them out in our van to the Italian, Swiss, or Spanish frontier. The more we spoke about it, the more it appealed to us. We joked about our van the rest of the time in Castel.

During *soupe de midi* next day, I realized why Abu had turned his back on me after our fight. "Titanium skull, *hein?*" said a Frenchman. "Abu broke his wrist on your fucking head."

Fighting was a punishable offense so Abu waited four days before reporting that he'd had an accident falling down the stairs.

While the platoon was practicing a chant that we were supposed to have learned by heart, I fumbled the words and made a bad attempt at lip-synching. *Caporal* Quandil called me outside, telling me to follow him into a building I'd never been in before. I expected him to give me the beating of a lifetime until I realized whose office I was in.

The *adjudant-chef* handed me a fax. It was from the Gestapo in Aubagne with a translation of the message I'd posted on the Foreign Legion public-forum site. "Where and when did you send that message?"

"While on leave in Castelnaudary, from an Internet café."

"Where exactly is that? Draw me a map of where that café's located. You were given a *nom de guerre* for a purpose, as you very well know. Have you forgotten that using your real name is a punishable offense? You've been sending messages about the Legion on an official basis, as a legionnaire—something you have no authority whatsoever to do! Here, you say that the Legion is full of *couillons* (assholes). And there you state that no one needs to worry about the drug test. What do you mean by that?"

"Well, drug as in narcotic," I said, tapping a vein in my arm.

"Oh, I see, you mean the inoculations? Well, that's not so serious. I'll let you off lightly this time but just listen to what I'm telling you—sending that kind of message to civilians is *strictly* forbidden!"

"*Reçu, mon adjudant-chef.*"

He turned to *Caporal* Qandil. "Make sure this man never goes into that establishment again."

I realized that his lack of computer knowledge meant that he thought I'd just sent a private email. He had no idea that I'd left a public message and my real name for the whole world to see. None of the NCOs had a clue about what a public forum was and rather than reveal his ignorance, *Sergent* Gagné never asked me to explain.

During *rassemblement* the next day, Captain Yudelevich addressed me. He was *chef de compagnie* and none of us had ever spoken to him before. I formally presented myself. "*Mon enfant* Sanchez," he said, smiling. "I understand you're familiar with Castelnaudary's Internet café."

"*Oui, mon capitaine.*"

He was an Oxford-educated man, and an excellent paratrooper. He'd also been an instructor for the Guyane commando training programme, one of the most demanding in the Legion. I admired him as an officer and a gentleman. He asked me which university I'd graduated from and what I majored in. Although French, his surname indicated that his grandfather had probably been one of the Legion's legendary White Russians. I could sense that he understood my desire to become a gentleman-soldier like himself. He was the only one who really understood the seriousness of what I had done, but no further action was ever taken.

Each year on Bastille Day, July 14, detachments from every unit of the French Armed Forces parade down the *Champs-Elysées* in a

Fascist-style show of military might watched by tens of thousands of enthusiastic spectators. The loudest cheers are always for the stately progress of the legionnaires bringing up the rear at the slow, arrogant marching speed of eighty-eight paces a minute compared to the French army's standard one hundred twenty.

This year the Legion was to be represented by the 4^e *RE*, and those selected were dispatched to Paris to rehearse. The rest of us were to take part in a smaller-scale parade along the main boulevard of Castelnaudary. We spent an entire week mastering the technicalities of marching in perfect formation with a Famas grasped across our chest. It was all too easy to fall out of step—not only were we marching to a regimental bugle fanfare without any time-keeping drumbeat but when an eight-man rank began to turn, the outside legionnaires had to adjust the length of their stride to keep up with the pivot man.

As the corporals kept stressing, the Legion's ceremonial march is quite natural—arms slightly bent, swinging to waist level, hands open, fingers and thumb straight, and chin always up. During one tricky turn I finally managed to coordinate my strides correctly but my swinging arm fell out of synch. This created a shambles behind me and the *caporal-chef* pulled me out to place me in the *mongol* group of nonparticipants. I was perfectly glad to be yanked out from the parade, for it would save me hours of ironing. The others went on to learn how to avoid the wave effect caused by minute cumulative delays working their way down the file.

On the evening of the fourteenth, the entire regiment was assembled to watch footage of the *Champs-Elysées* parade. In attendance, next to President Jacques Chirac, was King Hassan of Morocco. For the entire parade, glorious as it was, the president and king remained seated, but when the Legion appeared, they and the watching crowd gave a standing ovation.

One evening, *Caporal* Helm called me into his room to let me hear his latest Chemical Brothers CD. He'd picked it up while on leave in

Berlin during the infamous Love Parade, an annual event that began in 1989 just before the fall of the Berlin Wall, as a celebration of techno disc-jockey Dr. Motte's birthday. *Caporal* Helm, then a well-known DJ in his own right, had helped to organize it. In a few years, it grew into a street carnival with over a million participants.

As we listened, he told me about behind-the-scenes politics that we legionnaires were rarely aware of. "The *chef* is a control freak. He considers me a rebel, and, at the moment, he's trying to have me locked up. Don't believe anything you're told about the lieutenant being in charge here. It's only a year since he graduated from St-Cyr. The *chef*'s the one who's in charge; the lieutenant's frightened of him. As for that slob Gagné, the 2ᵉ *REP* colonel dumped him here rather than court-martial him for drunkenness. At first he was on his best behavior, but once he began drinking again all hell broke loose. I can't blame him though; he's not all there. And Galeski? He has his head up the lieutenant's ass because he's up for promotion to *chef* himself."

As a platoon, we were at a point where we were finding ways to cut corners at every opportunity. Because of my computer skills, the lieutenant put me to work entering data, which saved me from a lot of mindless *corvées*. It was a pleasure to get my fingers on a keyboard once again, although I was doing nothing more than entering names into Excel worksheets. Whenever possible, I spent the entire afternoon on a single document, and amused myself for the rest of the time drinking Pepsi and searching the lieutenant's hard-drive for pornography. After seeing Calderon spend hours stenciling the names of each room's occupants onto placards, I showed the *chef* that with Excel I could do the same thing in five minutes, even pasting in the Legion's flaming grenade emblem. I could also click and change occupants' names if they moved. To the instructors, this was black magic.

Now that I had access to the bureau, I could download sensitive files. Thinking I didn't understand French well enough, the lieutenant assigned me the task of entering his handwritten comments on each legionnaire. These were important because they would be included in our personal files and looked over by the colonel before deciding whether to send us to our regiment of choice. I printed them out and shared them with my friends.

"Here it says that Sadlowski 'must remain motivated to embody all that makes for a *bon légionnaire*.' Michaud is 'well-spirited, and a good *camarade*, but lacks toughness.' Let's see, Raducanu 'lacks maturity,' and Calderon 'could be a good legionnaire if he controls his temper.' And here, look at this! Sukhoi, of all people, 'one of the intelligent ones'!" The lieutenant had written that I was "intelligent but fragile," going on to say that I was a "well-rounded lad" who hadn't a clue why he had joined. It wasn't long before everyone, including my enemies, was begging to see what the lieutenant had written about them.

At Castel we learned that the Legion attaches special importance to water sport. The strongest swimmers are candidates for overseas postings to places like Guyane and the Congo. Michaud was in his element. Although awkward on land and still unable to master *la corde*, he'd kept quiet about being a former member of the French national swimming team. I, however, hated swimming even more than soccer. I was no good at it. My cardiovascular system worked superbly but for some reason I got out of breath after the first length of the pool and made a spectacle of myself in front of the lieutenant and captain who watched us in their Speedos and goggles.

High-diving was another thing I had never done before. *Sergent* Galeski decided that the best way to teach me was using the time-honored Legion method of ordering me to do it immediately, and sent me straight up to the five-meter board. I stood there looking down at water, which looked like rock-hard cement, until he started to climb up after me. I managed to propel myself forward into the emptiness. Fortunately my body aligned itself instinctively. My head hit the water and I felt my hair being plucked out before I resurfaced to the cheers of the platoon. Like marching raw recruits directly into combat, the Legion's baptism by fire often works.

We were now nearly at the end of basic training and what mattered most was how we were going to do in the tests covering everything we had learned. Every Monday morning, we had a twelve-kilometer run along the Castelnaudary Canal. As the tests approached, the entire regiment, led by the colonel, did the run in *tenue de combat* and *rangers,* with a loaded rucksack. As we ran we were pleased to realize that we were now in better shape than the corporals. *Caporal* Qandil stopped halfway into the run supposedly to piss and we never saw him catch up.

I knew that when I eventually returned to civilian life, I would never march or run again as I did in the Legion, so I took the final Cooper seriously. The glory of a solid Cooper would be a lasting testimony to my body's peak performance. When the one-minute warning bell sounded I forced myself to accelerate, swearing to myself that I would cherish the memory of the agony as a souvenir of what I had achieved. At the finishing whistle, I had done 200m better than before, making a total of 3300m in twelve minutes. Anything above 3200m was considered outstanding and duly noted in our dossier. Though I finished fifth, I was satisfied that I'd given my all.

During our French language test, the lieutenant came around to "supervise" the group of slower learners, which *Sergent* Gagné had included me in. Since the lieutenant was himself evaluated on his platoon's performance, he whispered the correct answers to Kapelski and several others. I finished early and *Sergent* Gagné called me outside. "I see you've been trying to fool me," he said, pulling my ear until it popped. "You act like a *mongol* who doesn't understand a word, but now I see that you scored a level four! You'll pay for this." Native French–speakers are considered to be level five, so level four was an excellent score for an Anglophone.

The next challenge was the commando march—not a march at all but a run, in full *tenue de combat* and a ten-kilogram rucksack.

This test identifies the legionnaires best qualified for the *Régiment Étranger de Parachutistes*. The others stuffed things into their packs any old way but I was determined to make scientific preparations. I carefully packed my pack the night before to make sure it would be perfectly balanced on either side of my spine, and wadded empty spaces with things like my sleeping bag to make sure nothing started moving as I ran. With my understanding of engineering dynamics, I knew that any lateral movement of my rucksack would waste kinetic energy, which would eventually transfer via my pounding feet into the tarmac. I therefore tightened my shoulder straps so that the rucksack felt like an extension of my body. To keep myself hydrated the next day, I drank a primitive electrolyte cocktail of sugar and salt.

It was a broiling day, and the *infirmerie* was on stand-by to treat anybody who passed out. Most men took off at top speed but I paced myself according to the discomfort I felt and distance before me. If my calculations were correct, I wouldn't feel totally demolished until just after I crossed the finishing line. Although I began with a full energy reserve, it was impossible to sprint with the load I was carrying. Before the halfway point, my back and thighs were aching and my lungs felt as if they were about to burst. I braced myself for the pain to get steadily worse during the second part of the run. Now I was passing a lot of the fast starters who had stopped in their tracks out of sheer exhaustion. Though I made superhuman efforts as I approached the finishing line, I was moving only at a trot. My legs simply wouldn't lift and extend any faster but I finished fourth in thirty-eight minutes.

"For a businessman," Sadlowski said to me, "you're a hell of an athlete."

Still pumping with adrenaline, I went for a shower. When I turned on the water, I yelped out in pain. The rucksack had scorched the skin off my back down to the secondary layer and before lights-out, the scabbing had glued my T-shirt to my skin.

Marksmanship carried special weighting in our final ranking. We were given nine rounds to fire at the target, with any miss resulting in *mort subite*—sudden death elimination. Dupont panicked and his first round went through the ceiling, resulting in a score of zero. To keep a steady hand, I'd abstained from all caffeine for the two days before the test and secretly drank a bottle of Kronenbourg before starting, hoping that the alcohol would steady my nerves. Perspiring with concentration, I fired three rounds in each position—lying, kneeling, standing—and achieved a perfect score. For the first and only time in basic training, *Sergent* Gagné congratulated me.

When the lieutenant announced that we were about to start the final seven-day endurance march, he added that a number of us could expect to suffer "some discomfort." Remembering how excruciating the two-day *képi blanc* march had been, I tried to cheer myself up by thinking how when it was over I would no longer have to suffer the company of *Sergent* Gagné. I was grateful that I'd never reported sick or missed a single one of our rigorous workouts.

We were dropped off to begin the march near the Spanish border. I paid particular attention to my feet, always avoiding puddles, which quickly bring on blistering. I wore two pairs of socks—acrylic dress socks to reduce friction against the leather and standard-issue wool ones to absorb sweat. Our first bivouac was near the Pyrenean village of Les Angles. When I checked to make sure that Calderon was okay, he admitted having problems with his feet. Szabo was also marching on raw flesh. I tried to help, offering them my Elastoplast and reassuring them that we were all going to come through in one piece.

The instructors allowed us a half-hour at a nearby café, so I took Szabo off to enjoy some quiet time over tea. The young waitress with endless legs caught my eye. "A legionnaire from America!" she explained. "I studied English and love speaking it."

"And I can speak a bit of your French too. Learned it on the job, you might say."

Caporal Qandil stuck his head around the door. "You might say you know how to speak English and a bit of French," he said and pointed at my *tenue de combat,* "but you don't know how to arrange your fucking collar."

I grimaced at the waitress and sat down.

Back at the bivouac as darkness began to fall, we listened to the sounds of a party going on and the voice of Edith Piaf singing in the distance. On sentry duty that night, I took a lengthy shit outside *Caporal* Qandil's tent.

By this time, our bodies had acquired a superhuman ability to repair overnight. When I woke up after a few hours of sleep, I was fresh and ready to go. Much of the day's march was on paved roads—even and smooth, but ruinous for the knees. I marched on the dirt shoulder whenever possible. During a pause, *Sergent* Gagné sent me to fetch his canteen and I realized how he was able to lead us on these agonizing marches—his rucksack contained little more than his sleeping bag. All his other heavier necessities were stored in the *chef*'s truck.

We bivouacked for the night by a lake nestling in the mountains and the *chef* made sure we were all well away from the bikini-clad tourists. Sitting under our tarps staring at them across the lake, we salivated at the soft flesh we'd been deprived of for so long. In the middle of the lake was a floating platform that some men had swum out to in their underpants. Knowing about my poor swimming ability, *Sergent* Gagné ordered me to join them.

It looked like it was kilometers away. "Keep an eye on me," I said to Sadlowski before taking the plunge. After expending enormous effort, I looked back and saw that I'd barely made it past the shoreline. *Sergent* Gagné bellowed with laughter. With each mouthful of green lake water I swallowed, I feared I would never make it. Exhausted and in a state of panic, I realized I was now at the halfway point between the shore and the raft. I'd little choice but to try to go on. I eventually dragged myself on to the platform and lay there panting like a half-drowned dog, knowing that I now had to swim all the way back.

The mountain phase of the march was the worst and, although most of us would have been happy to be left to die at the wayside, *Sergent* Galeski was hell-bent on making sure that everyone finished. He became exasperated by Kapelski's attempts to march on the outsides of his feet to avoid worsening his blisters. He made him unclip his Famas strap and fix it around his combat belt so that he could be dragged along. "I'll harness you like a horse if you don't keep up!"

Shortly later, *Sergent* Galeski attached another would-be dropout to the back of Kapelski's belt. Being pulled along mountain ledges like a two-man train, they were in constant danger of slipping and falling down onto the jagged rocks below. The other man was utterly exhausted and could hardly continue. Even Mikhailov, who was pushing, gave up on him. At midday, he finally passed out and *Sergent* Galeski shouted at him to stand up and stop play-acting. I wondered how it must have felt to be marched to death in *Afrique*.

Michaud, who had been joking with me about how much easier the march would be if we had our van, came under a viral attack and started staggering. When we stopped for a ten-minute break, he began weeping like a child. We were marching at a punishing two hundred paces a minute, from sunrise to sundown. Calderon was also suffering, and, in a fit of *cafard,* he'd begun the second day's march in his shower-sandals. Once we'd bivouacked for the night and Kapelski pried off his *rangers,* his feet looked like ground beef. I remembered how I used to sit comfortably all day behind my Chicago office desk and then complain to myself in my car on the way home about what a hard day I'd had.

The big advantage I had over the others was my knowledge of the human body and its functions. Since dehydration is the main cause of fatigue, I drank as much as I could. Even after downing five canteens, I allowed myself to piss only once a day. Sweat poured off my face and spattered my *rangers* with white crusty salt. Sweating at that rate, it was impossible to restore the body's sodium balance with our *RCIRs* alone but I'd done a bit of forward planning. I'd stolen from the *ordinaire* handfuls of salt and sugar sachets, which I mixed in equal amounts into every canteen—a poor man's Gatorade for endurance athletes, I explained to the others.

There was no doubt that the Legion had turned the fitter ones into efficient marching machines. Though I was struggling, my body had now accustomed itself to the weight of my rucksack and was fooled into believing its mass was part of me so I was able to march the steepest grades and up and down canyons. After taking an entire day to cross a mountain plateau, we were forced to make the dangerous descent at breakneck speed. With the others behind shouting at me to get a move on, we jumped from rock to rock like frogs, feeling pain from microfractures in our shins, knee cartilage grinding away as we landed.

With our bodies in such a state of hyperactivity, we were desperate for calories. Within one hour after the heartiest *soupe,* stabbing hunger and fatigue kicked in again. I'd invented a special *petit déjeuner* guaranteed to keep a legionnaire marching until midday—sugared bread washed down with a water solution containing three packets of instant coffee, three sachets of sugar, powdered milk, and cocoa.

Toward the end of the march, we entered a small mountain town that seemed untouched by the modern world. The mayor came out to greet us and invited us to billet in the relative comfort of the town hall. The townsfolk had arranged tables outside with food, Kronenbourg, and *pinard*. Showered and rested, Szabo and I enjoyed a drink and a few words that evening.

"I have two secrets," he said, "that I've never disclosed to anyone else here. Firstly, I want you to know that I used to be an *adjudant chef* in the National Police in Budapest. My brother was the same but he's unfortunately married with children, so there was no way for him to enlist like me. Then he got shot in the chest and his disability compensation amounts to no more than I get here in two weeks. Sanchez, if we ever make it out of the Legion, will you help me get to America?"

"I'll do anything I can for you as a brother."

"That means more to me than you can understand."

"And your second secret?"

"I'll tell you some other time."

By day seven, even the strongest were suffering. All my lower joints were aching and my legs felt like they were going to give up on me. Though we'd finished the mountains, we were now wading across sand and scrambling up and down bare dirt hills. Because the descents were so steep, we slid down on our asses even though we risked crashing out of control into the gullies. But though we all finished as wrecks, there wasn't one man who failed the march. The legion tradition of starting together and finishing together had been painfully upheld.

After four months' training, we could accomplish amazing feats of stamina on the most basic fuel—a full day's march on a bottle of Kronenbourg or a shot of *pastis*. We were fit and, more important, we were tough—which is not the same thing. An Olympic distance runner is physically fit, but, like a finely-tuned performance machine, a world-class athlete will falter when deprived of the right vitamins and eight hours of undisturbed sleep. He would be unable to finish the shortest march under Legion conditions. Fitter than most other civilians, I'd joined as a well-tuned Lamborghini, which the Legion had turned into a rugged 4x4 pickup truck, made in the USA.

With basic training officially over, the instructors, apart from *Caporal* Qandil, took off for two week's leave while we stayed on in Castelnaudary for military driving instruction. Though I'd brought with me photocopied proof of my U.S. driver's license obtained at age sixteen, I still had to take the course. After mornings spent scrubbing toilets and polishing corridors, we spent the rest of the day in the regiment's technical zone attending lectures and driving. Evenings were spent sweeping and mopping the driving school premises. We had little free time but we were allowed into the canteen to enjoy a Kronenbourg before evening roll-call. Michaud and the others were ecstatic that they now had access to as much tobacco as they could smoke.

Of course the Legion was unable to organize anything as elementary as a driving course without *sketch*. It didn't matter that I'd already driven for nine years; the *caporal-chef* instructor used his foul-smelling breath to scream at me for braking too late or muddling the military serial numbers we had to memorize for the oil, transmission, windshield wiper, and brake fluids. The cars we used were hilarious 1960s 2 CV Citroën contraptions, more appropriate in a Louis de Funès comedy film. The *chef* with his trainee sitting alongside him in the front seats looked like two apes in a sideways-on sardine tin.

Classroom time wasn't much better. Anybody caught dozing was made to hold a heavy wooden log above his head for the duration of the lecture, and our knuckles were rapped with a stick if we didn't answer correctly. We spent entire mornings going over slide after slide of the French driving code. I was bored out of my mind and spent most of the time daydreaming.

Also attending the driving school were legionnaires from other regiments. I met up with a *mafia Anglaise* once again—Sijfert, an overgrown South African with a sense of humor; Kulzer an articulate German skinhead, and a man from Tulsa, Woodman, a tall ham-handed former U.S. Army infantryman whose arms were tattooed in every conceivable color. Across his shoulders in Germanic font were the words: POLAR BEARS RULE.

"Things here wouldn't be so shitty if the Legion spent less money on Kronenbourg and more on half-decent equipment," Woodman complained.

Sijfert, an Afrikaner from a good family, had given up everything for adventure. He was a big talker with a strong accent, and though only twenty years old, he had some tall tales of life in the South African army. He'd already done one year in the Legion, and, apart from disliking the Brits for their involvement in the Boer War, he had a violent distaste for black Africans.

"What was Chad like when you were there on mission?" Woodman asked.

"It was black! How the hell else did you think it was like?" The *mafia Anglaise* roared with laughter. "I don't care where the Legion sends me, as long as I can kill *kaffirs*. Those savages have taken over my country and now nobody gives a fuck."

"Same thing in America," said Woodman. "We're invaded by browns from Mexico."

"How about you, Sanchez, how did they treat you in corporate America?"

"Not well."

"The thing I really like about the Legion is that they have toilet partitions. Unlike in the South African army, you can have a proper morning wank. How was your wank this morning?" Sijfert asked Kulzer, the paratrooper.

"Quite excellent," he replied in a sophisticated tone of voice.

Kulzer was a handsome man with bright blue eyes who spoke English fluently. He was extremely polite and was probably brought up in an aristocratic German family. When he went out on leave with Sijfert, he told any women they met that he was a male model, and Sijfert claimed to be a wildlife photographer.

Caporal Qandil made a point of letting us know that as far as he was concerned our basic training was far from over, by teaching us the electric chair and the duck walk. He laid into us when Dupont turned up late for midday parade. We were marched into the *salle de musculation*. "*En position!*" he barked. "*Pompes!*" We began doing push-ups, with him using his fists to keep our backs straight. After half an hour every man was flopped onto the floor like an exhausted fish.

"*En position!*" he shouted. "*La chaise électrique!*" For this we were made to press our backs against the wall, bend our knees so that our lower legs were parallel to the floor, and hold our arms straight out before us. Our muscles burned and trembled after only a few minutes.

"Very good Sanchez!" he shouted. "You're sitting just like your name—*sans chaise* (without a chair)."

As our sweat rolled, he shouted again. "*En position! Pompes,* you bastards! Up, down, up, down!"

"*Fatigué?*"

"Never, *Caporal*."

Then we were given the duck walk. With hands clasped on our heads, we waddled around in a squatting position for a half-hour. When we thought things couldn't get worse, he found a packet of milk powder on Calderon. We were marched back to our rooms. All cupboards were to be opened for inspection. He threw out everything onto the floor and pushed over the furnishings. Packets of sugar, cocoa, potato chips, and cookies were opened and scattered onto the *bordel* of clothes and personal belongings. The hallway floor was smeared with soda, yogurt, Kronenbourg, and wine.

"Hungry?" *Caporal* Qandil asked, handing me a box of cookies. "You have five seconds to eat this!"

Thinking I'd outsmart him, I opened the box and gobbled the cookies like Cookie Monster from *Sesame Street,* chunks falling out of the sides of my mouth. He wasn't impressed and punched me in the gut, making me spew up everything I'd just gulped down.

"I want this place spotless in fifteen minutes!"

That afternoon we arrived at the driving school drenched in sweat and smelling of cocoa for a further lecture on *Le code de la route.* Learning the European Rules of the Road was tricky, to say the least, with all the subtle differences between white or yellow, and dashed or dotted shoulder lines. I'd thought my university education would get me through anything the Legion could throw at me but I failed the written exam.

In the evening, just as we were cooling off after lights-out, Dupont decided to visit a neighboring platoon. *Caporal* Qandil beat him senseless and he was ordered to bed, to sleep in comfort while the rest of us were jammed into a tiny washroom.

"Thought training was finished, did you?" he shouted.

He turned out the lights and closed the door on us. "No one comes out of there until morning *reveille!*" We didn't even have enough space to lie down. In a few minutes, the room was not only steamy from our perspiration, but filled with farts and body odor. Hoping to get a few hours' sleep, I squeezed myself under a dripping sink and lay down in a puddle of putrid water.

*   *   *

Before leaving for Aubagne, we were paraded in front of the captain to discuss our regimental preferences. If we'd really been given a choice, most men would have chosen a posting to *l'Afrique* or Guyane, not to battle guerrillas but for the handsome overseas pay premiums.

I, however, had set my hopes on *la Musique Principale* that the Canadian sergeant had told me about months before. It was formed just after the Legion was created in 1831 and now doubles as a mortar-platoon. It consists of eighty musicians, many of whom began with no prior musical experience. *La Musique* has its own distinctive traditions—it's the only French military band still to use fifes, and side-drums are worn low with the base rim at knee height. In the rear ranks is the *Chapeau chinois,* a percussion instrument consisting of a conical copper plate hung with bells carried on a staff and surmounted by the Legion's seven-flamed grenade symbol. In spite of its name, the instrument has nothing to do with China. It is of Ottoman origin and is decorated with two horsetails, symbols of a defeated enemy. *La Musique* performs in France and abroad; in 1997 it appeared at the Royal Tournament in London.

"Sanchez," Captain Yudelevich said with a wry smile, "I hear many things about you. The latest is that you're an undercover journalist for *The New York Times*."

"*Oui, mon capitaine.* Most people here are baffled as to why I enlisted in the Legion. I didn't want to disappoint their expectations."

"And now we must decide where to send you," he said, looking over my dossier. "*Musique Principale?* Of all things in the Legion, you want to be a musician? What do you know about music?"

"Nothing, *mon capitaine.* But I want to learn. I've mastered the art of soldiering these past four months, and I'm confident that I'll finish well in my platoon. Having learned how to conduct war, I want to try something completely new. Traveling with the band, perhaps even to America sometime, is something I'd love to do. Music is my next big challenge."

"You never cease to amaze me, *mon enfant*."

On the train to Marseille, before changing for Aubagne where everything in the Legion begins and ends, I took the time to page through my dossier and discovered that *Sergent* Gagné had doctored my test results. He had taken a hundred meters off my Cooper and added six minutes to my commando march. But what the hell! By this stage I was accustomed to Legion injustice; it was just great to know that basic training was now over.

At Aubagne, waiting to go into the office of the 1er *RE* colonel, we were formed up in line in the order in which we'd finished basic training. The man who'd come first was a former French seaman—an excellent athlete and soldier but completely without any personality. After seven years in the navy, he was little more than an order-taking machine.

Sergent Gagné, back from leave, walked down the file handing out his appraisals. "Number one, Valent. Good soldier and marksman . . . Pierron. Should do well . . . Burnazian. Not bad . . . Number four, Krupa. Hard worker . . . Raducanu. Pit bull . . . And, oh, but what have we here? Sanchez? *Putain!*" In spite of his efforts I had finished sixth—not bad for an Anglophone civilian.

When I was marched in to stand *au garde-à-vous* in front of the colonel, he congratulated me on my posting to the 2e *REG*! Captain Yudelevich and the lieutenant were also present. The captain stared at me, subliminally telling me that arguing with the colonel was a bad idea.

"*Mon colonel*, I requested posting as a musician."

"My records don't indicate . . ."

"The Legion is like the good Lord," the captain put in, "and works its wonders in mysterious ways. I assume you've no further questions?"

Later, discussing our postings over a Kronenbourg in the *club compagnie,* we discovered half of the platoon had been dumped like me in the *2ᵉ REG.* Sadlowski was ecstatic about his posting to the *2ᵉ Régiment Étranger de Parachutistes.* I was glad for him; he'd earned it with his sweat and blood.

The *2ᵉ REP,* based at Calvi in Corsica, as far away from the mainland as possible, is considered the most professional unit in the Legion. It is split into four companies, each with its own specialization in night, mountain, urban, or aquatic warfare. On permanent standby, the regiment can move at company strength anywhere in the world within twenty-four hours and spearheads France's FAR, Force d'Action Rapide. It includes the crack unit formerly known as CRAP, *Commandos de Recherche et d'Action dans la Profondeur,* a pathfinder unit specializing in HALO parachuting, High Altitude Low Opening, which is open only to those with the rank of corporal or higher. CRAP understandably has since been renamed GCP, *Groupement de Commandos Parachutistes.*

The regiment has frequently been on four-month detachment to Djibouti, Central Africa, and Guyane. *Le sport* is its religion and annually the entire regiment performs a commando march across the length of Corsica—two hundred kilometers of rugged terrain. A lot of very pretty German and Italian girls spend their holidays on the island's beaches in hopes of meeting a legionnaire. Laetitia Casta, a French supermodel of Corsican origin, is the *2ᵉ REP's* official *mascotte.* Mikhailov and Sukhoi, who finished basic training just behind me, were also posted to Calvi. Calderon was delighted. "They should send all that Russian garbage to roast in hell on that island of the damned."

Szabo was one of only two legionnaires posted to the *1ᵉ Régiment Étranger de Genie,* based near the city of Avignon. The *1ᵉʳ REG,* a combat engineering regiment, includes *Détachement d'Intervention Operationelle Subaquatique* (DINOPS). Like the Navy SEALs and British SBS, they specialize in underwater explosives, beach reconnaissance, and sabotage. They provided support to the U.S. Army's 82nd Airborne Division during the Gulf War. The men in DINOPS must pass both the *Armée de Terre's* parachute school and the Navy's combat swimmer course. They are trained to arrive at their targets by land, air, or sea using submarines, Zodiac inflatable motorboats, and two-man Klepper kayaks. They may be armed with not only the Famas but, depending on the type of mission, Heckler & Koch MP5 Sub Machine Guns, 9mm Beretta pistols, mines, and other weapons.

Before we were sent off to regiment, *Sergent* Gagné walked past everyone but shook hands only with his favorite, Sukhoi. We were then formally inducted into the Foreign Legion by the *Général de la Légion Étrangère* himself, and taken for the very first time into the *Crypte*. The general was a small man with a battle scar above his left ear. Standing *au garde-à-vous* beneath the oil painting of the Battle of Camerone, he began with the story of that historic encounter. Afterward, we filed reverentially past the wooden hand of *Capitaine* Danjou. We finished with the oath to serve with *Honneur et Fidélité*.

As the *2ᵉ REG* bus pulled out of the *Quartier Danjou*, Sadlowski waved and flexed his arm, telling me to be strong. I remembered that Szabo had never revealed his second secret. I was already missing my *camarades* but I knew that the patron saints of the *2ᵉ REP* and *1ᵉ REG* would protect them. I never saw them again.

6.

SAINT-CHRISTOL

A very high percentage of [Foreign Legion] members have suicidal tendencies. An elite unite is only elite when the majority consider themselves already dead. That is the full evolution of the soldier. Dying is what the Legion is all about.

William Brooks

The 300km truck-ride from Castel to Saint-Christol d'Albion in Haute Provence took several hours. After leaving the *autoroute*, we ground along progressively narrower roads through a succession of ripening vineyards, which brought back memories of Nadine grape-picking in the region of Bordeaux. Before enlisting I had written to her in Canada to say that I was going through a difficult period in my life and thought the Foreign Legion might heal me. She had never replied.

By the time the trucks had groaned up to the Plateau d'Albion the temperature had dropped markedly and I was wondering what kind of eagle's nest quarters we were being taken to. The military base at 840 meters surrounded by snow-capped mountain peaks lies like an island in an ocean of rockbound breakers. The leaves were already turning brown, and though we were in southern France, winters at this altitude are frigid. Saint-Christol, a small place with a few hundred inhabitants, is the nearest village.

As we drove through the front gates and guards saluted, I was looking forward to what the 2ᵉ *REG* had in store for me. I'd persuaded myself that the *capitaine* knew what he was doing in posting me here. In Castel I'd become disenchanted with foot-slogging infantry combat and knowing that I was technically inclined, he must have assumed that I'd be of use in an engineering *régiment*. It included two *compagnies de combat,* and a CCL company, *compagnie de commandement et de logistique,* to which we were attached for a week until posted to our permanent *sections.*

We were welcomed with a hot *soupe* followed by a good beer buzz. With me were about half of my *section* from Castel, including Calderon, Michaud, Dupont, and Raducanu. Of the men already there, the only one I knew was my *paesan,* Woodman. Calderon and I were pleasantly surprised to find ample, on-tap supplies of civilian wine and Kronenbourg 1664, named for the year the brewery was founded in the Strasbourg district of Cronenbourg, modified to Kronenbourg to make it more Germanic. Normally both were reserved for officers.

Our first impressions however were misleading. It did not take me long to realize that we had been dumped in a *régiment* of chaos and peeling paint. Most of the buildings were run-down and abandoned, with the Legion occupying only a few key sites. The *cadres* were too busy to worry about the creature comforts of junior *légionnaires.* Their top priority was simply to make the place habitable. Though it was late autumn, the central heating system was still inoperative. In the Spartan quarters we were allocated it was difficult to find so much as a functioning *armoire.* If a *chambre* had any sink at all, the water the taps spewed out was brown with rust. The only good point about the base's decrepit state was that since all the surroundings were trampled and muddy, we were spared the gardening we had loathed in Castel.

As newcomers, we were given responsibility for cleaning up the entire *compagnie* but we had not so much as a bucket with us. We had to beg and borrow cleaning equipment from the *légionnaires* already there who were naturally reluctant to lend rookies their precious *matériel de corvée.* I developed calluses on my forefinger and thumb from constantly wielding brooms. Like a new inmate in a

State Penitentiary, I knew that I would have to fight for personal survival. Although *instruction* was over, we were all about to experience something just as bad, the *jeune légionnaire* period of our career.

The *Armée de l'Air* had given up the base after the Cold War but they still maintained a presence in the surrounding region where France's top-secret long-range nuclear missile arsenal was stationed. It was typical that the French Ministry of Defence should have solved the problem of what to do with a disused air base by handing it over to the Foreign Legion. By giving us the keys to the front gate, they'd transferred to us the responsibility for tidying up the *bordel*.

The *régiment* was less than a year old but morale was low. Fighting was common, and not just among *légionnaires*. Most of the *sous-officiers* were violent men from the 2ᵉ *REP* who had been transplanted into what was already becoming known as the *régiment* for fuck-ups. In the club *régimentaire des sous-officiers,* all-out brawls took place among the *chefs, sergents,* and *caporaux-chefs,* most stemming from "misunderstandings" over women in Apt, the nearest town. Ordinary *légionnaires* were taking their own lives at an average of one a month. The *mafia Russe* of all groups had organized a hunger strike in protest against the brutality of the Polish *caporaux*. The *Général de la Légion Étrangère* himself had had to intervene to bring it to an end.

The Legion's relationship with the citizens of Apt had been uneasy from the start but had seriously worsened after a *sergent* was brought back to base half dead after being knifed by two Arabs. Most of the *régiment* was about to be deployed to Kosovo but a covert call went out—the traditional rallying cry of *A moi la Légion!* Dressed in *tenue de sortie* to show everyone who they were, the 2ᵉ *REG* set off to wreck the town center. The Arab community must have heard of the intended reprisal raid for they were waiting for them and a desert outpost fight on French soil broke out between *légionnaires* in *képis* and their historic enemy. Woodman and his personal Wild Bunch slipped into town in civilian clothing carrying lead pipes and bats and committed some of the most vicious hooligan thuggery. The Gendarmerie was called in to quell the gang violence, and several *légionnaires* were arrested. One *sergent* beat an Arab teenager with a nail-studded two-by-four, and was sentenced to a civilian prison term—he was a Turk. Later a Russian psychotic on leave lost his mind outside Marseille. He car-jacked an Arab family and murdered them. The leftist press had a field-day that once more brought the Foreign Legion's very existence into question.

The 2e *REG*'s morale problem stemmed from its isolation. Out of sheer boredom, *légionnaires* resorted to degenerate ways of passing their time. Drug usage was endemic, but the establishment paid little attention, partly because many *sous-officiers* were themselves involved. Alcoholism was also rampant. I naturally joined Woodman and other Castel *camarades* at the *foyer régimentaire* for nightly piss-ups. Though I'd grown up as a boy who disliked the taste of beer, I felt myself slipping into the drunken lifestyle of a soldier for France.

The 2e *REG* colonel ordered club activities to be organized in order to keep his unruly brood out of mischief. Posted on the notice board were the bourgeois pastimes we were encouraged to participate in, including table tennis and painting. *La boxe anglaise,* regular boxing, and *la boxe française,* kickboxing, were specifically forbidden. The sport that came closest to allowing us to work off our aggression was judo, headed by none other than *jeune légionnaire* Raducanu. But if the *REG* was trying to persuade us to do something constructive with our evenings, it made a bad job of it. I ignored the order to spend my after-hours in remedial swimming courses by going into the makeshift *salle de musculation* to rebuild the kilos of muscle I had cannibalized during *instruction.*

To squeeze in time for work-outs, I skipped the meager *soupes du soir* and had to scrounge about my *section* asking for crackers from unused *terrain* rations to combat hunger and replace lost calories. Food was always a scarce commodity and my roommates had designated a spare foods shelf for collected instant coffee, the tinned mutton that everyone detested, and *sachets* of evaporated milk. After *petit déjeuner,* we smuggled back as many *baguettes* and marmalade pots as we could slip into our underpants without getting caught.

During the first week, my *section* went out on long runs with the personable *Capitaine* Gach, himself an accomplished runner. Though the farmstead-dotted landscape was frosted and our feet broke through ice-covered puddles as we pounded along the dirt paths, we ran in shorts and tank-tops.

"Quite a clever idea, really," the *capitaine* said to us as we paused for a breather. "Nobody would guess that France is concealing thermo-nuclear weaponry amongst these rolling hills and abandoned farmhouses. A satellite photograph would show little more than sheep."

"Does France have an intercontinental capacity?" I asked.

"Good question," he replied. "Most of France's arsenal is carried by Mirage bombers. You see, France has taken the Third Power position. Though they co-operate with NATO, they refuse to be part of the Anglo-hegemony. The phrase *l'exception française* expresses our determination to remain different. It originated in the fight to defend French culture, and has expanded to take in whatever is special or better. The French state developed the TGV and promotes the ideas of Jean-Paul Sartre, yet the undemocratic steamroller way it goes about it leaves many institutions unaccountable. France takes pride in protecting its identity against the influences of the outside world, yet internally it is confused about where it is going."

The more I engaged him, the more the *capitaine* enjoyed responding in kind. Not expecting a *légionnaire* fresh out of Castel to ponder such issues, he appreciated my conversation. While I was engaged in technical discussions with him, even the *sergents* remained silent.

"Take advantage of the good weather to train your bodies," he said as we started again. "We will soon be putting together an *équipe de cross* composed of the best runners."

* * *

On the day we were given our definitive postings, I found myself in the *colonel*'s bureau, standing at *garde-à-vous* beneath the penetrating gaze of Our Father, *Général* Rollet.

"Yes, I can operate a computer," I told the *colonel,* "and yes, I could assist an *officier* in an office, but I joined to be a soldier in a *compagnie de combat.*"

He let me have my way and I was posted to the 2e *Compagnie* under the command of a very young, likeable *Capitaine* Gach. He was a bit of a rebel and known as something of a playboy. He had caused scandal at St-Cyr Military Academy by dating a Negress and several *légionnaires* got to know former *petites amies* he'd had in Apt. I and Michaud were in a small *section* consisting of fifteen *légionnaires,* three *caporaux,* two *sergents,* and a *sergent-chef* who, having joined the Legion as a boy of eighteen, knew of nothing outside it.

Before being accepted into the *section* we were expected to formally present ourselves to our new *caporaux* and present them with a suitable peace offering, such as a crate of Kronenbourg. One of them was the Jekyll-and-Hyde character, *Caporal* Diagana, a clean-featured Senegalese REP man, notorious for enforcing Legion *sketch* to the last detail, from perfectly pressed creases in *tenues* to immaculately polished *rangers,* including the soles.

Another was *Caporal* Bendada, a North African Muslim but generally well liked and accepted as European. He was the son of an Algerian loyalist who had fought to keep Algeria French. He'd been in the only other unit in the French military to wear the Green Beret—in their case worn to the right—the *Commandos-Marine,* a secretive unit using false passports and discreet private accounts with the *Banque de France* to take part in France's covert operations. His violent behavior had led to his being thrown out of the *Armée de Terre* so he'd joined the Legion. He was obviously of superior stock. A chain smoker, avid drug-user and heavy drinker, who got by on little more than a few hours of hashish-induced sleep, he had been a tri-athlete as a civilian and was the *section*'s finest sportsman. In spite of his punishing lifestyle, he had the endurance of a Kentucky thoroughbred. In the chaos of the *régiment*'s early days, he had beaten the shit out of a *légionnaire*—shit was smeared on the floor. After leaving the infirmary, the *légionnaire* was moved to the CCL and later deserted. But brutal as *Caporal* Bendada could be, he was also an intellectual, and a gentleman of sorts. He had a university diploma in philosophy and could describe in detail any work of literature I could think of. He always spoke English to me and obviously knew something of my background. He was more a friend and guru to me than a superior.

I was put in a *chambre* with a Frenchman, a Bulgarian, and a Russian. Back in Castel the *section* had all got on together and I was accepted. Being thrown into a *chambre* with *vieux légionnaires* who disliked Americans as much as they disdained *jeunes légionnaires* was a different matter. I saw early on that I would have problems with the Bulgarian and the Frenchman who were both clearly determined to give me a tough time.

Andropov, the Bulgarian, was a large Muslim bully who had served in Bulgaria's punitive battalions. Sharing a room with a well-groomed, educated American raised in a proper family seemed to unsettle him. He often talked to himself and suddenly, out of the blue, he would ask me why his parents had abandoned him as an *enfant*. When I realized that he was an orphan, I managed to mingle a little sympathy with my contempt for him.

The Russian, Maximov, was the exception. He made for a good *camarade,* being one of the few Russian gentleman-soldiers. He had been a Battalion Commander but was now a humble ranker. An engineer like myself, he had a wife and two children in Volgograd, to whom he was able to send more money as a *légionnaire* than he had as an officer in his homeland where criminal violence had reached the level of Chicago in the 1930s.

"Russia was better off under the Tsars," he said. "I lied to them in Aubagne by stating that I was simply a chemical engineer. I told them nothing about commanding three hundred men and having more responsibility than our *chef de compagnie*. Every *caporal* knows that I don't give a shit about Legion *sketch*."

In his early days in the Legion the *caporaux* had tormented him relentlessly. He showed me the scar across his scalp. "The Legion did this to me, but they learned that a *légionnaire* can only be pushed so far. I remember drinking an entire bottle of Smirnoff and going for a *caporal* with a knife. But before blade met flesh, the *chef* broke a chair over my head. Vodka is the devil," he went on. "But things are better for me now. You *jeunes légionnaires* have still a lot to go through."

My roommates made it clear that they expected me to keep the *chambre* in spotless order. Being the *jeune légionnaire,* I was perfectly willing to do so as a good-will gesture, but I should have known better—it only made me look a weakling and a fool. In additional all *jeunes légionnaires* had morning and afternoon *corvée* nearly every day of the week. After waking, changing into morning *tenue,* and making our beds we had to sweep and mop forty meters of corridor, scrub out foul toilets, or do *corvée de bureau.* The *douche* corridor was always flooded with a centimeter of filthy water. There was no drain so we had to somehow mop it up with rags, and wring it into a bucket until the floors and *douches* were dry. Every task had to pass inspection by the *caporaux* before we could expect a slug of coffee or a bit of *baguette.*

After *soupe de midi,* a Foreign Legion *régiment* normally enjoys a brief siesta. This was the time when *jeunes légionnaires* were assigned afternoon *corvée.* The entire *compagnie* also performed *corvée de compagnie* twice a day, fifteen minutes before *rassemblement,* slowly filing our way across the parade ground, picking Marlboro butts from the road.

Most of the rest of our daily work was equally tedious. Because there were only three *compagnies* in the *régiment* to rotate onto services, every *légionnaire* had to devote one entire week out of every three to guard-duty, service in the *ordinaire,* or EIT duty anywhere the *régiment* needed a work squad. Those without duties at any given time were at the disposal of the *adjudant* responsible for assigning work in what has been termed the Legion of the Damned.

Because I was an American I was teased and abused by my French and Bulgarian roommates for being stupid enough to join the Foreign Legion. The more accommodating I was, the more they hated me. This nonsense had to stop and violence nearly ensued when I finally became fed up with the endless broom-work. "I'm not the only one in this *chambre!*" I said to Andropov, as he lay thumbing through his stack of cheap French pornography.

"You're the janitor in here," he snapped. "I'm the *chef de chambre* and I don't do shit!"

He got off his bed, grabbed me by the lapels, and ordered me to carry on sweeping. Twice my size, he was more than willing to scrap but rather than lash out, I warned him with a death-stare to never touch me again. When I returned the following afternoon, Andropov had swept the floor and cleared the trash. The next problem was dealing with a *vieux légionnaire* across the corridor, a hot-headed *REP* man.

"If I ever hear you arguing with your *chef de chambre* again, I'll personally beat the fuck out of you. Clear?"

Had it not been such a delicate point in my Legion career, I'd have been delighted to settle my account with the showman paratrooper. He'd more to lose than I in a brawl since I'd have been the *jeune légionnaire* who beat a *vieux parachutiste* to a pulp. But the political repercussions from the others for having the audacity to hammer a *vieux* was something I was unsure of, and I didn't want to have to sleep with a blade under my pillow for the next month.

"Our section doesn't like you," Michaud said to me, "especially the Russians. Funny thing, actually—it's only because you're an American."

"It'll pass. You need to worry more about yourself."

I was becoming concerned about his mood swings. Depending upon how much hashish he had at his disposal, he went from manic euphoria to deep depression, bad enough to want to slit his wrists. A contented and hard working *légionnaire* when he smoked reasonably, he readily admitted that were it not for Mister Brownstone, he'd have deserted long ago. One afternoon, he came into my *cham-*

bre with blood streaming from his nose and a sickening smile on his face.

"I think I like our fucking *caporaux!*" he said. "Real tough guys, proper *légionnaires*."

"You really need to stop smoking that shit."

When the official workday ended at 18.00 the Legion called *rassemblement,* then marched us to *soupe*. Other armies left it up to the men to decide if and when they ate, but not the Legion. Evening free time was short, since *extinction des feux* was enforced at 22.30. In theory, if we were in proper *tenue de sortie,* we could be off base until the next morning's *appel*. But the fact that having a bit of night life involved spending two days' wages on a taxi into Apt meant that most of us spent our free time on base. The few who found a *petite amie* in town, if possible one with a car, were the lucky ones. For the rest of us, we had nothing better to do than smash Kronenbourg bottles on the corridor floor and play rugby over broken glass with the latest hits in Euro-pop blaring out from the *chambres*.

Theft is common but any *légionnaire* found stealing purely for himself is punished mercilessly. In the recent past, petty thieves had ended up spread-eagled on a table pinned down with a bayonet through each hand. But stealing for one's *section,* even from *Madame la République,* is a completely different matter. During the First World War, Harvard *légionnaire* David King had been offended when he found shop-keepers locking their doors and running about in panic to warn others that *légionnaires* were coming. But he quickly realized that they were quite justified. When his *camarades* got back on the train, *baguettes, fromage, pinard,* and tobacco were spilling out from every greatcoat. Thieving was so celebrated in the Legion that the Americans of that time wrote a *chant*:

> We are the famous Legion that they talk so much about.
> People lock up everything whenever we're around.
> We're known for pillaging, the nifty way we steal.
> We'd pinch a baby carriage, and the infant for a meal.
> As we go marching and the band begins to play,
> You can hear the people shout,
> Lock the doors and shut the shop, the Legion's here today.

From the cellars of our block I stole an oak table and lugged it up to our *chambre*. But after one particularly violent orgy it went missing.

"Oh, yes," said Andropov casually, "*Caporal* Bendada broke it last night demonstrating a sidekick. Go and steal another one."

The French wasted little time organizing the inevitable *mafia fran-cophone*, making the non-French further resent their exclusivity and arrogance. The Legion was supposed to be for foreigners for Chris-sake! Michaud and Dupont joined without hesitation. Michaud's popularity amongst them was not just because he was a French-speaker but because he was able to supply the *compagnie* with hashish. *Caporal* Bendada, an honorary member, allowed Michaud and Dupont to buy and sell as they wished, until the day came when both showed up at morning *rassemblement* with black-eyes and bloodied lips.

"*Caporal* Bendada beat me up and banned me from doing busi-ness in the *compagnie*. I'm also on the *chef's merde*-list. He'll be lay-ing into me tonight."

"I told you to be careful with your popularity," I said to Michaud, "especially with the *mafia francophone*."

Maximov was a true camarade and arranged for me to become an honorary member of the *mafia Russe*. One evening soon after my induction, while we were watching old Russian war movies, he stuck an empty ballpoint pen into my mouth, then using a Camping-Gaz stove, heated a spoon red-hot and placed a speck of hashish in it There was a sudden knock on the door. "Go ahead and let him in," he said to me as I frantically fanned smoke out the window. "It's only *Caporal* Diagana."

"Perhaps Michaud's right," I said feeling pleasantly warm and euphoric. "This is the only *merde* that makes Legion life bearable. Now, hand me some of that there Smirnoff."

After *extinction des feux* we continued smoking and joking by flashlight. Those wanting to graduate to bigger and better things broke into the block's abandoned far wing, reserved for the yet to be formed 3*e* *Compagnie*. I now understood why during EIT duty weeks earlier the *chef* had ordered me to board up every entrance and window with scrap wood. By prizing out my nails, the Russian hard drug users had found a fine place to shoot up in, scattering every room with syringes, pornography, smashed Kronenbourg bottles, and window glass.

Weeks later, after assessing the building's suitability for the 3*e* *Compagnie,* the *chef* gave us a lecture. "I'll be brief. There is evidence of a life of filth in the *bâtiment* behind us. Not only have you been breaking into forbidden quarters but you have been indulging in banned substance abuse." His face flushed, his eyes narrowed, and the arteries in his neck bulged. "Drug-users are on a par with homosexuals, Jews, pedophiles and necrophiles! There's only one cure for pestilence like that. If I find anyone in there I'll crush his skull." He stomped heavily with his *rangers* and we could feel his blood pressure rise with each snarled out word. "There's only one place for junkies in the Legion—two meters under the earth . . . Have I made myself clear?" he screamed, staring Michaud straight in the eye.

"You heard what the *chef* said!" shouted the *caporaux* who regularly smoked with us. "Just don't let us catch you before he does!"

"Did you notice the *chef* glaring at me when he spoke?" Michaud asked me later. "He's nearly forty, and speaks of pedophiles! When he went out with the *cadres* to Apt last month he fucked a fifteen-year-old. If he ever buries me two meters under, I'll tell him to jump in with me."

That week, we were assigned to wash our *section's* amphibious VAB (*Véhicule de l'Avant Blindé,* armored car) while it was being used in a demonstration for *chefs de section*. As the various components were being pointed out, I hung around outside to hear what was being said. Instead of appreciating my interest in learning, the *chef* asked me what the fuck I thought I was doing.

"Just listening," I replied.

"Just listening, *CHEF!*" he bellowed and jumped out of the vehicle to kick me in the nuts and order me to do *pompes* until the demonstration was finished. But by now we had worked out a system for this kind of thing. I began by flogging myself up and down on the tarmac until the *chef* got back in the VAB then I stopped. Maximov gave me a wink whenever the *chef* looked as if he was about to poke his head out to verify what I was doing. Soon, I was lying comfortably on my belly and making regular grunting noises as if in great pain. As I was passing a count of two hundred, the *chef* finally barked "*Debout!*"

"This *sketch* is getting to me," I said to Maximov.

"He just wants to show you that he's the boss. I also had it rough when I was new. All I can say is that it'll get worse before it gets better."

When not binge drinking, I took it upon myself to improve my sport. I ran about the huge former air base and along the video-monitored fifteen-kilometer barbed-wire fence. Because I no longer had *Sergent* Galeski to compete against, I couldn't push myself at the same intensity, no matter how hard I tried. I often stopped to wander through parking lots full of rusted machinery and discarded *matériel de bureau* and into partially demolished buildings with old signs reading *"Ultra-secret"*. After going into one boarded-up building that was also surrounded by barbed wire, I suddenly noticed a nuclear hazard skull and crossbones warning. I sprinted back to my own block and scrubbed every centimeter of my body till it hurt.

In the middle of the wasteland we inhabited was a long runway and hangar used for France's Mirage nuclear armada. I wondered about the wisdom of stationing foreigners, some of them from actually or potentially hostile nations, on a nuclear base considered top secret. Some of these foreign *légionnaires* had science degrees.

Our barracks had been renamed the *Caserne Maréchal* Koenig, after the heroic World War II commander and lover of British Susan Travers, the first and only woman to serve in the Foreign Legion. We now had to prepare for the ceremonial parade celebrating the presentation of our tricolor, the *régiment*'s official announcement that it was open for business. For this, the rundown regimental base was to be made spotless—not only the buildings but also dozens of heavy vehicles. We spent days on end refreshing each vehicle's camouflage finish using kerosene, although this acts as a dissolvant on paint-work. The *caporal-chef* in charge then produced a can of grease and, using our boot brushes, we spread layers of it over every single tire. Finally the grease ran out and we had to resort to our own boot polish. When the high-ups decided they were unhappy with the location of one particular tracked vehicle, orders came to move it over the muddy ground. We then had to go over every detail of the now mud-encrusted rubber tracks again. Woodman complained of the "bitch work" he was assigned. Because the Legion was too tight-fisted to buy some rocks, he was forced to break granite with a sledgehammer to construct a base for the flagpole.

"Legion of the damned?" he grumbled. "Legion of the shammed!"

In addition to the endless bitch work, we spent whole mornings on parade ground drill. As in Castel, marching in perfect formation was no easy task, especially as we had to make several turns while marching in files eight men wide. The most difficult technical feat was the apparently simple one of getting several hundred *légionnaires* to take the initial step in unison. What would happen to a *légionnaire* who ruined the parade by getting out of step in front of an invited audience didn't bear thinking about. Desertion was probably the easiest option.

On the big day we all managed to get off in uniform step and commenced our slow, arrogant Legion pace. I fixed my eyes on the pivot man and colleague to my left. Though I was as nervous as hell, it was good to know that I was participating in the *régiment*'s tricolor presentation. Parading before the cheering crowd was like walking a tightrope. My heart beat faster with every counted step towards the edge of the parade ground, when we'd be out of sight of Colonel and spectators.

After the parade, we were allowed to attend the festivities in the *ordinaire* where the wine was flowing and food for once was plentiful. Dressed in *tenue de parade,* I was enjoying life and looking forward to a *campagnie de combat* posting when a Russian *caporal* came up to me. "*Jeune légionnaire* Sanchez, why don't you cut out the English and speak more Spanish?"

Despite this negative start, he seemed friendly enough. "My *petite amie* in Barcelona taught me the language." This was the first time I'd ever heard a Russian speak my mother tongue and he spoke it well. "I've been in the Legion for three years now," he added, "and I'm telling you from experience; there's nothing for you here, especially in this *régiment.*"

"I'll find something," I said idealistically.

"Speak to me again in a few months," he said. "You'll have understood by then."

Most of the officers were present, some of them with female

guests. I had the satisfaction of staring at their ladies as if to say: "Damn right, I'm undressing your *petite amie* with my eyes."

Running about preparing food was a mad but personable Australian. Beam was his name, so we called him Jim after the whiskey of that fame. He had served ten years in the British army. Originally posted to the 2*ͤ REP*, he had been dumped after an injury, like a worn-out car, in the 2*ͤ REG*. The Legion didn't like outsiders in its élite ranks and soft jobs such as cook, store keeper, or barman were only open to *légionnaires* with many years service, generally those disabled or near retirement. Every *légionnaire,* whatever his intended job, had to pass through the soldiering phase whether he wanted to or not.

We had the evening off and retired to the Legion *foyer* for beer.

"What happened to the new Englishman I met last week? He brought back some potent hashish from Djibouti."

"Already fucked off," Jim Beam said. "Don't blame the bloke. He'd just got back from doing four months proper soldiering. You know how much they earn in Africa? After a week back in Saint-Christol, he just couldn't tolerate the *sketch*. So he just fucked off back to England with a fistful of Legion pay."

"And the Russians? What are they like here?"

"As lazy in the Legion," said Woodman, "as niggers in the US Army."

Two more South Africans joined Jim Beam, Woodman, Sijfert, Kulzer and myself, to complete the handful of men in the *mafia Anglaise*. Lohmann was another South African army veteran who had seen considerable action during apartheid. Like every South African I met, he was well-spoken and well-disciplined with all the elements of an excellent soldier and anxious for the kind of action he'd seen in his homeland. I learned early that every Afrikaner shared Sijfert's opinion of Negroes, however polite or educated they were. It made sense, considering that most Afrikaners were raised on farms which had had to be turned into fortresses against rampant post-apartheid black-on-white violence.

South African Weber was the *mafia Anglaise*'s golden-boy idealist.

His problem was that he had no previous service and had no idea how a military was properly run. He was romantic about his new home and never found fault with the Legion, at least for the first few months. The rest of us, including Woodman, who had served in the democratic US army, were quickly fed up with our 2^e *REG* posting. We soon found that nobody in the *mafia Anglaise* had requested the *REG*.

7.

Montpellier

From the moment they enter the Legion, bonding takes place. They build a tremendous esprit de corps, and that, as we have learned throughout history, makes for a good fighting man.

Norman Schwarzkopf, US Army General

In Castel, we were always being told how different life was going to be *en régiment* but the free weekends we'd been looking forward to turned out to be only thirty-six-hour leaves from midday Saturday to midnight Sunday. And even those depended on whether we had guard, *ordinaire,* or EIT duty. However, one day the colonel was so impressed with the regiment's turnout that he rewarded us with a full forty-eight hour leave, and for once, I was not on duty! As usual the weekend began with a heavy ironing session. Other western armies do not allow their personnel to wear uniform while on leave because of the danger from terrorists, but legionnaires are expected to remain in *tenue de sortie* at all times.

Since the 2^e REG was located in the middle of nowhere, the *Compagnie de Commandement et Logistique* (CCL) operated a bus service to Avignon, leaving on Friday evening and picking us up again at midnight Sunday. The bus stopped outside the railway station, which was teeming with legionnaires from surrounding areas—the *1er Régiment Étranger de Cavalerie* in Orange, the *1er Régiment*

Étranger de Génie in Laudun, and the 2e *Régiment Étranger d'Infanterie* in Nîmes.

With forty-eight hours of freedom ahead of me, I felt a bit like a long-term convict on his first day out. What was I going to do with myself? Luckily, I came across Woodman and we decided to take a half-hour train ride down to a favorite Legion hangout, Montpellier. It is a university town with a student population of sixty thousand giving it a Bohemian atmosphere and teeming nightlife, very different from the other villagelike cities of Provence.

As we stood downing beer surrounded by fellow Kronenbourg-guzzling legionnaires in the *buffet de la gare* in Montpellier, I told Woodman where we were going to stay. "One of those hostels I used to stay in during my backpacker days. Full of attractive, intelligent women from around the world. *Action!*"

Legionnaires were banned from most of the region's hostels but I got us beds at the Hostelling International hostel where I knew their night man, a Spanish *ancien*. The first thing we did was to change into the civilian clothing that we'd sneaked out in our sports bags. I'd borrowed all mine from Calderon. After a hot shower, we were ready to get the drinking started again. Once we got to the *Place de la Comédie,* it didn't take long to find a suitable watering hole. The London Tavern had the right-sounding name and it was full of female English exchange students.

Heavy drinking fosters male bonding but did not appeal to the tall English catwalk model I found myself standing beside. When I was a civilian, my approach was gentler.

"Can't remember what I do for a living right now," I slurred. "Ah, yes, I think somebody told me that I'm a wildlife photographer. Woodman here is my colleague. We work in the same office, in fact. Understand?"

"No."

"Oh okay, we're both in the French Foreign Fucking Legion! You know, white-capped bastards running about the desert. That's what we are. Yeah, but come to think of it, I used to be a professional, a man of respect. You know with a suit and tie and all that nice shit."

"I'm sure you were," she said and walked away.

"*Putain!* Why the hell did you scare her off?" I shouted at Woodman. "Get me a beer, you bastard."

Though I tried my hardest, I soon realized that I was no longer welcome to the sort of girls I used to meet in my backpacking days and I resented it. I was sitting at the bar just before it closed, when another English girl accidentally jostled my arm. She apologized in French. When I replied in English, she introduced herself and I kissed her on both cheeks as the French do. She had been drinking, too, but seemed sincerely interested in getting to know me.

"And what brings you to France?"

"If I tell you, either you won't believe me or you'll run away."

"Oh, come on," she said. "I'm sure it's something interesting. The suspense is killing me."

"What if I tell you I'm an engineer and that I work for the French Ministry of Defence?"

"Like something out of a James Bond film?"

"Kind of. I'm in the Foreign Legion."

"Don't be daft," she said. "Go on, tell me what you're doing here in this lovely part of France."

When I handed her my ID card, her face went white and she disappeared.

"I'm a legionnaire!" I howled after her. "And I'm proud of it! Does any other woman in here have a problem with that? Damn you all. To hell with you!"

"Now you're really sounding like a legionnaire," said Woodman.

There was a 02.00 curfew at the HI hostel we were staying in. Just before 04.00, we rang the buzzer and spoke into the intercom, hoping the night man would open up.

"Antonio, open the door for your fellow legionnaires," I said, speaking Spanish. "It's cold out here and we ain't got nowhere to sleep."

"*Joven legionarios,*" he said unlocking the gate. "Don't you know about the curfew?"

"Yes, but . . ."

"Step inside."

"*Señor,* it's an honor to be in your presence."

"Follow me." He opened the reception door and picked up a liter of *vino.* "Care for a glass?"

"A legionnaire never turns down a drink from an *anciano,*" I replied, though I was on the verge of passing out.

"Yeah, you bring back memories of my time in the Legion. It was very different then, a real family. Though I certainly appreciate that it's more democratic now, I don't agree with what the French are doing to our Legion. They're trying to bring it into line with the *Armée de Terre.* Well, it won't work; it just won't be the same."

"Antonio, I know that you went through the same as us, and sure as hell more." He had a huge scar running from the back of his neck to his thigh from a parachute jump gone terribly wrong. "I only hope that after this first weekend off, I'll be returning to *regimiento* more sane than when I left."

"You should know by now that the Legion is *mierda,*" Antonio said. "But to understand it, you have to first understand the French. If they see a pile of *mierda* on the floor, they don't clean it up; they place it on a silver platter and decorate it with garnish and lettuce."

After we'd emptied the bottle, Woodman and I said *Bonne nuit,* and stormed upstairs to the dormitory where Antonio said there was already a group of Swiss backpackers. We turned on the lights, and lay on our beds trying to see who could fart the loudest. Before we finally passed out, the Swiss had moved into a different room. Woodman fell asleep snoring noisily, with his feet on the headboard, still in his Timberland boots.

We were awakened next morning by the cleaning staff who tossed us into the street before the 10.00 lockout. Still drunk and staggering, we made our way into the city center and slept on a bench in the *Place de la Comédie.* That afternoon, while Woodman went off to spend his savings on having his arms tattooed again, I tried to find an Internet café. As I was coming around a corner, somebody grabbed my arm.

"Hey, forget about the fucking Internet," Sijfert and Kulzer said. "You're coming with us."

"Okay, where're we drinking?"

"Hold it. I've just noticed a pair of underage fifteen-year-olds staring at me."

"Piss off, Sijfert," I said. "I don't give a shit how young they are. What the hell are you talking about anyway; you're only twenty."

The young *Françaises* dressed in Adidas and Levi's were on the other side of the street, whispering together. They came across to us.

"And what is this *Légion Étrangère* they tell us about?" one of them asked.

"Better you don't know, *chérie*," I replied. "Aren't you supposed to be in school?"

"Oh, I can't be bothered with it," said the other, spitting on the pavement. "What are you doing here in the *Place de la Comédie* at four o'clock in the afternoon?"

"We're just about to have a drink somewhere where you birds are too young to go," Sijfert answered.

"*Ah nous, nous préférons* other drugs. You like smoking *chite*?" she asked, meaning hash but sounding like something else. "*Suivez-nous.*"

Three English-speaking legionnaires crowding along behind two teenage *Françaises* must have looked suspicious to the locals. We smoked up, crouching between two parked cars in an underground carpark, but nothing came of it. It must have been the squatting position. Sijfert let out a long, loud, stinking fart and the girls ran away.

That evening, I met one of Sijfert's Irish comrades—Ellison, the boxer. We were sitting in The Fitzpatrick, when he came roaring in still wearing *tenue de sortie* and *képi*. "Now that's a man's fookin' sport," he said, pointing at the France-England rugby match playing on the television. "Who's got the next round then? Get that bollocks barman over here before I start breaking shit."

The Fitz was a recognized meeting point for the *mafia Anglaise* from various regiments, so we were soon joined by another Irishman and a Kiwi.

"It's great to get away from all those Russian bastards," Ellison continued. "If one of them comes through these sacred doors, I'll smash his teeth in!"

The pub was beginning to fill with students. "Looks like tonight we're going to have some Legion birds," Sijfert said.

"Where?" I asked.

"Over hyewp the bar." He hiccuped into his glass.

"That skinny pair?"

"No, two slappers behind them. I know you're an engineer used to shagging Ally McBeal types, but I don't give a toss if they're heavy. Grab me another Guinness and they'll suit us fine."

He managed to get one of them to come over and join us.

"Hey, Ellison, show us how you slap your old fella on the table!" the Kiwi shouted.

Ellison stood up to unfasten his trousers and the girl, giggling with both hands clamped over her mouth, jumped up to push her way through the crowd back to her friend. "What?" he howled after her. "You taking the piss outta me? Get back to the bar where you belong, you worthless whore."

"Lads," said the Irish bartender, coming across to us, "could you quieten it down a bit and kindly watch your language."

"You hear that, lads?" Kulzer yelled. "Now everybody shut the fuck up!"

Ellison noticed Woodman chatting to a young American guy in a Berkeley T-shirt. "Get that wanker over here," he bawled.

The student came over and sat down apprehensively.

"We're going to show you how the Legion drinks."

"Er, what's the Legion?"

"You never heard of the Legion? Steady on, you little runt. You taking the piss outta me too?"

"It's kind of like Hell's Angels on camels," I put in.

Surprisingly, nobody touched the American. He got drunk with us and we taught him all about Legion traditions and customs—how to get on the piss-train and how to fuck portly dames.

Toward the end of the evening Ellison was at the bar making out with the overweight girl he'd called a whore, but after a few more stouts he went limp and sat there staring vacantly into space. "Yeah," he said, "now I think I had enough. It's time for you guys to take me home."

Sijfert made sure Ellison had his wallet and ID card, and took him out with a supporting arm around his shoulders while Woodman and I went back to Antonio's *vino* and stories about the Legion.

"After finishing my first contract in the seventies, the lieutenant paid me a surprise visit. They knew I wasn't feeling at ease as a civilian. In return for taking part in the black ops prior to the Kolwezi paratroop drop, he said I could keep whatever I laid my hands on. There's diamonds down there, you know, and gold. Well, I've always been blessed with *baraka*—that's Arab for luck—so I said yes."

Sunday morning we joined the *mafia Anglaise* for an Irish breakfast at The Fitzpatrick. Though it was far from what an American would consider a real breakfast, I ate my sausages and sautéed mushrooms with relish. Sijfert was behaving sickly sweet with the stunning *petite amie* he'd picked up. When she went out to the ladies' room, he said she'd licked his ass the previous night, but I told him I didn't want to hear the details while washing down my food.

We did nothing else that day and evening but drink ourselves silly.

"I should've joined the U.S. fucking Marines," Ellison said, "but some bastard told me that the Legion was better."

"Come on, Ellison, they wouldn't let you in," I said. "And anyway I'm certain that those guys back in Camp Lejeune, North Carolina, are thinking the same thing about us. Let's face it; we've got Nice and Cannes just down the road. We can jump on the TGV and be on a Mediterranean beach in thirty minutes. Can you imagine spending the weekend in a town like Jacksonville full of people like Woodman here?"

At midnight the bus took us back to Saint-Christol.

*   *   *

"I'm pissed off with this Legion of *sketch*," I said to no one in particular as I was mopping the floor one morning.

"I understand your problem, Sanchez," *Caporal* Bendada called out. "You think too much for your own good. You question the Legion because you don't understand the system. Just bear in mind, next week we have our regimental cross-country trials. If you make the team as one of our *crossmans*, life will get very different for you."

While cleaning the showers next morning, I noticed a pair of underpants hung up to dry. Assuming the owner would soon be coming to retrieve them, I let them be. But when *Caporal* Diagana inspected my work, he flew into a fit of rage that I hadn't taken them down and told me that I was confined to barracks.

I was ordered to sweep and mop an entire company wing and clean the duty office. Whenever I reported to the orderly corporal to say that I'd finished, he always found something else for me to do. After I'd finished washing the trashcans with a sponge, he pointed out that I'd neglected to scrub the insides. I was sent outside again in the freezing cold with a toilet brush and a bucket of water. While the company slept, I was perched up a ladder in pitch darkness and icy winds, cleaning windows. Working efficiently was pointless—no matter what or how much I scrubbed, I'd have to go on working until the corporal tired of watching me toil.

The London publishers of *Rough Guides* publish music, too, so I'd mailed them a book of *chants de la Légion*. In return, they sent me journals on the Languedoc-Roussillon region in a large envelope, which had been torn open for inspection before it reached me.

"These'll come in handy," I said to Weber, "if we ever get a chance to see anything besides these mountains."

"Please yourself but they don't interest me. I hate this country. It produces nothing but *mongols* called Frenchmen who've made the Foreign Legion into a shithouse."

Weber had a touch of brilliance and, in spite of his negative attitude, within a couple of months he had been earmarked for the corporal training course. I challenged him to try to beat me in the regimental cross-country race. As we waited for the starting gun, I was nervously eyeing him on my left. Though I loathed Legion *sketch*, when legionnaire was pitted against legionnaire in mano a mano competition, I became electric. For the others this was just another sporting activity, but I was determined to win a place in the regimental team. I was going to show everybody what I was made of.

The ten-kilometer race took us all the way around the perimeter fence, and through the neighboring woods and hills. The adrenaline rush of competing reawakened my pride in being a member of an elite fighting unit. I passed Weber early on, suspiciously easily. Halfway into the race, I spotted the leader and counted five runners between us, with several behind closing the gap. I had the same distance again to run and my lungs were bursting and my heart thumping out of my chest. I was soon no more than a running zombie with a grimace. A technique that helped me gain on the leaders was throwing myself down the descents. I relaxed, flailing my legs in a zigzag motion and swinging my arms as if losing my balance, thus managing the steepest grades without falling over. I finished sixth, just missing the five-man winners' podium but at least I'd made my presence felt. Not surprisingly, no cross-country team ever materialized.

I consoled myself with the thought that my athletic skill might earn me a slot in the 2e REG's *Unité de Recherche Humaine* (URH), a mountain reconnaissance group providing support for the 27e *Brigade d'Infanterie de Montagne*. One requirement was fluency in English.

"Don't even think about trying for the URH," *Caporal* Diagana muttered to me, eyeing my naked body while I was in the shower. "You're fast, but you'll never be this platoon's sportsman. I know your kind well; you'll turn into a deserter before long."

*   *   *

Though I now had a military driver's license, I still needed to have it "confirmed" by driving across France with a psychotic adjudant. Following behind us, was *Caporal* Chung, a Chinese with a long service record—one of the more likeable corporals. He spoke English with me and told me about the colorful life of adventure he'd led before joining the Legion, including a stint as dishwasher in San Francisco. He never took the training course for corporals but earned his rank during service in Lebanon. He had saved the life of a wounded comrade under fire and was awarded his stripes on the spot.

We began with my driving for five hours up and down the *plateau d'Albion,* along cliffs and over fallen rocks, with the adjudant beside me filling in a form on his clipboard with red ink. "Take off your *képi*! Can't you see we've left *régiment*? . . . No, *mongol*! Shift to second gear first! . . . Now what the hell does that speed limit sign say? Did you learn a damn thing in Castel? You probably don't even know what that solid yellow line means."—I didn't!

Very early on the following morning we drove up to the *Armée de Terre's* base in Lyon and spent the rest of the day loading *Caporal* Chung's truck. After hours of backbreaking work in freezing weather, we had stopped for *soupe de midi*. The quality and quantity of the *Armée ordinaire* food amazed me. And there waiting in line to be served was a female colonel! Mind-boggling! High-ranking officers were eating in the same quarters as the rank and file. When I passed the colonel's table, I saluted her smartly. She eyed me up and down with suspicion, as if saluting in those circumstances was unnecessary, and simply nodded.

"I told you not to look over your shoulder when changing lanes!" the adjudant howled as I was driving back to Saint-Christol. "What do you think rearview mirrors are for? Right now, it's me talking. The next time you do that, it'll be my fist!"

I struggled to explain, but couldn't work out the French translation for blind spot.

"Now, pull in here to this service area."

As I was switching lanes, I glanced over my shoulder again and was rewarded with a punch in the ear.

A few kilometers from our base, on a bend in the narrow, winding road, a Peugeot suddenly pulled out from behind an articulated truck and came within feet of a head-on collision. With lightning-quick reflexes, I applied the brakes and, veering dangerously close to the bordering cliff edge, allowed the offending driver to cut back in. The adjutant had no time to curse and grudgingly praised my immediate reaction. Regardless of the red marks on his clipboard form, he passed me.

The Legion's workhorse is the GIAT Industries *Véhicule de l'Avant Blindé* (VAB) multipurpose armored vehicle. The main difference between *régiment de génie* VABs and those of the infantry regiments is the additional engineering goodies they carry, such as shovels, axes, pulleys, and heavy cables. Mounted on every VAB is the aging, but time-tested 12mm U.S. Browning a LRAC, *Lance Roquettes Antichar* (LRA), an anti-tank rocket launcher. The Dragar turret with a 25mm gun with a firing rate of up to 400 rounds per minute is an optional extra. The steel hull is nuclear-blast-proof and NBC protection is integrated in the air conditioning system. The VAB's 300 hp high torque turbo diesel engine, with a fully automatic gearbox, independent suspension, and large wheels give it high tactical mobility and a top road speed of 110 kph. It enables Legion units to carry out lightning strikes to kill and destroy, before making off like bandits in a getaway vehicle.

The Legion's blitzkrieg tactics caught the eye of Stormin' Norman Schwarzkopf, the commander of U.S. forces during the Gulf War. Not only was the Foreign Legion given special mention after the war, but the general invited a detachment to march through Times Square for the victory celebration—the only foreign army to parade on American soil since World War II. In return, the general was made an honorary legionnaire, First Class—a rare honor not given even to France's premier statesman Charles de Gaulle. In addition, Schwarzkopf was given a wallet-sized card with the Legion's telephone number and an accompanying message stating that should he ever be bogged down in a no-win situation, the Legion would go anywhere in the world to bail him out. Schwarzkopf's five-star field cap is on display in the Legion's museum in Aubagne.

We traveled by VAB to the village of Sissonne, one hour north of Paris for training exercises. The chaos and disorganization in the final hours before departure were typical Legion. *Jeunes legionnaires* like ourselves were ordered to load the trucks, but not before we'd finished our usual morning cleaning duties. The corporals ordered me to fetch the mops, brooms, and buckets that were to accompany us and I left my rucksack lying on the tarmac. It was already in the truck when I returned. Andropov had been told to load it, so he greeted me with a blow to the chest. But this was no time to begin a fight—I still had to sprint over and sign for the LRAC launcher then back to the VAB, where I sat panting and double-checking that I had my pistol, gas mask, helmet and, just as important, my beret stuffed in the pocket of my combat fatigues. Forgetting any of the dozen items that were checked and rechecked not only resulted in severe punishment from the instructors but a second beating from the others in the platoon who were made to suffer, too, in order to build up *cohésion*. I sighed with relief once the convoy finally began to move north.

I had to put up with Raducanu during the trip. Though a tiger on the battlefield, he had a child's mentality and spent his time calling me names, and shouting, "Are we there yet?" every half hour. I was trying to ignore him by thumbing through the latest issue of *Képi Blanc,* the Legion's monthly magazine, when shots rang out and the VAB halted dead in its tracks. We leapt out to deal with the enemy. *Caporal* Diagana shouted, "Gas!" as artillery opened up and I realized that I hadn't properly adjusted my mask. My jaw was painfully pried open but there was no time to fumble with the straps in the middle of a firefight. We made a sprinting retreat through the forest and waited for a half hour to rendezvous with the vehicle. I was gasping for air and could barely see through the misted visor. Then, to make matters worse, I jumped into the wrong vehicle. Thinking I was the first one in, I waited for the others to join me, until the *chef,* acting as an observer, grabbed me by the lapels and dragged me out.

We finally arrived at Sissonne to find we were to be used as guinea pigs for the newly commissioned lieutenants in the *Troupes de Marine,* some of them women! The Legion is often expected to prostitute itself to the needs of the *Armée de Terre,* who know that legionnaires are trained to accept *sketch* and traumatization.

As we were lining up for *soupe, Caporal* Diagana ordered us to push and shove our way to the front of the line. "Put on your legion war face and get those *Troupes de Marine* out of the way. If any of them don't like it, I'll deal with them." It was astonishing for us to see male and female *Troupes de Marine* sitting and chatting together. They must have felt the same about the Legion gang of green-bereted thugs speaking Russian, Czech, Polish, English, and thick, bastardized French.

A duty cook made the mistake of raising his voice when a Bulgarian took one baguette too many. *Caporal* Diagana was furious that any French soldier had the audacity to speak like that to one of his men. That evening, with his neck veins popping, he lectured us on how we should behave. "You are legionnaires. Allow nobody, I repeat *nobody,* to treat you with disrespect! Is that clear?"

Though our maneuvers were routine, they caught the attention of the U.S. Army brass and two combat engineering lieutenants who were sent over as observers. Before we returned to base that night, while painstakingly loading the trucks once again, I ran into them.

"Purdue," I whispered to them as I passed.

Though they were American officers, they were from a foreign army as far as I was concerned. I had no idea whether to address them as Sir, *mon lieutenant,* or just dude.

"Ohio State ROTC," one whispered back.

Caporal Diagana and the *chef* bawled at me to get the fuck away from them, "*Imméd!*" For having said a couple of words to my fellow countrymen, I was made to scrub the showers and the hole-in-the-ground *chiottes turques* before joining the others to clean every piece of kit that we had been using. I scrubbed the canvas straps of my LRAC carrying case three times, because dust had settled on them, and used a Q-tip to wipe my gas mask visor. Then, an hour before our time of departure, we were screamed at and made to do *pompes* until we were flailing like beached whales because a bit of pillow down was found underneath an instructor's bed.

The *REG*'s principal task with the new intake was to crank out legionnaires with battlefield skills. A *jeune* legionnaire's first year is spent getting enough specialized training courses under his belt to be useful. The first three were the *Brevet de Ski Militaire,* the Heavy Vehicle Driving License, and the de-mining course MINEX 1.

Back in the days when I was still dithering about joining the Peace Corps or the priesthood, I got to thinking about the mathematical ratio of effort to propagation of good. Land mines are indiscriminate weapons that prevent the return of refugees, damage the environment, and jeopardize peace. Of 26,000 civilians killed and maimed by land mines every year, ten thousand of them are children who often mistake them for toys. If the Legion could teach me about mine clearance, I'd willingly accept what it demanded of me, whatever the cost to myself in personal suffering. Furthermore, the technicality of the MINEX 1 was a refreshingly intellectual challenge for me.

In just two weeks, I learned how to detect, identify, and remove land mines with my hands using a shish-kebab skewer. More refined demining techniques exist but the Legion, true to form, resorts to the most old-fashioned, unsophisticated, and dangerous methods. In freezing weather, we prodded the earth with our skewers, waiting to hear the distinctive click. It was a painstakingly slow process, requiring three legionnaires to advance together along meter-wide paths. The skewer needs to be carefully inserted into the frozen ground at an angle so as not to detonate the mine. Each centimeter has to be combed to detect antipersonnel land mines the size of a man's thumb. Depending on the terrain and weather conditions, clearing no more than three meters by ten per day is common. In Kosovo, we were told, there were land mines designed to kill the deminer himself and there was nothing we could do about them except, "Hope you don't come across any."

At morning parade one day, the captain announced that a Belgian army general, accompanied by a photographer from a major Brussels newspaper, was coming to observe our expertise. He invited us to remove our Velcro nametags and said that if we did not wish our faces to be photographed, we should arrange to be bending down to pick something up just as the photographer snapped his shot.

We all put on our mine-clearing kit weighing over forty kilograms—Kevlar trousers and vest, helmet with heavy visor, and what looked like inflatable Eskimo snowshoes. It was bitterly cold and our hands were going numb so, to warm us up, a corporal sent Dupont waddling up a hill and we were made to run after him to bring him down with a rugby tackle. Then Rhee, a South Korean, was ordered to play a wounded deminer lying at the bottom and I was detailed to rescue him. Walking like a drunken duck, I stumbled to where he lay, and with superhuman effort, managed to heave his body over my shoulder in a fireman's lift to stagger back up the hill with him.

Classroom theory lessons, which lasted until lights-out, were given by *Caporal* Sperazzo. Dressed in our spotless *tenues de sortie,* we had to pass around oily demo land mines. When he inspected our notes he flew into a rage whenever he found someone who had written illegibly or hadn't used black ink. We were punished by being made to lie facedown on the floor and do *pompes* under the desks and chairs and between each other's legs.

When the course finished, I came out second.

Not all *jeunes* legionnaires took part in MINEX 1. One platoon rotated onto *métro* duty. After years of Islamic terrorist bombings, France uses armed soldiers to guard railroad and *métro* stations. Michaud went off on a swimming course. Woodman, who'd almost killed the adjudant during his automobile driving course in Castel, was assigned to the heavy vehicle equivalent. His driving was so bad that when his instructor, a kickboxing champion, bellowed at him to drive to a secluded area of the forest, he expected to be kickboxed into the next millennium, but he was told to pull over and get out to hunt for mushrooms. Maximov failed the heavy vehicle course twice and was given five days in the lockup for wasting Legion time and money.

Just as we were all becoming thoroughly pissed off, we were given a forty-eight-hour leave. Many of my *camarades* were too broke to do anything but stay in the barracks to drink and smoke themselves stupid but I needed to get out. I almost blew it, though. That Friday evening the duty *caporal chef* wanted to cancel my leave because my socks were a shade of green too dark. Our kindly captain, however, walked by as I was being put through the wringers and ordered the *caporal chef* to cool it. I borrowed a fermenting pair of socks from a Bulgarian and I sprinted onto the bus with seconds to spare.

I checked into the Avignon Youth Hostel. The only other person there was an Anglo-Canadian girl. "But you're American," she said, "so why are you in uniform?"

"Don't you recognize the white cap?"

"No, but it looks cute."

"Something to do with the French army." As I sat down and placed my rucksack on the floor, it gave out a distinctive Kronenbourg clink. "Mind if I drink? It's been a long week in the office. Care for a bottle yourself?"

"Oh, no," she replied. "My tummy is kind of upset. A lot of the food over here doesn't agree with me. I've been away from home for weeks now and I'm getting a bit homesick. How about you?"

"Well, I suppose I've been away from my family for quite a long time as well."

"Fair enough," she said. "I think I'll just have one of those French beers after all."

After a few more bottles she'd forgotten all about feeling under the weather.

"I know *centre-ville*," I said. "Let's go out for a stroll along the medieval battlements and stop by somewhere for a *pastis*."

"Okay, but don't you want to change into something more casual?"

"Civilian clothes are in the pipeline, but, for now, my *tenue de sortie* will have to do."

Walking through a back alley, we encountered two skinheads wearing leather jackets and black Levi's. Seeing I was a legionnaire, they just nodded to me. When we went into a crowded *bistrot*, the barman served us two *pastis* before I'd even placed my *képi* on the bar. "For you and the mademoiselle, from the gentlemen across the bar."

I looked over and saw an unmistakable group of leather-faced, shaven-headed men in civilian clothes. I nodded at them in gratitude but before we'd half-finished our drinks, the barman delivered another round.

"See those roughs around the bar?" I said to the Canadian. "Legionnaires. I am one of them."

"But why are they buying all the drinks?"

"Difficult to explain."

"From the new *régiment, n'est-ce pas?*" one of them called across. "Welcome aboard. How is it going up there at the 2e REG?"

"*La ferme* (Shut up!)" another said. "Don't bother the *jeune* légionnaire when he's with his *copine*." He spoke with the authority of a corporal and sent over another round.

He and the drink made me feel quite sentimental. Life in the Legion is hard and exasperating but undeniably special. As a legionnaire you become a life member of a worldwide secret society. Though I walk through the valley of the shadow of death, all I need do is call out, *A moi la Légion!* and fellow legionnaires armed with rods and staffs will spring out from the back alleys and *bistrots* to come to my assistance.

Next morning I woke up with a thumping hangover and left the hostel early so that I wouldn't have to meet the Canadian again after unsuccessfully running my hand up the inside of her jumper the night before. I got on the TGV and within hours I was in Paris. There was nobody there to greet me and all the hostels in the city center were fully booked, but it was like a homecoming for me.

*   *   *

I rode the *métro* out to the Arab neighborhood of Barbés in the 18ᵉ *arrondissement*, known as Montmartre, a center for crime and prostitution. Broad avenues sweep past narrow, winding streets, some of which tail off into stepped alleyways leading up to the Basilica of the *Sacré Coeur*. Before the North Africans arrived, it was home to the city's art colony, including jazz-age expatriates like Picasso, Modigliani, James Joyce, and F. Scott Fitzgerald.

The run-down hostel I took a bed in wasn't listed in any tour book but it had no evening curfew, checkout was at noon, and it cost only seventy francs per night. At first I didn't much like the look of my roommate, a stunted Algerian wearing leg braces, but we got talking.

"I'm here to find work," he said in fluent English.

"Doing what?" Imagining that he was a thief or a pimp.

"A year ago I was awarded an advanced diploma in IT but I've been looking for work ever since and have found nothing. Before coming here, I had such high expectations of France and the French but I'm beginning to think they just don't want me."

"That's sort of how I feel myself," I said and went out for another trip on the *métro*. I remained standing in my *tenue de sortie* while slouching civilians with their feet on the seats looked me over with suspicion. I got off at *Maubert Mutualité* and wandered around the Latin Quarter.

My first stop was my old Paris watering hole, the *Violon Dingue*, an all-American bar with the Green Bay Packers playing Kansas City on the tube.

"Are you a milkman wearing a hat like that?" asked a drunken girl with a terrible American twang.

"*Viens,*" her French boyfriend muttered to her. "He's an Englishman in the Foreign Legion. Let's go somewhere else."

Just then, a huge Arab bumped into me without making any attempt to apologize. I dismissed it and finished my drink. Minutes later, the same thug came up to me again, but this time he went so far as to take my *képi* and place it atop the bar!

"You a legionnaire, too?" I asked.

He said nothing.

"If you're a legionnaire, you'll shake my fucking hand!" I growled, staring him straight in the eye and waiting for him to make a move. But it was obvious that he could flatten me so I wasn't going to take him on bare-handed. My peripheral vision was scanning for near-at-hand beer bottles that I could smash over his head. The more I brooded about disfiguring him, the more frightened I became of myself. I left the premises before my id took control.

That took me along the cobbled street to The Hurling Pub, with an older, more affluent clientele. Standing at the bar was an elderly moustachioed gentleman who smiled and bought me a beer "for services rendered to *Madame la République*."

"I had a legionnaire friend several years back. I met him when he was in Paris for the July 14 parade down the *Champs-Elysées*."

"Cool. Any chance of another drink?"

"I'm a well-known journalist."

"Oh yeah? Well, buy me another beer, you rich old bastard."

"Please, order whatever you want. Drink as much as you like."

"What?"

"Yes, I always bought a lot of drinks for my other legionnaire friend. He was a very good-looking young Asian. As a matter of fact, we became lovers . . ."

"Bullshit. No legionnaire would degrade himself to that!" I snapped.

"Young man, there's nothing wrong in it. It's society that has brainwashed you into thinking about sexuality like that. Underneath your bourgeois attitude you may well feel the same way about men as I do."

"You disgust me."

"I compensated him well for his services."

"I'm nobody's toy."

"But you're so poorly paid for everything you do for this country."

"Any enjoyment you may have with me will be very expensive. I'll want half payment now and half tomorrow morning."

After living as a posh Chicago yuppie, this was what I had come to! Not only was I prepared to fool a randy pervert into thinking I'd sleep with him but I was about to take the half-payment and kick the piss out of him in a dark alleyway.

"How much are you worth?" he asked.

Just then, his cell phone rang. He excused himself, ordered me two more beers, and went outside. Before he returned, I sculled them both down and sneaked away to Polly Magoo's, a Bohemian hangout that Jim Morrison drank himself oblivious in. There I got talking to an attractive Swedish girl named Annika.

"I've seen documentaries about the Foreign Legion. Tell me," she said fluttering her eyelashes at me, "how many men have you killed?"

"Well," I grinned, "not very many, only the really bad guys."

There was another girl eyeing me farther along the bar. When she passed behind me on her way to the ladies' room, she gave my right bicep an approving squeeze.

"So why did you join then?" asked Annika.

"Well frankly, if you tell me that something's dangerous, stupid, that I can't do it, or that I'll get killed trying, then guess what I'll do?"

"Barman!" she squealed. "This man deserves another drink."

On Sunday before taking the train back to Avignon, I paid my soul mate Katarina a visit. We were enjoying polite conversation over an elegant lunch with much better *pinard* than that in the Legion, when the phone rang.

"Mother remembers you from Berlin a couple of years ago," Katarina said. "Come over here and say hello."

"Dear boy," Frau Wunder said, "Katarina tells me you've joined that *Fremdenlegion*. You used to be so bright and positive about life! What are you punishing yourself for? Have you done something terrible?"

"*Nein,* Frau Wunder, it's a bit more complicated than that."

I put down the phone. "Katarina, I don't want to go back. I know that wearing the *képi blanc* is something very special, but the price is high, way too high. Tell me to stay here in Paris with you."

She smiled and shook her head.

At thirty minutes to midnight waiting for the *REG* bus in Avignon, I was chatting to the bargirl in the *café de la gare*. "Is the road to Saint-Christol still closed?" I asked, admiring two perfectly rounded tits nuzzling together under her open-necked blouse.

"The weather's always pretty bad up there on the plateau."

"I love France and French women," I said, feeling pleasantly buzzed, "This would be my favorite country in the whole world, if we could just get rid of all the Frenchmen."

"Cheeky monkey," she said, blushing.

"Yup, I'm cheekier than a fat ass."

"Careful, that's my boyfriend at the table over there. We're moving to Miami in the spring and he doesn't like me getting into conversation with other men."

"Typical fucking Frenchman," I said, turning around to leer over at him. "He isn't saying much at the moment."

"Mon dieu," she said. "He'll really scold me. But I must admit that I'm attracted to that type. I don't want someone who's too gentle, if you know what I mean."

"Somebody a bit dangerous, huh?"

"Hmmh, yes."

"A mercenary type?"

"Did you do something terrible in your homeland to end up in the Foreign Legion?"

"Maybe . . ."

"Do you have an assumed name?"

"Yes."

"What's your real name?"

"If I told you that, it wouldn't be a secret, now would it?"

I suggested that she follow me around the corner for a quickie but, just then, the corporals began shouting and I had to gather up my things. *"Au revoir, ma petite.* Send me a postcard from *la Floride*!"

*   *   *

We were mopping the platoon office when a Polish skinhead named Czarneski presented himself to the *chef* to explain why another Pole had failed to return from long-term leave. "He hasn't deserted. They stopped him at the border and found his ID card with his *nom de guerre*. You can go to prison for joining the Legion in Poland."

Although only twenty years old, Czarneski was a hard-nosed brawler no corporal dared touch. There was a warrant out for his arrest for almost killing an antiriot policeman during a fight at a Warsaw football match. But in spite of his background, he was neither a bully nor a showman. He kept very much to himself and threw his weight around only when he needed to.

"There are niggers and Jews everywhere, even in Poland. Look at what's happened to France, full of blacks and Arabs. But then, the French are just as bad as niggers anyway."

"Don't you think you're a bit racist?"

"Not at all. I hate the Germans, too."

I could only laugh in astonishment.

"You're from Kentucky, right? You're a member of the Ku Klux Klan then." He slapped me on the back. "You and I are Aryan brothers."

What made him think I was in the KKK, or even a Caucasian, was beyond me, but from then on he was a *camarade*. Friends are invaluable assets in the Legion and I couldn't afford the luxury of picking and choosing them according to their code of moral conduct.

Czarneski already had a long service record. Some of the men he had done basic training with were now corporals but he had always been in too much trouble to win promotion. In crude Spanish, he explained, "I *mucho* like the *mucho caliente* (hot-blooded) women of Spain." He and a band of Poles had spent their first long leave in Barcelona. They used their hotel room for sleeping in during the day and for drunken orgies at night. In town, when they weren't brawling, they collected various items of combat gear. To try out a new commando knife, they slashed their window drapes into ribbons and Czarneski carved up a new room door with a samurai sword.

At the start of another forty-eight hour leave, I was with Woodman and our unruly mates on the TGV. I opened a rucksack full of Kronenbourg and the others enthusiastically helped me lighten my load. We were well buzzed by the time we pulled into Montpellier. In perfectly pressed *tenue de sortie,* we made our way to Antonio's hostel. Remembering *Caporal* Diagana's instructions about putting on a Legion war-face, we strode along glaring aggressively at anyone who didn't quickly get out of our way.

Woodman and I changed out of *tenue,* finished our remaining Kronenbourgs, and made off to look for Sijfert and his 2^e *REI* bunch in The London Tavern. Sitting at a table with four young Swiss women, I realized how long it had been since I'd had any intimate female contact. I always found it easy to be charming when I was in a good mood and sufficiently drunk. I flagged Woodman over and prayed that he wouldn't begin speaking about disassembling his assault rifle.

We took the girls to the nearby Fizz disco. In spite of his redneck chat lines, Woodman was making good progress with one of them, until he spotted the Stars and Stripes hanging upside down in a row of national flags above the discotheque entrance.

"Ain't having that," he said with a drunken stare.

"Woodman, don't start shit now," I pleaded. "Think of the lovely girls we're with. Can't we fix it some other time?"

"How dare they!"

"Oh, fuck it!" I bent over and let Woodman stand on my back. He was taking down Old Glory when I suddenly found my head enveloped in a mist of chemicals; Woodman fell down, writhing in pain after being maced in the eyes point-blank by the doorman.

"Get up!" I said, trying to lever him from the ground. "Keep your eyes shut and get up."

I wiped my own eyes and ended up squirming and rubbing

madly like Woodman. We were saved by the girls. They led us down to the city fountain and dunked our heads in the water. It was half an hour before we could speak again; by then, the girls had gone.

We met up with Weber after midnight.

"I actually like that discotheque," I said to him. "Now, thanks to Woodman, we're blackballed from yet another fine Montpellier establishment."

As we were walking back to the hostel, a group of Arabs bumped into me. I turned around and confronted them. One of them pulled a knife.

"Put away the blade!" I snarled. "I'll disembowel you with my hands alone."

As the man was about to leap forward, Weber with his enviable IQ asked: "By the way, do you happen to know where the McDonald's is?"

Caught completely off-guard, the Arabs pointed down the street and walked away in confusion.

"Works all the time with the *kaffirs* in South Africa," he said. "They never know what hit them."

"Though I've tried," Woodman said, "I cannot think of a single thing that I like about Arabs— nothing at all."

"Hungry?"

"Yeah," he said, "let's go eat some *couscous*."

Before departing for Paris the following morning, I did some forward planning and stopped at the local Monoprix. I stuffed my rucksack with the enough baguettes, cheese, Dijon mustard, sliced ham, yogurt, ruby-red, and Kronenbourg to last Woodman and myself until Sunday night. I had learned that with a bit of effort, a legionnaire can have loads of fun on little money. I spent a tenth of what other legionnaires threw away on drink by pissing-up in the hostel before heading out to the bars.

Before settling down for a nap on the TGV, I gave Woodman a plastic goblet of *pinard*. He had his nose buried in Dostoevsky and assured me that he only needed a sip or two. I woke as we pulled into Paris's *Gare de Lyon* station. Woodman was wickedly drunk by then, his coat on the floor and his *tenue de sortie a gros bordel*. We'd just gotten off when he threw up like a volcano all over the coach door.

"Don't you know we're in *tenue de sortie*, you stupid cunt?" I barked. "Let's get outta here before a *sergent* sees you."

"I know I'm just an embarrassment," he slurred as we walked into the street. "You go on ahead and leave me here."

"I'd just love to leave you on your own vomiting on yourself all weekend, but I won't. We're supposed to be legionfuckinaires. Now, shut your ass and try to walk straight. We're going to take a room in this hostel here."

He was so drunk that he signed in with an X. When he got up to our room he stripped and went into the bathroom. I heard him gagging and running the shower but he came out looking just as dirty as when he went in and lay down on his bed to sleep it off. When I went in to have a wash myself, I found the shower drain clogged and overflowing with his swill.

"I'm tired of messing around with women," he said when he woke. "All that time you have to spend chatting them up and getting to know them before you get to have sex. I know you're fed up with me, so just tell me where I can get a quick lay and I'll get out of your hair."

"Fine, if you're hell-bent on getting laid, I'll take you to Pigalle. Now, let's get into our civvies."

The first place we went into was a red-lit lounge with shag carpet and curtained booths along the wall. "That's a cute blonde in the corner over there," he said as we sat at the bar.

"Right," I said. "I'll wait here. Just remember to ask how much before agreeing to anything."

But without any bargaining, he handed over a third of his month's salary, for a short time and a complimentary bottle of cheap champagne. Moments after he was escorted behind the velvet curtain, a fat Negress perched herself on a barstool beside me.

"I'm a Christian," I said. "I don't pay for sex."

"I make you feel good." She started rubbing my leg and crotch. "Young man need good woman."

Somehow, she managed to give me an erection. I politely told her that I would allow her to take me behind the curtain for a free blow job, but that there was no way I would forward a single *centime* to screw her fat ass.

"Get one in for me!" I shouted to Woodman as I finished his champagne, "and one for General Rollet!"

"She let me do her twice," he said, coming out in better spirits. "She'd get fired if her madame found out she was double-dipping."

"Was she French?"

"Well, no, but it's just as nice to screw a Russian after they've been screwing us in the Legion for so long."

I took Woodman on to the *Violon Dingue*. He darted straight to the bar while I scanned the establishment and spotted a woman sitting alone, reading a book. Such a peculiar charade in a rowdy, smoke-filled bar told me she was looking for trouble. She found it.

"You couldn't pick somewhere a bit quieter to read in?" I asked. She told me she was Rachel, a Londoner in Paris on business.

"Me?" I said. "My friend over there and I happen to be soldiers. We're in the Foreign Legion."

"The Foreign Legion! Those men in funny white caps with hankies down the back?"

"What you call the hankies went out of fashion a long time ago."

She pulled up a seat for me and I could see there was something on her mind. After a couple of quick drinks she was already telling me that I could walk her to the *métro* station. Woodman was still at the bar but I forgot about the Legion's creed of never leaving one's *camarade* behind. I winked at him and left.

"Well, thanks for walking me to the *métro,*" she said.

It was not difficult to persuade her to let me escort her back to her hotel. We got off at Ecole Militaire and walked past the Artillery Academy where young Lieutenant Napoleon was trained.

"Doesn't night guard-duty suck?" I asked the young cadet sentries over Rachel's shoulder when I stopped to neck her. We sat down on a bench in front of a statue of General Morand.

"A perfect view of the Eiffel Tower." She sighed. "Lovely, isn't it?"

"Watch this," I said and snapped my fingers. ". . . Oh, *putain!* What time is it? The tower lights were supposed to turn off!"

"I think you've seen too many movies."

She leaned back on the cold granite and closed her eyes. We kissed tongue-to-tongue until she pulled back to breathe. "So, besides killing, what is it that you all do in the Foreign Legion?"

"When we're not pillaging African villages, we sing."

Looking up at the heavens, I felt like the legionnaires of yesteryear gazing into the African sky and thinking back to *la belle Europe*. "*En Algérie* is a sad song, but a touching one, of a sentry in Algeria who speaks of his untimely death." I sang out into the frosty night sky:

> *en Algérie un Képi blanc*
> Repels the Kabyle band.
> His comrade, shirt awash with *sang,*
> Lies dying on the sand.

> "Farewell fair France and you, my friend.
> This death is naught to me—
> In Honor served I to the end
> With true Fidelity."

> When legionnaires in battle fall
> And draw their final breath,
> No salvoes sound, no bugles call—
> A cross salutes their death.

The temperature was dropping rapidly and I was dressed in nothing more than a tight *Le Coq* soccer top and Levi's.

"Aren't you cold?"

"I've experienced worse."

"By the way, where are you sleeping tonight?"

"Er, I . . . I haven't quite figured that out yet."

"You naughty legionnaire," said she, nuzzling me. "You come to Paris with little more than the clothes on your back and go out searching for somebody like me to sleep with. You think I'm going to let you get away with that?"

Minutes later, she was telling me to run up the stairs while she distracted the hotel *concierge*. We stood in her room tugging at each other's clothes. "You've persuaded me to have sex after all," she whispered as we fell on to her bed, "but only with a condom."

I rolled over onto my stomach and lay there without speaking. I'd gone to war without bringing my helmet!

"Don't get angry."

"I'm not. I'm working out a battle plan." I mounted her breast and placed my old fella on her lower lip. When I came it was the orgasm of a thousand sunburned men.

I woke up at exactly 06.00. At first I couldn't figure out if I was in Paris dreaming that I was in the Legion or in the Legion dreaming that I was lying next to a naked woman. While Rachel showered, I made my way back to the hostel.

Woodman was half awake, sprawled on his bed, scooping yogurt with his fingers. Cheese, beer, and *pinard* were strewn about the floor. After giving him directions to the nearest tattoo parlor, I packed my affairs, changed into *tenue de sortie,* and this time grabbed a fistful of condoms.

"Oh, dear," Rachel said when she opened the door, "you really are in the Foreign Legion after all!"

Before she caught the Eurostar rail service to London's Waterloo, we spent the day on the *Champs de Mars* under the Eiffel Tower. We gave exhibitionist displays of affection in every café we went into. Legion *képis* have a clear plastic inside support lining, and by tradition, a lover's photograph is placed behind it. I planned to retire Nathalie from my *képi* after developing the photographs I'd taken of Rachel.

*   *   *

When we got back from permission I was surprised to hear that four of the Russians had spent the entire weekend at EuroDisney. "And what about you?" I asked Maximov.

"Fucked a whore in the Bois de Boulogne."

"Your wife and kids won't mind?"

"Don't be a soft cunt. Screwing a whore is no worse than wanking."

The others burst out laughing.

"You've never had a whore? Are you a faggot?"

"No, a Christian. I still nail the chicks but I figure that if it's free and consensual, it's only half wrong."

"So, because you come from a rich country, you feel superior to uneducated animals like us, eh?" Andropov said. "You won't drink with us, you don't go out with us, and you don't screw whores with us. *Achtung!*"

But we had little time for chatting. The depot was to be spruced up for the general's visit the following month. Growing along the ten-kilometer-long barbed-wire perimeter fence was a jungle of trees, undergrowth, weeds, and stubborn vines. When not on guard or *ordinaire* duty, we were ordered to clear it. At first we had little more than our engineering hand axes and saws to work with. Some had to try to uproot thick bushes with garden hoes. Then we discovered a decrepit weedwhacker and attached a blade to it to chop through the bushes, smaller trees, and, occasionally, parts of the fencing. Within minutes of using the leaky machine, men's combat trousers were drenched with gasoline but that didn't stop them puffing at cigarettes as they worked.

Incredibly now that we were *en régiment,* everyone was pulling his weight, Russians included. Slacking off and finding ways to get out of work had been commonplace during basic training but *en régiment* it was anathema. The Legion had taught us that the man who succeeds in evading his share of the work is simply increasing the workload of the others. Kangaroo court justice was applied and slackers risked bodily harm. For many of us, work had become something like a sexual obsession—we wanted it heavy and intense.

We were given less clearing work at weekends but had little more free time because the 1ere *Compagnie* had gone off on field exercises, so we were on service duty every second week. The corporals assigned me to Guard, EIT, or *Ordinaire* duty every weekend. Michaud worked out that none of us would be getting any leave for the next three months. I began fantasizing about being a Gary Cooper character in a 1930s Foreign Legion film. At a prearranged time, a Ray Ban–wearing Nadine would come crashing through the gates in a convertible to rescue me. When my daydreams became overly vivid, I was brought back to reality by a slap on the back of my head from *Caporal* Diagana shouting, *"Action!"*

Officers mess duty was some relief because we could get smashed on unfinished bottles of superior wine and stuff our faces with left-over *filet mignon* and *moules marinières*. One Saturday I was in the coolers with Jim Beam, scarfing down French pastries while he chopped celery.

"Do you have *plein les couilles,* too, like me?" I asked, leaning against the refrigerator. "Alcohol doesn't seem to be the cure it used to be."

"I've been in this shithole long enough to know that the only long-term remedy is desertion."

Weeks later, I learned that old Jim, who constantly slagged off on the Legion, had signed on for another five-year stint! The Legion had a way of getting soon-to-be-civilians pleasantly drunk, dangling the promise of an NCO training course before their noses, and asking them to sign on the dotted line.

I hitched a lift into Avignon from a sergeant who carried a photograph of Adolf Hitler in his *képi* lining, and took a train to Montpelier. It was good to see Antonio at the hostel again. After a night of heavy drinking, I enjoyed a long chat with him in his *bureau* as I finished his wine. Like a true *ancien,* he was always ready with fatherly advice.

"There are several men I have problems with," I said. "It's only a matter of time before we'll resort to our fists."

"*Niño,* I know that at times the Legion devours its own. See your *capitán*; he's usually an understanding sort of man."

"You know the system—there's no way his subordinates will ever allow me to speak with him face to face."

"*Si,* but occasionally you've got to break the rules just to be heard. I once had to make myself heard after coming back from leave a month late. I knew I was in serious trouble but I thought ahead. I hid a hand grenade under my *képi* before I was marched in to see the captain. When he sentenced me to the *compañía de disciplina,* I grabbed the grenade and pulled out the pin with my teeth. 'Tear up those papers you just signed!' I said. 'Now, take your pen and sign a new document stating that I returned late from leave for medical reasons.' While he pissed his trousers, I nearly shat mine laughing. After he handed me my documents, I tossed him the grenade. He dived under his desk, cowering like a child until he realized that I'd pulled the pin on a practice grenade! Now finish your *vino* before you go out to find yourself a *chica guapa.*"

When I left I took the TGV up to Paris. Hours later I was walking into my Arab quarter hostel. Maumi, the *concierge,* was a lovely Berber girl who by then knew me on a first-name basis. "Juan," she said, "you look so handsome in your *képi blanc.*"

"Will you smudge the books for me and give me a room with a shower and toilet?"

"Anything for you, Juan."

"Now, tell me, when are we two going to get together for a *pastis*?"

"All in good time, *mon petite* legionnaire."

I later found myself wandering the streets near Notre-Dame, very drunk and alone. I stumbled into Polly Magoo's and got into an intimate chat with Annika, the young Swede. "Yes, I gave in to my lesbian tendencies after we met last time," she said. "I slept with several women, but I can now say that I prefer men . . . not that it wasn't a lot of fun though." She waved at another girl chattering noisily at the next table. "Hey, Ellen come and meet Juan."

"Heard your not-so-beautiful upstate New York accent miles away," I said to Ellen.

"You got a funny mid-Atlantic accent yourself," she responded. "What are you doing in France?"

"I'm in the Foreign Legion."

"Oh, right, I've heard something of that."

"No worries," I said, "most Americans haven't."

Ellen was on exchange from the exclusive East Coast Tufts University, and lived in the posh 16ᵉ *arrondissement*. Like many wealthy Americans, her parents hoped that for a handsome fee, France would groom their daughter into an elegant society lady. We arranged to meet the next day in the Jardin du Luxembourg.

"I like your hat," Ellen said as we were sitting on a park bench. "How do you keep it so white?"

"By one, not touching it, and two, not letting anyone else touch it either." I lifted her hand away from my *képi* and held it in mine. "How are you getting on with your French studies?"

"Oh, it's such a pain in the ass and French people get on my nerves!"

"But you can't have anything against Paris as a place to live in? I always look forward to coming back. After weeks of soldiering, I'm delighted to be able to immerse myself in some culture."

"You said your parents are from Mexico?"

"Yeah." I moved over slightly to rub my knee against hers.

"Both? Because you don't act like a Mexican. I mean, you speak perfect English and are well-educated and stuff." Her knee was nudging back at mine.

"Ellen, I'm beginning to wonder if you can really be a student at Tufts. Hey, I just thought of something interesting to do. Come on."

We got up and walked over to a plane tree where I stood with my back against the trunk and put my arms around her. She stretched up to whisper in my ear. "Know what I did after I met you last night? I got myself off thinking of you in my bath, not just once but twice." I could feel my old fella stiffening. "You wanna know my fantasies?"

"Sure."

"I want you to strip off my clothes and tie me to a chair, blind-folded. I can't see you, but I can feel you teasing me with your penis. You're running it between my legs, along my breasts, and then along my face. I want to suck it but you won't let me. When you untie me, you get me on to my knees and do me doggy-style, tugging on my hair like riding a wild mare."

I licked her ear and unbuttoned her trousers.

"Just before you climax, you pull out and let me suck you off . . . That was great!" She sighed. "Now tell me your fantasy?"

"I'm a writer." I chuckled. "But I don't think I'm as creative as you!"

Her long coat provided us with perfect camouflage. I slid my hand down the back of her Levi's and tugged at her g-string from behind.

"Want to feel how wet I've become?" she gasped.

Over her shoulder I could see mothers pushing baby carriages along the paths. She unzipped my fly. Anybody who looked over would see both our bodies rocking and her arm jerking to and fro.

We had strolled off to the Champ de Mars, when we were passed by two Arabs. "I wouldn't sacrifice my blood for a foreign land," one of them muttered just loud enough for me to hear.

"Why do these North Africans always want to fuck with me at the least convenient times?" I breathed into Ellen's ear.

"From what I heard, it seems you guys did a lot of bad stuff in their country."

"That's a load of crap! Wherever Legion boots touched North African sand, water flowed and wheat fields grew. It was thanks to us that decent people there could live happy and sleep sound." Ellen gave me a blank stare. "Sorry! Look, I didn't mean that. That Arab just pissed me off. I sometimes forget that I'm a Christian, like you. I didn't come into the Legion with these attitudes. Fact is, the jury's still out on what I really believe."

8.

LONDON

What difference does it make if a hundred thousand rifles fire in Africa? Europe does not hear them.

King Louis-Philippe

By this time, I was beginning to understand how the Foreign Legion system works and had begun bullying other *jeunes* legionnaires more junior than myself. Like everything in physics or mathematics, the Legion has observable patterns. Once these are understood, the system begins to make sense. I now understood why a man with a mortgage to pay off, car payments every month, and screaming children might wish to live as a Foreign Legion monk.

Though our wages were meager, I'd managed to build up a small war chest by simply applying the first law of dollar-dynamics—if $\$_{out} > \$_{in}$, then $\$_{savings} = 0$. The easiest way to reduce $\$_{out}$ was to abstain from Legion staples such as Ray-Bans, Rolex watches, cigarettes, hashish, and whores. I was still wearing the *képi* issued to me during basic training and still had several unused Aubagne-issue tins of shoe polish. My moneyman reputation spread throughout the company and had the pleasant effect of earning me special treatment even from the corporals.

I often had to make loans to the Bulgarians who hung around in my room late into the night playing CDs like *Bulgaria's Greatest*

Moments in Folk Music. It was a relief to meet up with the *mafia Anglaise,* who gathered whenever possible in Woodman's room. He displayed an encyclopedic knowledge of military matters in his discussions with Weber about battle tactics and riot control.

"Just spray them all with a machine gun."

"No way," Woodman insisted. "Use your riflemen to pick off the leaders; then they don't know what to do."

"Hell, yeah, and even rubber bullets can kill, too, if properly used," Jim Beam put in. "In Belfast we aimed directly in front of their feet. When the bullet bounces off the ground, it picks up velocity and slams into the bloke's chest."

"Ever played Hunt the Sniper?" Woodman asked. "Great fun! In Bosnia, we'd send out a *jeune* legionnaire running in zigzags to draw fire while a second legionnaire watches for the muzzle flash and pots the sniper."

"Hey," Weber said, "doesn't Sijfert talk a load of shit about what he did in South Africa?"

"You forget that he was a lieutenant at age seventeen," I said sarcastically, "and blew a platoon of Cubans in Angola to kingdom come."

"Sijfert doesn't know what he's talking about," Lohmann said morosely. "I wish I could forget the horrors of South Africa. Men died in my arms, mates of mine, murdered by the *kaffirs.* Sijfert's never been into Zimbabwe on search-and-destroy missions. After the bushwars, I worked as a township paramedic. Have you ever seen a man burnt alive? The *kaffirs* were using the Winnie Mandela necklace on any blacks they thought were helping the whites. They put a tire around their necks, filled it with gasoline, and set it alight. I've had to tend to blob things that are still alive, but there's nothing you can do, nothing!" He began weeping.

"I just saw Brad Pitt in *Fight Club* this weekend," Jim said to change the subject. "If my girlfriend comes around with the Peugeot, let's go looking for Arabs in Apt."

"You feel like an angel of death," Lohmann sobbed. A few weeks later, he deserted.

I spent a fair deal of time philosophizing with Woodman in the *salle de musculation.* He spoke at length of books, including Joseph Conrad's *Heart of Darkness,* which Coppola adapted into the film *Apocalypse Now.* Originally a Polish seaman, Conrad signed onto a French ship in Marseille and spent most of the next twenty years before the mast. He would have been ideal Legion material—the sort of writer with loads of spunk that I strived to be myself.

Back in my room, Woodman handed me two books that he'd just finished, one on Einstein and the other on quantum physics. He was always a mystery to me—a mad genius, a soldiering monk who had banished himself to the rifle and tattoo artist's ink. Had events in his life been only slightly different, he could have been lecturing in one of the world's great universities.

I won grudging respect from the NCOs by taking it upon myself to run in my free time. Although this was good for my cross-country performance, I wasn't just keeping fit for the Legion, my drinking was beginning to give me a bit of a belly. All the same, I was proud of my *crossman* status, for I wasn't a born runner. I ran on guts and determination.

My personal duel with *Caporal* Diagana continued on our next commando run wearing full fighting kit. Whereas I preferred to remain in cruise mode for the entire race, he started slow and gradually increased his pace. Although I looked silly, I was running with the legs of my combat trousers pulled up to my knees, helping me to gain precious seconds. With two kilometers to go, I passed the captain, who a week before had beaten me in the Cooper.

"Go for it, Johnny!" he called.

I thought I'd finish second in my company but in the last kilometer *Caporal* Diagana nudged his way past me, sneering as he did so. For days after, my lungs ached and I was coughing up phlegm.

Caporal Diagana had bested me as an athlete but I got my revenge on the rifle range. I needed a lot of time to adjust my Famas sights. On several occasions, my shots were well grouped but off;

other times, they drifted low, then high, then low again. But once we began the competition, my shots were on the mark. At two hundred meters, with the naked eye, I shot a man's head off in eighteen out of twenty shots. *Caporal* Diagana was nowhere. The only other man who tied with me, instructors included, was the Russian army captain, Maximov.

One weekend afternoon, I ran into Antonio in Montpelier. He now had a second part-time job as a cook in a *bistrot* and offered me and my *camarades* a free meal whenever we wished. We sat down in a café for a drink, and a chat.

"I know *Noël* can be a lonely time for a legionnaire if he's out on his own," he said. "If you have leave during the holidays, I'll see to it that you don't eat alone."

I placed my *képi* on his head while I went to the toilet. When I returned, he was arguing with the barman over the bill. "You're trying to rob me. This is scandalous. I refuse to pay!"

"*Monsieur,*" said the barman, "your *ticket* shows exactly what you've had and what you owe."

Antonio erupted into a drunken rage. "I won't stand for this!" he roared.

The barman began manhandling him. "There's your money," I said, giving him a fifty-franc note. "Show the *ancien* some respect and take your paws off him. If you'll just stand aside, we'll be on our way."

"*Joven legionario,*" Antonio said as soon as we were outside, "I beg you to buy us another round. There's a better bar just up the street."

When I went 'round to the hostel a week later, I was saddened to learn that Antonio no longer worked there. Eventually, they told me that he was in the hospital in a critical condition. While working as a doorman at a discotheque on an off-night from the hostel, he'd been beaten, stabbed, and left for dead. Had I known of such dangerous side work, I'd have told the old tiger to retire. I was certain he'd put up a hell of a fight though.

Antonio was typical of what many a legionnaire comes to, often after impeccable service. "Depending upon how he is led, a legionnaire can be the best of soldiers or the worst of brutes," a general said in the nineteenth century. Nowadays, the *anciens* become either model citizens or aimless vagabonds. After years of Spartan discipline, being discharged into a civilian world where there is no one to tell them what to do is a trauma that often creates a feeling of worthlessness.

I went on to wait for Sijfert, Kulzer, and the Irish thugs at The Fitzpatrick. There was an attractive Frenchwoman sitting at the bar and I got talking to her.

"Legionnaire, are you? How very interesting."

"There are several of us in here—the ones with the *boule-à-zéro* haircuts and leather jackets. The man sitting next to you is one."

"Oh, no, he's my boyfriend, an *Armée de terre aspirant* (officer cadet)." She turned to him. "Meet my legionnaire friend."

He was training to become a lieutenant but we were both in civilian clothes and there was no way I was about to salute or address him with the polite *vous*. We shook hands for several tense seconds, staring into each other's eyes, like two rams about to charge each other for the ewe.

"*Un légionnaire, vraiment?*" he asked.

"Yes, got a problem with that?"

"No, I just wanted to thank you."

"What?"

"I know what it takes to be a legionnaire," he said, waving at the barman to refill my glass. "The Legion has served France well. You won't hear it often, but *merci*!"

I was stunned. Neither I nor any of my *camarades* expected gratitude from the country we'd sworn to defend. As far as our adoptive homeland was concerned, we were delighted to be the priests of a dead god. But simply being thanked like that was a morale booster.

Another man I got into conversation with that evening was an American businessman with an important French oilfield services company with a German name. It wasn't long before he was asking me to join his team. "So, how long are you in this Legion army you speak of? If you can get out of it, I'm certain that with your Purdue degree, French fluency, and experience you'll fit well in our corporate hierarchy. You'll get to travel to Chad with a briefcase instead of a rifle."

I thought of how many hours I had to work in the Legion to earn the price of one pint of Guinness. Getting back into a suit and tie, or blue, fireproof coveralls, and practicing the fine art of engineering again was very appealing but it wasn't as easy as that. "If I did manage to get out of my job here, I'm not sure how welcome I'd be in this country. Look," I said, "I'm kind of undecided about the way my future's going right now. Just leave me your card."

Along with Camerone Day, *Noël* is a holiday when the iron discipline is relaxed for the most part and replaced by the Legion's nurturing side. A politically incorrect Catholic culture takes over to persuade men who have cut themselves off from their family and country to see the Legion as home. Every man from the *jeunes* legionnaire to the most senior officer spends *Noël* with his immediate family—the Legion.

Christmas required weeks of preparation. Teams were organized for the regimental sporting tournament and the entire depot was given a face-lift. The barracks were repainted and the company offices remodeled. Pine trees had to be cut down, decorated, and arranged inside the entrance. A *club compagnie* was to be built entirely from scratch, and each platoon was to construct a nativity crèche.

The corridor where one of the Christmas trees was to stand needed touching-up, so *Caporal* Diagana volunteered me for the task. It took an entire morning simply finding paint and brushes for the job. As I sorted through the half-empty cans, it became obvious why the walls were painted in twenty different colors.

Caporal Diagana was dissatisfied with my off-white shade choice of latex paint. After further hours of searching for a sufficient quantity of another color, I made the revolutionary suggestion that we could mix in small amounts of other paints to achieve the desired shade. Minutes later, *Caporal* Diagana returned with two cans of enamel. I tried politely to explain. "Oil and water don't—" but before I could finish, he flew into a rage because I was "wasting time arguing." Without further protest, I poured the enamel into the off-white and ended up with an interesting lavender hue, which I slapped on the walls.

Next day, we were all perched atop chairs, using spoons to scrape paint from office doors and windows. There were years of paint layers caked on the glass and the order was to remove it by any means possible.

"Have they ever heard of paint remover?" I asked Maximov as he walked by.

"Too easy, *mon ami*."

The tedious process went on slowly, square millimeter by square millimeter. I was a third of the way finished by *soupe de midi* when I pressed too hard on the glass and the window shattered.

We had a welcome change from scraping paint when the NCOs ordered us to tear down a brick wall. Each of us was handed a chisel and we began chipping away at the mortar. Suddenly, a Spanish sergeant barged in with a sledgehammer and an orgy of violence began. Other sergeants attracted by the noise also wanted to have a go. A Calvi kickboxing champion began smashing the wall with sidekicks, and other sergeants who couldn't find sledgehammers joined in by running up to land flying kicks. When the dust cleared, I was detailed to remove the rubble.

The Legion has always had its own plumbers, carpenters, painters, even engineers and lawyers. A *caporal-chef* carpenter magically appeared and helped us build our *club compagnie* from little more than 2x4s and plywood scrap. With it halfway completed, I was assigned to work under the company barman, *Caporal* Chung, preparing a hundred baguettes *au jambon*. They were sold for fifteen francs each, with the profits going into the fund for *Noël* supplies of Kronenbourg and *pinard*.

I came back to find the clubhouse finished but with completely bare walls so I suggested to *Caporal* Diagana that I could brighten it up a bit by painting a mural. He simply grunted that he would mention it to the *chef*. Nothing came of my suggestion until I showed the captain a sketch I'd done and offered to transfer it on to the walls. His eyes lit up, and in no time, the officers were abuzz at the thought of a muralist in the ranks.

"Why didn't you mention your abilities before?" the captain asked. "I'll provide what you need for your project. It must be finished by *Noël*, though, so the colonel and civilians can see it when they're judging the crèches."

Next day, a wooden-faced *Caporal* Diagana ordered me into the platoon office. When I walked in and formally presented myself, the *sergent-chef* ordered me to close the door. I turned around and he leapt out of his chair at me. He slammed my head against the door and clenched my windpipe, cutting off my breath.

"Sounding off again about your fancy skills!" He bared his teeth in a snarl. "Always trying to get yourself special treatment. Well this time you won't."

"But . . ." I gasped and he squeezed tighter.

"Have I made myself clear?"

"Permission to explain," I croaked.

"No!"

Curiously, after being choked by the *chef,* I felt pleasantly drunk and euphoric. Though I was only half-conscious, he continued lecturing me, but it was as if his voice was coming at me from inside a tunnel. I almost thanked him for the psychedelic buzz but he told me to leave. I straightened my *tenue de combat,* picked up my beret, and properly dismissed myself as if nothing had happened. As I was walking past the captain, he saw obvious signs that I'd been beaten. He demanded to know who had done it.

"Fell down the stairs after drinking," I muttered.

"Who did this?"

"But, *mon capitaine,* I don't want more *merde*. I'm already—"

"*Mon efant,* who was it!"

"*Le sergent-chef*."

"I'll deal with his personally," he said and walked away.

Next morning, I was again summoned to the platoon office. I expected the worst, but instead the *chef* just ordered me to get busy on the *club compagnie* mural. *"Action!"*

It was the first time I'd been able to enjoy a few stress-free days while on duty. My first mural was a strong figurative work, inspired by communist and fascist visual propaganda. I painted the face of a singing legionnaire, using black to accentuate the shadow under the peak of his starch-white, wall-encompassing *képi*. The captain was so impressed that he demanded I create another mural of a Legion mountaineer wedged in a crevasse.

The difficulty in painting the second mural was that I had no paint thinner, so I couldn't wash out the encrusted brushes. With the captain pushing me to finish the job before the colonel came around, I had to paint the entire mural with my fingers. I added a decorative edelweiss growing on the crag face and used gold-metallic for the exploding grenade emblem on the legionnaire's beret.

The captain astonished me by shaking my hand. "If you keep up your *sport*," he said warmly, "you'll do fine in this company." Had he not been a captain, he'd have been a fine mate to share a pint with.

With *Caporal* Diagana overseeing crèche construction, we went to great lengths to produce a scale-size model of the Legion's last stand at the battle of Dien Bien Phu, complete with a silty river. The tedium didn't bother me much and I spent entire afternoons quietly twiddling cardboard into a red-green Buddhist temple, which should normally have taken a half hour to make.

Noticing that I was underemployed, *Caporal* Diagana put me on to building a bunker with 2x4s, in which we placed a figure of the Virgin Mary cradling the Christ Child in *tenue de combat* and *képi,* with an Indochinese assistant in black spray-painted pajamas and Adidas shower sandals. Where on earth the baby doll came from nobody could understand. The bunker was reinforced with sandbags and camouflage netting. Jungle sounds were broadcast by a hidden cassette player. It took a month to assemble but when it was finished, it was breathtaking.

When *Noël* arrived, the officers and their families were invited to tour the barracks and judge each platoon's efforts. To begin with, the children were taken out to the drill square for a special surprise. Suddenly an intimidating VAB roared up and out of it popped three clowns in wigs, makeup, bath gowns, and bozo-shoes who tried to balance balls on their noses and threw buckets of water over one another. Then the three trained killers, Michaud, Androprov, and Dupont, jumped back into the VAB and drove several times around the square, waving and shouting *Joyeux Noël!* to the children while their *camarades* hooted and hollered back.

After this the officers and their wives and children filed past the *crèches*. When they came to ours *Caporal* Diagana, in immaculate *tenue de parade,* retold the story of Dien Bien Phu.

After World War II, France had reimposed a colonial regime in Indochina, but in 1946 the communist Viet Minh movement led by Ho Chi Minh started a guerilla war for independence. In 1953 French commander General Navarre set up an important military base in the valley of Dien Bien Phu with the dual purpose of cutting off enemy supplies and reinforcement routes from Laos and luring the Viet Minh under Vo Nguyen Giap into a large scale battle that he was confident he would win. But the French made the mistake of assuming that the Viet Minh would be unable to get batteries of artillery up the surrounding mountains.

When Giap launched his offensive on March 13, 1954, over two hundred artillery pieces, including numerous batteries of Katyusha rocket launchers, had been disassembled and manhandled in sections up the hillsides. Dien Bien Phu's outlying strong points were overrun days after the initial assault and the main garrison came under heavy artillery barrage. When the Viet Minh bombardment eventually destroyed the airstrip, *jeunes* legionnaires from Algeria, many using parachutes for the first time, were dropped into the cauldron. Colonel Piroth, the French artillery commander, finding himself unable to silence the enemy guns, went into his dugout and committed suicide. Having lost an arm in World War II he was unable to cock his pistol, so he lay down and exploded a grenade on his chest. Half of the defenders were legionnaires. On May 7, after a siege of fifty-seven days, when the base was finally overrun, the surviving legionnaires in true Camerone style fixed bayonets and charged.

Our platoon won an undisputed first place in the crèche competition.

On Christmas Eve, we put on a comedy sketch. This was the one day when we were free to mock, tease, and imitate any superior, regardless of rank. To mimic our captain, who held his arms motionless at his sides when he walked, we had a legionnaire striding about the stage with two giant *papier-mâché* hands hanging from a string around his neck. But all the laughter, male bonding, *camaraderie*, *pinard* and *chants* were things I heard about later, for on *la nuit de Noël* I was stuck in an EIT guardroom. The closest I came to the celebrations was poking my head into the frosty air to hear the singing.

In charge of our EIT squad was *Caporal-Chef* Green, a pioneer sporting a full beard and handlebar moustache. The story was that he'd served as a young USMC lieutenant in Vietnam, where he beat up his commanding officer after his platoon was wiped out. He had escaped to France and had one of the longest service records in the Legion, with battle decorations to match. After serving in the *REP*, he'd transferred to the Legion's new mainland regiment. It was hilarious to hear him speak French. Even after nearly two decades of service, he still spoke unintelligible, bastardized Texan-French. Unlike other NCOs who drove miniature Peugeots and Renaults, *Caporal-Chef* Green drove a rusted 1980s Range Rover.

"A Hoosier? I'll be damned!" he said. "Say, how are things back home?"

"Fine."

"I wish I could return, but Uncle Sam and I just don't get along. No matter, my old lady and I are planning on visiting as soon as I retire. With the French passport I'll get, I'll be taking the old truck with her and the dog to Canada by sea. Then I'll try to slip across the border. I'll keep away from the big cities to avoid him."

"Him?"

"Who d'ye damn well think? The FBI, the attorney general, the Alcohol Tobacco and Firearms Bureau. Hell, they're likely to send one of them black helicopters after me. So, how are you enjoying the Legion?"

"I'm suffering from crippling *plein les couilles*."

He burst out laughing. "Old boy, I've had them for over fifteen years! Haven't you figured the system yet? This is a *gros bordel* of an army. It's been like that since I came on board, and it's gonna be like that until the Socialists close us down. Just take your analytical mind, wad it into a small ball, and throw it in the trashcan."

What had initially sparked my interest in the Foreign Legion was an early 1980s *National Geographic* article describing it as a career for adventurers who wanted to live dangerously. It outlined the Legion's traditions and history and included an interview with an unnamed Texan. The accompanying photograph showed him in *tenue de parade* on the Champs-Elysées. "I was the only one in my platoon to make it back," he had said to the interviewer. "I decided, hellsbells, if we're gonna do it, let's do it now."

I realized that *Caporal Chef* Green was the legionnaire I'd read about.

"Saw an article about the Legion years back," I said to him. "There was a photograph of a legionnaire on the Champs-Elysées. Could that have been you?"

"Don't know what you're talking about," he growled.

Suddenly there was a loud tap at the guardroom door. It wasn't Santa Claus but the colonel in *tenue de sortie* bearing a bundle of gifts. We formally presented ourselves and he handed each of us a wrapped present. He stayed for a quick drink, then carried on hand-delivering gifts to every other legionnaire in the regiment. Though we were stuck on EIT duty, *Noël* cheer abounded. Our commanding father had come to give his children presents.

We came back to reality the following morning, when we were noisily awakened for an 08.00 roll call. We dragged ourselves out of bed with poisonous hangovers to be informed of a problem with the perimeter fence and ordered to gather as many picks, trenching spades, and other tools as we could carry.

Earlier that morning, *Caporal* Chung had finally been relieved. Not only was he exhausted from working the bar twenty-four hours straight, he was also drunk. He had jumped into a P4 jeep, fallen asleep at the wheel, and driven through the fence. We were marched off over the frost-covered ground like gulag prisoners to repair forty meters of heavy-duty perimeter wire. We began by chipping through the frozen earth around deeply cemented fence posts. Then, with our bare hands, we somehow managed to drag out the concrete stumps.

We hung around for hours in the cold, waiting for a new roll of fencing to arrive. Before fitting it, we had to set up new posts, meaning that old posts for a distant area of the barracks had to be dug out, hauled along, put in with bleeding hands, and anchored with cement mixed on-site. That night we clawed and pulled the new fencing into place in the light of truck headlamps. Though this was a typical day's work, what rankled was its timing. During the millennium celebration of our Lord's birth, we were laboring like slaves. The hardship of Legion life began getting to the idealistic Weber.

"Do you know what my friends told me before I joined?" he said as he hacked at the earth with a pickax. "That if I joined the Foreign Legion, I'd be posted to some desolate garrison to dig holes. I told them they were crazy."

"I know what you mean," I said, wiping slushy mud from my face, "but it's too easy to complain, and it does no good."

"It's pitch-dark out here and freezing. We've finished our work but now have to wait hours for the damned officers to finish their coffee and come along to announce that we're done. It's maddening! Mark my words, I'll get my revenge on these French bastards even if I have to knife a corporal. I know all about *kaffirs* in South Africa, but now I realize that the French are worse. Try as they may, they fail at everything. Look at the *bordel* they've made of what used to be a German Legion. Why didn't I listen to my mates?"

*   *   *

When we were at last dismissed, covered in mud, I went back to my room and found a sheet of manila paper on my bed. It was my first five-day leave, from December 29 to January 2! I was overjoyed to think that I was going to be free to join in the millenium celebrations. Others were less fortunate. Because of the danger of terrorist attacks, the Legion was placed on high alert. Even those on leave were required to leave a contact address and telephone number, so without telling Katarina, I gave her number as my contact.

Weber and I decided to share a taxi into Avignon. When he turned up at the gates he was carrying an enormous rucksack packed so full, one of the straps had broken.

"Weber, where in God's name are you going with that?"

"Holland," he replied. "I've had enough."

"*Putain*, Weber! You can't desert now. You're down for the corporals training course, an honor for any *jeune* legionnaire! Christ, then we have weeks of free skiing on our ski course."

"Thank you very much. The Legion's too good at fucking up a good time in the Alps. The Legion's for people like Woodman."

When we got into Avignon we shook hands and I wished him good luck before catching the TGV to Paris. My plan was to celebrate the millenium in London but I had no passport. In any case, it was strictly forbidden to leave metropolitan France and I was supposed to be on military alert. Well, that wasn't going to stop me. I decided it would be easier to avoid passport controls by crossing the channel through the rail tunnel rather than by ferry, so when we arrived in Paris I transferred trains and headed for the Gare du Nord. I had just handed over a fistful of cash for my ticket and was walking along the platform for the Eurostar train when I ran into a spot-check passport control. I'd changed into civvies but I was still wearing my Legion parka and *boule-à-zéro* haircut.

"*Passeport!*" the policeman demanded.

I explained that I had only my ID card and tried to pass myself off as a Frenchman by speaking French as well as I could. When he saw *"Nationalité: États-Unis"* printed in the corner, he handed it to his superior. "Do you realize that what you're attempting to do is strictly forbidden under *Légion Étrangère* regulations?"

"Oh, I didn't know about that. I must have misunderstood," I exclaimed, switching into *Caporal Chef* Green Texan-French.

"Perhaps I should notify your regiment."

"*Chef*, I'm not trying to desert. I simply want to spend the millenium with my *petite amie* in London and . . ." Before I could finish, he handed me back my ID and pointed toward the downstairs exit.

I refused to give up and boarded the next TGV to Lille. From there I hitchhiked to Calais and took the Sea France ferry bus to the dockside. There everyone got out and went into the terminal, which also serves as a customs and passport checkpoint, while I walked around the back to the feeder road where automobiles were waiting to drive into the ferry hold. I went along the line asking for a lift. Eventually, two workmen made a place for me in a van marked KENT BUILDERS and packed with cases of Kronenbourg, Marlboros, and ruby-red.

There remained the problem of British passport control. I bought the driver and his mates drinks at the bar and they agreed to let me hide behind the crates of wine when we landed at Dover. Though standard procedure is to stop every motorist, when the passport officers saw two men in dungarees driving a local work van, they simply waved them through, and me with them. They took me around to their firm's office and arranged for me to ride in a mate's van going up to London.

I went to the fifty-five-pounds-a-week hostel I knew in Earl's Court and slept with three men and a woman in a room that smelled like a pair of *rangers* after a long march. I got up just before noon and went along the corridor to the washroom. British plumbing standards are rudimentary, but for a legionnaire in need of a shower, it was luxury.

Funnily enough, when I went outside I missed being told what to do and spent most of my time wandering aimlessly through London's cold streets and around Hyde Park. I cheered myself by stopping at

pubs but Kronenbourg was expensive, so I purchased two-liter bottles of 5 percent Strongbow cider to take back to the hostel. I was
sitting in reception wearing my Legion sweater and parka when one
of the hostel's long-term tenants, an unshowered, unshaven Englishman stopped to chat. "Interesting insignia on your chest."

"Yeah, I'm in the French Foreign Legion."

"Well done, lad. My contract ended in '87. How are things
there now?"

"Oh, well, I'm in the new regiment, a *gros bordel* of chaos since
I've been there. You a member of the British AALE (*Amicale des Anciens de la Légion Étrangère*)?"

"No, but they celebrate Camerone Day every year here in London. I might just go along sometime to see some of the blokes I
served with."

"*Mafia Anglaise* comrades?"

"No, the ones I've got a score to settle with."

"I thought the *mafia Anglaise* back then were all buddies?"

"Don't you believe it. I remember a Welsh cunt who went home
on leave and talked a lot of shit to the local press. Well, there were
more Welsh *anciens* than he thought. When he got back from leave
the *mafia Anglaise* took his sorry arse into the *ordinaire* for a kangaroo court. They decided to hang him. They were putting the noose
'round the bugger's neck when the *chef d'ordinaire* walked in."

"The Legion's changed a lot. There are only four of us in our
REG's *mafia Anglaise* now that my South African mate's fucked off.
Anyway, if you still have contacts in the Legion, don't tell them that
I came over here to Britain."

"No probs, mate. I did exactly the same, though I spent a little
more time away than you will; several months in fact. When I went
back to Aubagne I got the standard forty-day jail sentence for going
AWOL."

"And then you finished your contract?"

"Sure. We all get to a point where we've had enough and there's
nothing that will keep you from going mad except disconnecting for
a time. You fuck off, get your head straightened out, and work out

if you want to return and face the music or spend the rest of your life as a deserter."

Those were words I remembered.

I met another former legionnaire at the hostel on the evening before New Year's Eve. Robert turned out to be a South African with dual nationality now serving in the Royal Marines. I took him to the rowdy pub I knew around the corner, O'Neil's, an Aussie-alley hangout where the English were rare and financially challenged individuals like myself plentiful. I went to the bar to get him a drink and found myself standing next to an attractive woman with a glass of vodka cranberry in her hand.

"*Est-ce que vous êtes française?*" I shouted over the music.

"What?"

"Sorry, I live in the South of France and was admiring your Latin profile."

"Partially right. I'm a Londoner but mother is French-Italian."

"From the side your face could be Roman," I said running my forefinger lightly down her forehead and nose. "You come here often?"

She smiled and blushed. "No. My Swedish flatmate's just back from a month in Gothenburg. I thought we'd go somewhere a bit different. Why not come over and join us for a chat later?"

"What do you mean later? I'm on my way right now."

I found out she was named Gwyneth and lived in trendy Islington. She owned her own beauty salon and did pretty well for herself. Christina, her flatmate, was an advertising executive. Later Gwyneth took me to a West End café that both she and her friend frequented. We sat there drinking the English excuse for coffee with our legs entwined and exchanging open-mouthed kisses. The video jukebox was playing the Robbie Williams classic "Millennium."

"And this is Soho Square," she said when we went back outside.

"Nice." We were standing in front of a darkened shop entrance. "Let's go in here out of the chill."

I slid my hands up her jumper and felt her nipples stiffen. Without meeting any resistance, I unfastened her trousers, and slipped my hand inside her undergarments. She didn't flinch from the frosty touch when I inserted a finger. She unbuckled my belt and slid her own hands down my Levi's. Then I took down both her trousers and my own and penetrated her. Christina, who had been around to the café, too, came by just as we were buttoning ourselves up. I knew it was wise to get on the right side of Gwyneth's flatmate. "Christina, *hur mår du*?"

"You speak Swedish!?"

"Just a bit. I could speak a lot more when I was at the Royal Institute of Technology in Stockholm."

"He might be coming 'round to our flat for a nightcap, if that's fine with you," Gwyneth said.

We all got into a cab to Islington.

"Don't be put off by the outside," Gwyneth said. "It's a council flat."

"Council flat? You're paying rent to the person who's leeching off the state?"

"Exactly. As you can see," she said opening the front door, "it's not so dreadful inside, now, is it?"

It was ultramodern with wood floors and a courtyard view. The three of us split a bottle of Boredaux. "This is *magnifique*," I said. "The leather softener we drink in the Legion is from the lesser known *Pays d'Oc* region."

After a few glasses, Christina could see that I would soon be giving Gwyneth a good shag, so she excused herself for the night.

"*God natt,*" I said, winning a smile of approval.

In no time, Gwyn and I were on the sofa heavily petting to the Chemical Brothers. I put my glass on the floor and she mounted my lap in nothing but her underpants. After half an hour she explained that her bedroom was just down the corridor. As I got up, I knocked my ruby-red onto her virgin carpet. The stain would have all night to set but she hadn't noticed and I said nothing. We had sex several times before passing out from alcohol and exhaustion.

At 06.00 I woke up in a sweat, recognizing nothing and panicking that I'd overslept morning parade. I had to lift the covers and look at the curve of her hips to reassure myself that I was still on leave. I ran my already stiffened penis along the crack of her rounded bottom. She smiled and slowly woke up to full-on intercourse.

We lay quietly for a while in each other's arms and started chatting about British politics. "In fact," Gwyneth said, "the Labor party has transformed itself into something very much like Lady Thatcher's Tories. It was all very clever political maneuvering toward the center by Tony Blair. The government's challenge now is reconciling traditional Old Labor with pro-Euro New Labor."

"Wait a moment," I interrupted, "how do you know so much about what's going on, just being a hairdresser?"

"I'm not a hairdresser!" she said, spanking my bottom. "And why are you running about killing people in the Legion of French Foreigners?"

"I pray that the Legion never asks me to kill anyone. I didn't join to kill people. I thought I'd have a try at making the world a slightly better place instead of living out my life as a consumer. In a few months I'll be clearing land mines in Kosovo with my bare hands. That is God's work. It's all very basic, my fair lady. The important things are always simple, the simple things are always hard."

I stared up at the ceiling as Gwyneth prepared tea, and told myself that we had become each other's millennium lovers. When I got up, Christina had come back and was sitting in the kitchen. I noticed that the wine stain was partially gone. She must have given it a good scrub so I greeted her with a fond kiss. Gwyneth started rushing about to get ready for an appointment with her girlfriends. They had plans for an elaborate millennium party.

"Gwyneth, I'm alone in this big city tonight. Why don't you take me with you?"

"Don't be daft," she said. "What would I tell my friends?"

"Tell them the truth: that you found me on the street, and felt sympathy for this down-and-out legionnaire."

"I'm not taking you," she said, putting on lipstick, "even though I find your pouting adorable."

"But, Gwyneth, what am I to do alone on this most important night?"

"You'll manage."

"Fine," I said, removing the pushpin from a photograph on her corkboard, "but I'm placing your photograph under my *képi*. Oh, come on, Gwyneth, don't throw me out in the . . ."

As I walked through the morning cold, I cursed her for throwing me out. I got back to the hostel and fell into bed. When I got out of it again in the middle of the afternoon, I came across Robert in the vestibule. I made my excuses for not getting back to him with his drink in O'Neil's and we decided to ring in the new millennium together. I prepared for the evening by filling my rucksack with bottles of beer and cans of Strongbow. We went outside and were swept along by the crowd to Trafalgar Square.

At fifteen minutes to midnight, I started worrying about the millennium bug. Was something terrible going to happen? Would I have to return to France? A drunken reveler bumped into us, asking why we didn't look as if we were having a good time. "There's birds all around this place searching for a new millennium shag. You're not a pair of poofters, are you?"

"Look," I said, placing my forefinger on his chest, "my mate here is a Royal Marine; I'm a Foreign Legionnaire. Do we look gay?"

He turned and disappeared, but he'd been right enough about so far not having much of a great time. Then with five minutes to go, we came across a red-haired woman pouring out Martini-Rossi to a group holding plastic cups. I grabbed a cup and stuck my arm over her shoulder from behind. "Some for me, too." As the last seconds ticked away, I tossed Robert my camera. "Take a picture of this," I said gathering the redhead in my arms and kissing her deeply. Fireworks exploded around us and in my mind. The millennium had arrived!

Holding her hand firmly in mine we followed the movement of the crowd, which stretched as far as the eye could see. With the redhead was an attractive black girl. She asked me where Robert had disappeared to.

"Didn't you notice his South African accent?" I said.

After hours of singing and drinking in the streets, the redhead and I were standing outside the entrance to the Tube around the corner from Buckingham Palace. She slid her icy hands up my T-shirt. "I don't think it would be right if I took you home."

"Why not?"

"You're a charming young man, and I'm sure we'd do great things behind closed doors—but I can't. The spirit is willing but the flesh just isn't up to it. Don't worry, you'll find somebody else soon enough."

New Year's Day, after the partying, was a somber letdown. The day was gray and frosty, and I was feeling lonely again. I took myself out for a walk through the empty, trash-littered streets and realized that I actually missed the Legion. I missed the charm of Provence, drinking with *camarades,* and knowing exactly what was expected of me every day.

9.

VALLOIRE

The air conditioner, crippled and exhausted, has stopped again, shuddering and wheezing like a desert trooper who has dropped his pack, fallen to his knees, surrendered to the heat. So far I've gotten a good idea why its called the "Legion of the Damned," because I'm in Djoubiti, Africa, billeted in the guest quarters from hell.

Alan Richman, GQ Writer

Back in France, we were getting ourselves ready for the upcoming ski course and a chance to win the coveted *Brevet De Skieur Militaire* (BSM). Only a handful of us had been on skis before but somehow, in two weeks the Legion was going to transform us into trained mountain troops and arctic-weather survivalists. Learning how to ski would be more exciting than our routine work, but I knew that things in the Legion never turned out to be quite as we expected.

The ski course was one of the very few occasions when the Legion supplied us with equipment that was new. Like children waiting to open Christmas presents, we lined up for our Austrian Koflach ski boots, Italian trekkers, Gore-Tex overalls and jacket, and a light modern rucksack with plenty of zippers. There was no way, however, that our standard-issue, cotton sleeping bags would provide much protection from the alpine winter. Almost everyone else purchased a civilian sleeping bag with Gore-Tex cover but I refrained on principle.

Skis and snowshoes were waiting for us at the *REG*'s chalet base in Valloire, a village at an altitude of 1,500 meters in the Savoy Alps, close to the Italian frontier. It took a chilling, one-day drive in open trucks to get there. At morning parade, we stood *garde-à-vous* in the freezing wind, our skis in front of us, neatly arranged in a tripod with the slats slung through the straps of our poles, and waited.

When the instructors inside had finally finished their *café au lait* we were marched off to the beginners' slopes to practice staying on our feet, making gentle turns, and braking. After *soupe de midi* back at the chalet, we were told that our introductory training was now over and we were whisked up by ski lift to tackle the ten-kilometer *piste bleue*. It ran down mountainsides where an error of judgment could slam us into jagged rocks and along cliff tops where any fall was certain death.

Not yet having learned how to brake efficiently, we descended the *piste* with our skis inclined inwards in the snowplow position. It wasn't long before connective leg muscles that no one knew existed began to ache. Every so often, the ski tips crossed, pitching us head-first into the snow. Sometimes, we took a curve too fast and were forced to abandon ship onto the ice to save ourselves from going over the edge. As if downhill skiing wasn't difficult enough, we were also taught how to go uphill using sealskins on the soles of our skis—an old-fashioned but effective technique that allows the skis to glide smoothly forward while preventing them from slipping back.

Carrying fully packed rucksacks, we embarked on our first cross-country march using general-purpose touring skis with adjustable bindings that can be loosened to allow the heel to rise when climbing or traversing more level areas. After a few kilometers, I realized how taxing ski-marches can be. As in the endurance march at The Farm, I had difficulty in keeping up with the others but more worrying was the tingling sensation in my feet that precedes blistering. We were soon above the tree line and facing a sheer mountainside. We couldn't march up directly but had to climb in a zigzag, using awkward 180-degree ski-kicks to change over from zig to zag and picking our way across perilous ice slopes, balanced on our ski-edges to follow the centimeter-wide tracks made by those ahead of us.

At one particularly steep patch, the entire company slid to a halt.

Trying to get across, one man after another lost his balance and went crashing several meters down the face. When the time came for me to try, I had got halfway across when my skis lost their grip in the ice. I skidded down headfirst in a tangle of poles and straps, legs flying in all directions with my face pressed into the ice by the weight of my rucksack riding up my back. Our skis never detached properly when we fell so it was often difficult to get up again but that day, an ankle strap tore loose, and my ski darted off down the slope on its own. Knowing that it was a cardinal sin to lose any piece of Legion equipment, I threw myself after it and had to struggle back up to the others, one ski on and one ski off.

Skis can take a lot of getting used to but I quickly realized how efficient they are for getting about on the snow. We managed several kilometers, including one of nearly vertical ascent. In summer conditions wearing *rangers,* the average legionnaire would cover only a fraction of the distance in the time. Fifty meters below the summit, one of my skis snapped in two so I again had to sweat my way through deep snow, my skiless leg sinking in up to my crotch.

We were allowed a *soupe de midi* break in the brasserie at the head of the *piste bleue.* I finished my slushy chicken and carrots on the *terrasse* with its breathtaking view and went inside for a shot or two of cognac antifreeze. It went down so smoothly that I continued warming up until it was time to ski back down to the chalet.

I was given a replacement ski and felt pleasantly buzzed until I realized what I was doing. Drunk skiing is infinitely more dangerous than drunk driving. The fear I felt skimming wildly along cliff edges soon sobered me up but I still couldn't get my body to do what I wanted it to. I realized that falling was inevitable and simply concentrated on lessening the impact. Falling even in the smoothest snow was like being dragged bodily over a bicycle rack. As I hit the ground, high-velocity snow invaded my body, bursting into my shirt, trousers, socks, and up my nose. Then suddenly the world would stop and I'd lie there listening to the snow crunch below my battered body. The bruises I got from crashing onto my poles and skis stayed with me for weeks.

I was out of bed early every morning to prepare the instructors' breakfasts and spent my evenings filling officers' wineglasses. Whenever I had a few spare minutes, I watched morning music videos on the state channel M6. The one I really liked was the luscious Belgian Axelle Red singing "Parce que c'est Troi." The slow, rhythmic sway of her hips mesmerized me—a brief warming fantasy before going out again into the cold. She was my new millennium Edith Piaf.

Everyone dreaded the upcoming bivouacs that began and ended with a punishing march. As we marched out of Valloire in early morning darkness, the awesome cold hit us within minutes. The right pocket of my combat trousers was caked with ice from the handkerchief I used to wipe away mucus dribbling from my nose like water from a leaky faucet. My hands and feet were achingly numb but it wasn't the pain that bothered me; by then I could simply unplug it. It was the danger of frostbite.

We were all wearing pajamas under our trousers and a double pair of wool socks, yet heat was escaping through the tightest seams. The relentless cold felt like a malevolent presence intent on slowly destroying us. Shuffling our feet or rubbing our hands together only made it worse. Every movement had to be calculated. Simply bending forward brought our thighs into contact with our frozen trousers, resulting in further heat loss. Perspiration seeped out through our leather Legion-issue gloves and froze in less than an hour. "Acclimating to temperature change," was what the Legion called it. Like everything else, we learned how to do it by doing it.

We zigzagged up the mountain face at a snail's pace, tumbling tits-over-toe attempting the ski-kick crossovers we'd not yet mastered. During the occasional breaks, I concentrated on wiping my nose, drinking from my canteen, warming my hands, and getting my rucksack back on before *Caporal* Diagana started beating me about the head and shoulders with his ski pole.

Our instructors were experts at picking out innocent-looking slopes prone to avalanches and areas containing snow-hidden crevasses. We traversed such hazards one man at a time, while others stood by with probe poles in case they needed to poke around for their *camarade*.

During one break, the *chef* ordered us to strip off our Gore-Tex jackets to check that our avalanche beacons were correctly switched on in transmit mode. I had made what *Caporal* Diagana considered an unforgivable mistake by wearing my transceiver outside rather than inside my T-shirt. When the platoon was out of sight, he took me aside and without saying a word, belted me a punch in the gut and followed up with another to my eye that laid me out on the snow. I squinted up at him and felt Legion *sketch* pushing me to the breaking point, but there was nothing I could do about it. I simply struggled back onto my skis and slid off to catch up with the others.

When we reached our objective, a mountain pass nestling between the peaks a thousand meters above the chalet, we began digging in for the night. There was nothing but rock and virgin snow as far as the eye could see, not that we could see that far, for our eyes were suffering from days of looking at nothing but fluorescent white. Two of the sergeants had served with the mountain troops of the German army, the descendants of Hitler's *Gebirgsjäger*. They demonstrated how to cut out blocks of snow using the ends of their skis to build an igloo. This was one of the various types of shelters we were taught to make, depending upon equipment available, how many men were to be quartered, and battle conditions.

Then we were ordered to dig trenches and place blocks of snow as roofing atop our skis—not an option in combat conditions because of the time it would take to retrieve them. Three-man teams working in relays set about digging trenches as deep as a legionnaire is tall, with a lower entrance tunnel sloping upwards and a trough for trapping the cold. We started in the afternoon and worked feverishly while temperatures and daylight were still favorable. While I shoveled chunks of snow out of the trench, my Japanese comrade, Yokoyama, crushed and packed them on to the roof. We used our probes to punch airholes in it. Each snow cave was connected by an uncovered trench to the others. Finally we smoothed down the inside walls with our hands to prevent droplets forming and dripping on to us while we slept.

After hours of toil, we had carved out a space we could crawl about in and big enough to accommodate our three-man team and a sergeant. We lit candles to heat up the interior from minus 4 degrees to a cozy zero degrees. Now that we were ready to get some well-deserved shut-eye, I regretted not having purchased a civilian sleeping bag. To make my frigid slumber slightly more bearable, I got into my sleeping bag fully clothed, Gore-Tex and all, and wrapped up in my rubber poncho. Strangely enough, I slept well, except when I had to crawl out onto the windswept snow to piss.

We were woken in the morning by *Caporal* Diagana screaming that we had fifteen minutes to prepare for parade. I scrambled around fitting every piece of equipment back into my rucksack and strapping on my retractable shovel. As we formed up on the snow, I went down on one knee to adjust my ski bindings. *Caporal* Diagana came up behind me, yelling and beating me about the head with his ski pole. The humiliation I felt in front of my *camarades* was ten times worse than the pain. As we moved off to begin the day's march, he stuck a hand radio into the side pocket of my rucksack. I didn't have time to adjust my straps correctly and, as he expected, at my first heavy fall the radio was tossed into the snow. He beat me about the head again, screaming that a mistake like that could cause the death of an entire platoon. We put on *couteaux à neige,* ski crampons, to get up the 400-meter ice sheet below the summit. When we finally got there, we had to use our arms to shield our faces from the stinging blast of ice crystals whipped up by the howling wind.

That night, instead of bivouacking in snow tunnels, we were to sleep in tents, portions of which each of us was carrying. When we reached our objective, we set about assembling the tents, partially burying them in the snow and using our ski poles as tent pegs. *Caporal* Diagana insisted that we insert the poles handle-first. I pointed out that when morning came, there was a danger that the poles would come out without the rubber handles. "Shut the fuck up, I'm the *caporal*," was his predictable response. Huddled in the tents after nightfall, we had to prepare our sleeping bags, arrange our ruck-sacks, oil our Famas, and eat and drink, with flashlights wedged under our chins to see what we were doing.

When I took off my boots, I realized how damaged my feet were. Blistering had begun during the first march, and since midday, I had felt as if I was walking on water cushions. Our Koflach boots were made of plastic, which, unlike leather, cannot stretch and mold itself to the feet. Not only had the blisters burst by the time we bivouacked; my heels were now bloodied. But there was nothing I could do about it three thousand meters up a mountain. Blood and blisters are to the Legion what childbirth is to women; both are prac-tically inevitable and have to be endured until they go away. Though warned against it, I covered my blisters with Elastoplast, which of-fered some protection but was extremely painful because raw flesh stuck to it and was gradually torn off.

In the morning, simply getting my boots back on was a major operation—not only had my feet swollen but I could only use my un-gloved hands five seconds at a time before they went numb. I had to use my nuts to thaw them out again. Yokoyama and I struggled to fold and pack the frozen tent flaps back into the narrow nylon car-rying bags. As I had expected, when I pulled my poles out of the hardened snow, they came up without the handles. *Caporal* Diagana ordered me to dig them out with my hands.

By this time, we were all suffering from exposure, dehydration, and exhaustion. I had to scoop handfuls of snow into my mouth be-cause the water in my canteen was frozen solid. All we could think of was being somewhere else, anywhere but atop a mountain sur-rounded by blinding whiteness, tens of kilometers from the nearest civilization. I stared back defiantly at the menacing peaks, and thought how much worse winter combat in the mountains would be than fighting in the desert or jungle. Up here the deadliest enemy is the relentless cold. Blood flowing from minor wounds, especially of the hand or foot, freezes and often leads to frostbite. Nowhere else is a fighting man so dependent on special equipment. Losing a ski, a snowshoe, or even a glove during mountain warfare can mean death.

After only a few days on the slopes, many legionnaires had become proficient skiers. I gained confidence with each passing day, and was soon venturing on to the *piste rouge* just for the hell of it. I was back to my old daring self, transformed from a scared, over-cautious beginner into a reckless *piste* hog. I cut in between women and children, and was fond of knocking over my own *camarades* if they didn't "get the fuck out of my way." Even when the steel edging on one of my skis started coming off, making cornering at speed highly dangerous, there was no way I was going to waste slope time by getting a new pair.

The ski course culminated with a two-day climb up the 3,400-meter *Mont Galibier*. By this time, like everyone else in the company I was as sunburned as if I'd spent the summer on Devil's Island, and my mouth was covered with cold sores. We were marching on *neige tôlé*, snow covered with an ice crust, which our skis kept breaking through. The grades on the harsh, lifeless mountain were so steep that I was using my gloved fists to help myself up. I was sorely mistaken in thinking my reserves of body fat would suffice to keep me moving. My stomach began crying out for nourishment and my blood sugar levels were deathly low. I had some sweets in my pocket, but then had to decide whether it was hunger or thirst that I was suffering from most. My water was frozen and I knew that any sugar would make me even thirstier.

Fifty meters below the summit, a rock face made it impossible to continue on skis. We had to take them off and finish the climb on all fours. It was exhausting but when we made it we felt on top of the world, with a forest of snow-capped mountains, including *Mont Blanc* on the horizon at our feet. We huddled together for a platoon photograph, which ended up in the next issue of *Képi Blanc*. Although the others were very pleased with themselves, I reminded myself that, like a child climbing a tree, getting up was only half the battle.

We managed to slow our descent to some extent by keeping on the sealskins. One after the other, we skied down the deep, narrow, zigzag tracks we had made on the way up. Lateral braking was impossible and our heavy rucksacks made for awkward weight distribution. In order to brake for the changeover from zig to zag, many men sat down and were crashed into by the man behind. Nobody could go five meters without falling over. We spent almost as much time on our backs as on our skis.

After several close calls, I met the slope with my name on it. Trying to avoid crashing into a rock, my left ski wedged itself deep in the snow and my body weight pitched me forward. My boot failed to detach and my knee bore all the torsion stresses. There was a sickening crack as I collapsed. I was lying in the snow in agony when Michaud ran into me and broke his hand.

When I was able to sit up and feel down my leg, I was relieved to find I hadn't fractured anything. I'd torn a portion of my anterior cruciate ligament and sat there biting my lip as the others careered past. Finally I got up and continued my descent. There was no way I was going to complain to the instructors that I had a boo-boo on my knee. I knew what they'd say: "On your feet. We can look at your leg when we get to the bottom."

Before starting the cross-country stretch of our march, we found ourselves at the top of an almost vertical ice slope. We had taken a wrong turn somewhere. After checking their maps, the instructors decided that a detour would add another ten kilometers to the march. We were ordered to take off our skis and, holding them across our chests, slide down on our backs with our testicles leading the way.

We attacked the final kilometers of rough, thickly wooded terrain by following a streambed. Then, my left binding locked up, making progress near impossible. Just behind me was *Caporal* Diagana. "Get your ass moving!" he howled, whacking me repeatedly with his ski pole. "You're always the fucking last! You can't even ski, you worthless cunt!"

"*Reçu, Caporal,*" I said, fantasizing how I could rip out his tongue with my bayonet.

Night was falling and it was obvious that we had to make it back to Valloire soon. Yokoyama, the smallest legionnaire in our platoon, was hardly capable of standing. Exhausted yet determined, he fell every ten meters, forcing us to stop and wait.

"Get the fuck up!" everyone shouted. "Why in hell do you have to keep falling over!"

We ended up carrying his Famas and rucksack but he was still useless. He was so limp that he couldn't even address the instructors correctly.

"*Oui.*"

"*Oui,* what?" the *chef* bellowed. "*Oui, CHEF!*"

"Okay, okay."

The *chef* struck him with his ski pole. "Put on your *raquettes,*" he ordered.

Yokoyama finished the march on snowshoes, even more exhausting than doing it on skis. There was nothing I could do to help apart from pleading with the others to have some compassion. "Can't you see he's trying? There's something wrong with the Legion when we prefer to crush our own weak rather than give them a hand."

"He's a hopeless cunt!" Andropov responded. "He doesn't belong in a combat unit."

Next morning at the chalet, I hobbled over to the *chef* and told him that I had injured my knee. Always wanting to be the superman, it was the first and only time in my Legion career that I was prepared to go to the *infirmerie.*

"You can walk on it, right?"

"Yes, but . . ."

"Then what the fuck are you complaining about?"

The hours before lights-out were the only moments of peace. Maximov buried himself in a Spetsnaz training book. The pictures were crude, but the message was clear. "It's really pretty simple to get prisoners to talk. Just tie them up with their arms and legs stretched out like this," he said, showing me the illustration. "If that doesn't work, you cut off a finger. If you don't want to leave marks, you attach electrodes to the ears."

"That's the kind of thing the Nazis used to do. I assume the author's never read the Geneva Convention."

"You're talking *merde*, Sanchez," Czarnecki said. "You know nothing about the Nazis. You've been brainwashed by CNN. Hell, the whole Holocaust thing was a propaganda story to get America into World War II. The Third Reich's policy toward Jews was emigration, not extermination. Not a single official document has been found ordering the extermination of the Jews. All we have is postwar bullshit from a few so-called survivors. And hardly any of them have said anything about gassing."

Suddenly, Andropov crashed into me and I fell over like a rag doll. "I told you to not leave your gear on my bed!" he roared.

"Andropov," I said, getting up, "I like you but I don't like your dark side. You and several others in this company enjoy nothing more than bullying the weaker ones."

"Bullshit. I'm tough but I'm fair. That's the law of the Legion. If you can't take it, then that's your problem."

"The challenge here isn't being the toughest bully on the block, it's gaining the respect of your *camarades*. Yoko and Michaud do as you tell them to, but they don't do it out of respect."

"Oh, I know, I know," he admitted. "I know I've got a dark side, but I can't help it. Anyway, as a legionnaire, I'm just as willing to give my life for my *camarades* as the rest of you."

"If you remember nothing else from me as the university man in this platoon, never forget that grace is far less expensive than force."

Days later Andropov was preparing to use a sledgehammer on his jammed combination padlock.

"Sanchez," he said, "you like to think you're an intelligent schmuck. Try to get this contraption open before I smash it to bits."

"You haven't turned the dial all the way around." I clicked it open with a flick of my fingers. "There you go! Remember what I said about grace and force?"

*   *   *

One of my favorite pastimes in the Legion was drinking tea. Whenever I had the chance to go into Monoprix, I came out with delicious packets of Chinese green tea, Earl Grey, Lipton yellow, darjeeling, or royal ceylon. Like a heroin addict, I crept away to my room between cleaning duties and brewed up some on my camping stove. In the evenings I had teatime chats with Maximov and Yoko.

". . . Yeah, one more cup. Thanks. As I was saying, Rasputin was a mad monk hell-bent on bringing about civil war. They say he had a dick as long as my forearm, a bit like one of those VAB pistons you were talking about."

The others resented Maximov and me discussing Russian history and engineering. They saw us as snobs—the Russian officer and the American intellectual.

"How long before you desert?" *Caporal* Diagana asked me as he draped his socks over the radiator. "What the fuck are you doing in a combat company like this? A worthless cunt like you should have stayed in Aubagne behind a computer. That's the only thing you're good for—high-tech bullshit. Soldiering's beyond you."

"With all due respect, *Caporal*," I responded, "like everyone else, I've thought of fucking off from the Legion more than once. It's thanks to all your thoughtful encouragement that I have been able to stick it out so long."

In reality, there was only one of us who had certainly never thought of deserting—little Yokoyama. The others found him likeable enough but a bit of a goofball. This was largely because of the difficulties he had expressing himself in French. Everyone forgot, or perhaps never knew, that Japanese is not an Indo-European language and has none of the easy-to-remember words that in English, French, Spanish, and German are the same or similar. In fact he was far from being feeble-minded, and I enjoyed listening to his ideas about life and honor.

"If I desert Legion," he said, as we were cleaning our Famas, "I not complete man. You must understand; I give my word. I look officer in eye and tell him that I serve with *honneur et fidélité*. If I break word, then me not good legionnaire here," he said, placing his hand over his heart.

"Hold on a minute, Yoko. What about what the Legion promised you? They claimed this would be like a family for you. My family doesn't steal from me. My family doesn't stab me in the back, or get their kicks by humiliating me. They promised you a life of adventure but instead they stick a mop in your hands and tell you to clean semen off the toilet seats."

"It not make difference, for I bound by honor. I nothing in Japan. I before am fish butcher, and boss exploit me. Make me working twelve-hour day just for living. My father, he gambler and alcoholic. I speak with my mother once since I come to Legion. You know I kill one man?"

"What?"

"I speeding with Kawasaki outside Tokyo. He not see me coming."

"Why is it only the world's good people who suffer?" I wondered aloud.

"Not feel sorry for me, please. This life I choose."

Our final march, a 1,300 meter ascent through pine forest to the top of the ski lift, followed by coming down the blue *piste*, was to be completed in less than two hours. So as not to waste time changing my clothes, I set off in the deathly cold without a parka or even a sweater over my regulation long-sleeve shirt. After half an hour I had pleasantly warmed up. The only nourishment I'd packed was two tins of rice pudding stolen from the *ordinaire*. Though many took the attitude that this was just another pointless race, I felt it important to maintain my reputation as a company sportsman.

My face was smeared with mucus as I cut through the forest out onto a manicured ski slope. Holidaymakers skied past and children cheered me on as I struggled upward, grimacing with every pace. I was now passing legionnaires who had set off before me at two-minute intervals. At the top, I stripped off my sealskins and launched myself down the *piste bleue*. I skied standing upright leaning slightly forward, allowing gravity to do its work, and managed to edge past Maximov at the finish line. A quarter of the men in the company were suffering from broken bones and other injuries and hadn't taken part at all.

That Saturday night, we were given leave until the next morning. The Legion was slowly coming into line with the *Armée de Terre*, so we'd been issued camouflage denims instead of the traditional olive-drab combat fatigues, and were allowed to go out wearing them and our *képis*, thus avoiding having to press our *tenues de sortie*.

The chalet was equipped with a fully-stocked bar open to legionnaires, provided they presented themselves properly to the instructors who hung around all day on the piss-train. Yoko and I had several beers before leaving to hitchhike into the village. We behaved like rowdy animals in the car that picked us up. It was only when we were getting out that we realized that the driver was a sergeant in civilian clothes. He winked and wished us happy hunting.

In no time, sleepy Valloire was overrun by camouflaged roughs searching for trouble. Most of us ended up in the village *discotheque*. A large part of the bar was occupied by the regiment's newly formed *Unité de Recherche Humaine* (URH) special forces, all proudly sporting the Legion's mountain warfare insignia on their chests. There were plenty of young women who provided easy pickings.

"Now you're an honorary legionnaire," I said drunkenly as I placed my *képi* on the head of a pretty young Danish tourist. "Say cheese for the camera. And now, you give me a kiss!"

With drink and women, even the strictest NCOs behaved like children. The first and only time I ever heard two of the sergeants speak English was when they were drunkenly trying to pick up a couple of Scottish birds with double chins.

The *mafia Russe* were outside roughhousing in the snow and singing their heads off. I joined them and took a swig of their

Smirnoff defroster. Then the *gendarmes* arrived. They simply asked us to quieten down but the Russians reacted as if they had spat on their mother's grave. Fast losing patience with us, the *flics* took out their truncheons. Maximov was in one of his rare but ultraviolent drunken rages. "Come on then! Take a swing at us, you French faggots!"

Before a free-for-all ensued, *Caporal* Sperazzo stepped out to defuse the situation. He tried to explain to the Russians that the French authorities had to be obeyed.

"But they're not legionnaires!"

"Doesn't matter. You'll all end up in jail."

The Russians crowded around him. "What the hell are you talking about?" Maximov shouted. "You *caporal de merde!*"

I was delighted to see fear creeping into the corporal's face. Earlier that evening, Maximov had told me how much he would like to use his knife on someone but hell, this wasn't the place for it! "Look," I said, pulling him aside, "you can't do it in the open. He knows who we are and so do the *gendarmes*. Just let him go for now. Later, you can trail him back to the chalet and put the mark of Zorro on his face in the dark."

I sneaked back to the *discotheque* for a last drink and got to talking to an attractive young *Française*. She told me that she was from a nearby village, and agreed to meet me for coffee the following Sunday afternoon.

When I staggered back to the chalet early on Sunday, I saw a trail of blood on the stairs. Several men mumbled that somebody had hurt a corporal. My stomach sank. Maximov had done it. I found him sound asleep in his bunk. He had not only done it but seemed to have got away with it. I lay down and fell into a deep blissful sleep, but not for long. The corporals stormed into our rooms, screaming, and tipping us out of bed. *Caporal* Diagana struck me across the mouth for no reason whatsoever. Regardless of rank or mano a mano skills, I was ready to beat him into pudding. I was very lucky that I didn't.

An Italian corporal came in, his face bruised and bloodied. Oh, *putain*! I thought. Maximov and his gang have beaten up the wrong man!

"Where's your self-discipline?" *Caporal* Speri shouted. "You're supposed to be able to control each other enough to prevent this sort of thing. Well we know who did it and we're going to teach you all what it means to be part of a unit. Now get outside, *immed*!"

With the corporals hollering, swinging their fists, and kicking everywhere and everyone, we were thrown out in bare feet and pajamas into the penetrating cold.

"Run, you bastards! . . . Now, *en position. Pompes!* Down, up, down, up!"

While I was in the *pompes* position, *Caporal* Diagana bent down and struck me across the chops again. "I said, keep going!" he barked with breath that still reeked of wine. "Guess what, Sanchez; the *chef* himself gave me permission to kick the shit out of you whenever and however I want to! Are you loving this as much as I am?"

"*Oui, Caporal* . . ."

"Seeing you sprawled on the snow disgusts me. Get over to the Dumpster and pick up all those cigarette butts in the snow. *Action!*"

"What the hell are you doing here!" *Caporal* Bendada shouted minutes later. "I told you to do *pompes,* you bastard. *Action!*"

I stretched out again *en position.*

"Trying to cheat your way out of some *sport,* were you!" he howled and landed a brutal kick in my ribs.

When the orgy of violence ceased, we were made to grab mops, brooms, and rags to clean everything up. We were forbidden to speak and any legionnaire who wasn't working up a sweat scrubbing was kicked until he did. The corporals swaggered around, muddying the floors and tipping over trashcans.

We spent the rest of the night on our hands and knees. While cleaning the in-between crevices on the radiator, Czarnecki muttered to me. "My KKK *camarade,* I see you're having it a bit rough these days. How did you manage to get on *Caporal* Diagana's bad side?"

Out of nowhere, *Caporal* Diagana struck me again with a right cross, leaving my head ringing like a bell. "I said *action,* you bastard!"

"*Reçu, Caporal.*"

Then, we were all corralled into one room and the door was slammed shut. "Keep it shut!" the corporals yelled and tramped off down the corridor. Nobody knew what was happening until we heard screams from Rhee, the Korean. The Italian corporal had been picking on him without realizing that he was a South Korean Marine Commando and a tae kwon do expert who could land whirling heel and flying sidekicks with surgical precision.

Rhee could easily have defended himself against one or two men but here he was cornered by over a dozen corporals. We couldn't see anything but we could hear it. Listening to a grown man, a commando, crying out like a child for mercy made my blood curdle. Though we were all made to suffer for Rhee's attack on the corporal, we respected him for having the guts to do it.

After *soupe de midi, Caporal* Diagana barred us from leaving the chalet and went away to sleep off his hangover. I, however, had to get out to meet the young *Française.* I persuaded Yoko to risk sneaking out with me for a quick drink.

We got to the café and sat drinking *pastis.*

"Past two o'clock now. Think she'll show?"

She didn't or she'd been there earlier and left. "Chalk up another victory for *Caporal* Diagana," I finally said. "You know, Yoko, I'm really getting a bad attack of *plein les couilles,* more now than ever before. I must've been German in another life. I can take hardship easy enough, but chaos and injustice I just can't put up with. Do you think anyone'd miss me if I just wasn't around any more?"

That evening with a *quart* of hot tea in my hand, I was looking through the ski course results.

"Hah," *Caporal* Diagana said, "ten men finished ahead of you. *Fatigué?*"

"*Oui, Caporal.*" I just couldn't care less about the Legion anymore; something had snapped.

My first priority was to call in all the money I was owed. Dupont had a debt of a good few thousand francs but payday was over a week away. I had a plan for collecting at least part of it but it took me over an hour to get the Russians to understand.

"Look, I'm selling you my debts for less money than they're worth."

I drew them a picture with boxes and numbers. "Dupont owes me 4,500 francs, right? If you give me four thousand francs, I'll tell him to give you the money that he owes me. That means that you'll be pocketing five hundred francs for nothing. Understand? No? *Merde!*" I went out to find Czarnecki. "For god's sake, help me explain."

"Sanchez, I can see you're thinking about doing something very stupid."

"Oh, you can, huh?"

"Why are you leaving us?"

"*Kurwa,* Czarnecki, I'm not deserting for good, see? I'm just fucking off for a while. I need a break from the Legion. I'll get my head screwed back on after a week or two. I'm sure you've felt this way at some point or another."

"I'm not saying I'm against it. But we've a forty-eight hour leave coming up. Whatever's bothering you will pass. I know how you feel about Diagana. Stick around; it's only a matter of time before we all give that nigger a good stomping."

"It's not just him," I said. "The fact is that I came into the Legion searching for something, something that I now realize I'll never find . . ."

When we got back to the barracks late on Friday, most of the others quickly pressed their *tenue de sortie,* and disappeared into the night. As they left, they grabbed a free baguette sandwich from the *club compagnie* compliments of *Caporal* Chung, just released from the lockup. Those too broke to go out couldn't understand why I was staying in, too. I took my time arranging my cupboard and polishing my *rangers,* and then enjoyed a long, hot shower.

Yoko was the only man in the *ordinarie* on Saturday morning. I told him what I was going to do.

"But you come back one day?"

"Don't know," I said, dunking a baguette in my coffee. "I just need to get away for a time to think. I came in to try to give my life some kind of purpose, a sort of searching for redemption. My existence before I joined seemed meaningless and it still seems that way today. Yoko, we've been pals. Wish me luck."

I walked out through the barrack gates and gave the duty sergeant a crisp open-palm salute. The bus was nearly empty and I sat alone, leaning the side of my head against the frosted window.

On the TGV, I concentrated on draining and crushing cans of Kronenbourg in the bar. I was swapping rounds with a former *REP* corporal, who had just been posted to the 2^e *REG*.

"No need to use *vous* with me," he said. "I'm in civilian clothes and we're off-duty."

"I wish all the corporals in the *REG* were that relaxed."

"I just got out of jail last week after a fight with a sergeant. When I went before the colonel, I requested a transfer to Aubagne. He looked at my file and said: 'Bullshit, you're going nowhere but the 2^e *REG*.' I've been there for three days and hate it already." He rolled himself a cigarette. "Discipline in the *REP*'s tough but the *sketch* in the *REG* is unbelievable! And that's speaking as someone with five years' service . . . Next round's yours, right?"

10.

PARIS

The legionnaire is a volunteer, first and foremost a man of action, brave in combat and eager for change. He disdains idleness and routine.

French Embassy in Washington DC

By the time we pulled into Paris, I was feeling uneasy about what I was doing. Did I really want to be labeled a deserter for the rest of my life? I could still get back to the *REG* by Monday morning and no one would be any the wiser. When I got to my hostel, I placed my *tenue de sortie* neatly folded with *képi blanc* atop on the shelf above my bed and sat down naked with a beer in my hand for a serious think.

The *concierge* came in to open the windows. "Won't you join me for a drink, my lovely Berber lover?" I asked.

"Juan, you're just as cheeky as ever."

"Oh Maumi, why don't you come over here and sit with me for five minutes?"

"My mother always told me never to sit with legionnaires if they haven't got their trousers on."

Later, I tried phoning Ellen but her American artificiality put me off.

"I'm, like, totally glad that you're in Paris again. I really hope you have a good time."

"Sure, but I was wondering if we could meet for a drink."

"Oh, I'd love to, but lately I kind of started realizing that all this partying and stuff is just distracting me from my studies. And I got a friend visiting from Tufts, but I do hope you have a totally fun weekend."

While drinking at Polly Magoo's that evening, I came across Annika again. She introduced me to her girlfriends as her Foreign Legionnaire. They were already well-fuddled and started taking the piss out of me.

"Just feel him," one giggled, poking me in the abdominals. "Come on soldier, entertain us!"

Another grabbed my ass so tight I had to remove her hand. "Look," I said, "I'm a legionnaire, not a toy!" The more irritated I became, the more they harassed me, until I finally left.

I made my way to the Violon Dingue. Before even ordering a drink, I noticed a slim redhead sitting with another girl and what looked like two *Armée de Terre* soldiers. She was about thirty years of age, wearing jewels and a business suit with black stockings. She was sitting on her stool with her knees primly together, saying little and smiling faintly when the others laughed. With flaming hair like that, there was no way she could be French.

"Well what brings you to a place like this?" I asked. "American, by any chance?"

"No," she replied coldly in excellent English. "French, like so many people in Paris."

"Always lively and chatty like this? Come on now, the French are never that uptight. You're behaving like a schoolteacher."

"But that's exactly what I am. I teach English in Versailles."

She fell silent again, while her girlfriend kept the soldiers entertained.

I bent forward to whisper in her ear. "I see you as a flower," I said holding out my upturned fist and slowly unfolding each of my fingers. "You only open when you feel the warmth of the sun."

She flashed an understanding smile and we leant toward each

other for a deep kiss. The soldiers were amazed to see me embracing a woman five minutes after having met her. Her girlfriend got up and moved away with them.

"I hope you weren't with those guys," I murmured.

"I was, but I know them no better than I know you."

"It's stuffy in here. Come on, let's go outside for a walk by the Siene."

I'd finally found my own Axelle Red. I knew it was only going to be a matter of time.

"My name's Marianne," she said.

"Mine's Juan . . . Well, it has been for a while."

She had a strong nose with a bend in it halfway down and she was taller than me, but I was fascinated by her slender elegance. "Look, we'll take that cab." I waved at the driver. "Come on, I'll take you back to your place to make sure you get home alright."

We got out at a tall building near the Gare d'Austerlitz where she said her mother had offices she no longer used. The place was spotless but a bit empty. We lay down on a sofa and I wasted little time in groping up her legs to pull down her black stockings. I began softly and slowly gratifying her with my fingers.

"All right then, we'll have sex," she said, "but first promise that we will see each other again."

I pulled her dress over her head and she lay back with her eyes closed and her freckled face gently flushed. We began with full-on sex, and then I turned her over, and penetrated her from behind, one knee on the floor and the other on the sofa. Before I fell asleep, we had sex once again.

Early next morning, Marianne woke up whimpering about what a fool she was for letting me sleep with her. Then she threw her arms around me and hugged me.

"Marianne, you're not quite right in the head."

"Don't be silly. What makes you say that?"

"I know all about it. I've been serving in an army of men who are not quite right in the head."

"So why did you join that army of mercenary psychos?"

"Oh I guess it's like why Sir Edmund Hilary wanted to conquer Everest—because it's there."

I'd stiffened again. I took her hand and placed it over her pubic hair, manipulating her fingers over her clitoris until she continued unassisted.

"Why do you make me do such strange things?" she moaned.

It was sheer pleasure watching her please herself. For fifteen minutes, her right hand fluttered about while she stimulated her breasts with the other.

"I'm not being successful." She sighed and beckoned me to mount her.

Just before sex, I slipped my hands under her buns and realized she had already drenched the sheets.

We fell asleep and when we woke up her mood had changed again.

"I've let you have exactly what you wanted."

"And so?"

"And so you don't deserve it. You're too clever for your own good and mine." She started pulling on her stockings. "You left the toilet seat up last night and you snore like a pig."

She went off saying she needed to fix some coffee and came back wearing a blue dress. She twirled herself around. "What do you think?"

"Stunning."

"Glad you like it. It is a Dior I picked up at the Galeries Lafayette. Now, drink this coffee down, I've got things to do."

"Look, I don't have anywhere to go and I'm running low on funds. You said your mother no longer uses this place, right? You wouldn't mind if I stayed here, would you?"

"Don't be ridiculous! What would *maman* think?"

"She won't have to think anything. I'm invisible. I don't pick up the phone and I don't answer the door."

"Out of the question. Drink up that coffee, it's time you left."

"Feeling ashamed?"

"No." She was checking her eyeliner in a hand mirror. "I'll simply put it behind me."

It looked as if my warrior's rest was coming to a premature end.

"But don't look so sad."

"Why not? There's a lot I wanted to tell you about."

"Why didn't you tell me last night?"

"Oh, I don't know, perhaps because I don't like speaking of things like that when I'm about to get laid."

"Don't use that language around me!"

I walked her over to the Gare d'Austerlitz so she could get out to her parents' place in Versailles for lunch. Incredibly, she was still living with them.

"I like you, Juan, but you're too aggressive."

"Yes, I'm aggressive, because I love life! That's the real reason I joined the Legion. Would I've sat down beside you last night if I were timid? Would we have had sex if I'd waited for you to make the first move?"

"Maybe you're right," she said as we boarded the metro. "I like your rough-cut image. I imagine that you got thrown out of school for unruly behavior, that you've been in trouble with the law, and your parents can no longer stand you. I think you wanted to try to become a better man by running away and joining the Legion. It's quite romantic, really!"

I wasn't about to destroy her fantasy. "I'm coming back with you and having lunch with you and your parents."

"Oh, no, you're not. *Maman* thinks I was out with Charlotte last night."

"Come on, come on! It's cold and gray and both of us have fuck-all to do anyway. If I was able to charm you, I'm sure that I can charm *maman*."

As we got near Versailles, I asked her how much it cost to visit the château.

"Almost nothing, a few francs. Why?"

"Because that's why you're bringing me out here."

"*Hein?*"

"That's how you'll explain me to your mother. You met me this morning in the Latin Quarter and wanted to show me around the château."

"You'll understand what I mean about *maman* when you meet her. This is our stop, St. Cyr-l'Ecole."

"Is that the military academy where they turn out officers for the Foreign Legion?"

"It was, until the allies bombed it during the war. I live just across the road. I'm from an army family myself. My uncle is a colonel with the *Troupes de Marine* in Kosovo. *Papa* was a lieutenant in Algeria. He'll be really interested to hear that you're in the Legion."

The more she spoke of the military, the more I cringed at the thought that I was about to go AWOL. I glanced at my watch and realized that I still had a few hours to catch the last TGV to Avignon.

"And who might this be?" Marianne's mother asked when she saw me.

"This is Juan Sanchez. We met this morning in a *bistrot* and I decided to bring him out to see the château. Juan, my parents, *Monsieur et Madame Galleaud*. Juan is a legionnaire."

Her mother's jaw dropped.

"*Bravo!*" said her father. "I worked alongside the Legion in Algeria. Stationed at *Fort de Nogent*?"

"No, I'm in Paris on a week's leave. Seeing how Marianne's an English teacher, we had a lot to talk about. France and French history fascinate me."

"Well, you'll enjoy seeing around the *château*," *Madame* Galleaud said. "But first of all lunch, *à table tout le monde*."

I sat down opposite Marianne.

"And what did you do before you joined the Legion?" *Monsieur* Galleaud asked.

"Well," I said, looking Marianne straight in the eye, "I was a mechanical engineer in Chicago." Her eyebrows shot up.

"Marianne will have told you," *Madame* Galleaud interrupted, "that I'm a bit of what they call a mother hen. There's nothing about *ma petite chérie* that I don't know."

"Ah, aren't mothers lovely!"

"How did you two meet? This morning, wasn't it? Seems rather early on a Sunday to be out and about having a drink. What *bistrot* was it you met in?"

"Er . . . Marianne?"

"The Victor Hugo, *maman*."

"*Ah bien*. But, Marianne, you were with Charlotte yesterday evening, *n'est-ce pas*? Did you spend the night with her?"

Marianne's father knew exactly what a legionnaire and a lovely woman like his daughter had been doing the previous night. Like a good soldier, he lent a comradely hand. "Why so many questions, *ma chérie*? These young people are here to have lunch and admire the glories of Versailles. There is no need to subject the *jeune* legionnaire to a cross-examination."

My palms had become sweaty, not from nerves but at the thought of food and *pinard*. It was twenty-four hours since I'd last eaten.

"*Oui,*" I said, "*un verre de Beaujolais sera très okay avec moi.*"

"But you speak French so well," *Madame* Gallot said.

"*Merci,*" I grunted with my mouth full.

"And I do believe I hear a slight *Marseillais* accent," *Monsieur* Gallot remarked approvingly.

I muttered and nodded throughout the conversation, not giving fuck-all if I made a bad impression or not. When *Madame* Gallot went out to fetch another bottle of wine, I stretched over and grabbed the last lamb chop.

After lunch, Marianne drove me in her mother's Renault to the château. She knew its history inside out. ". . . and in 1919, the *Triple Entente* and the Americans, who'd just entered the war, drew up the peace treaty to end all wars. It was here that it was signed. If your people had not been so demanding of Germany, the world would never have had to suffer the Second World War."

Here, in the sophisticated elegance of the Château de Versailles, I felt much better about getting out of the Legion. I pictured the last TGV departing from the Gare de Lyon, packed with my *camarades* but without me.

That evening, Marianne and I ended up back at her mother's offices.

"But we can't keep using *maman's* apartment," she said. "She worries about me when I don't come home. And she doesn't like me getting mixed up with dangerous men. You don't understand the control she has over me." She put her arms around my neck and began to whimper. "Oh, you're driving me mad . . . and now you're going to have your way with me again." She undressed. "Kiss me here," she said, spreading her legs apart and pushing down my head.

I woke up with a cold sweat at precisely 06.00. My *camarades* would be getting out of bed and realizing that I wasn't there. In a few minutes, the *chef* would be opening my armoire with steel cutters to confiscate my belongings. I fell asleep again and had a nightmare about the shame I was bringing on my family. It went on like that for over a week. I did little more than sleep all day and get up to wait for Marianne in the evenings.

One night she asked me to take her out to dinner at an upscale restaurant, Fouquet's, on the Champs-Élysées just down from the *Arc de Triomphe.*

"Why do you have such small teeth?" she asked, gazing at me from across the table.

"Civilization," I replied.

"You've got small hands, small ears, and a small smile. You're a very compact man; small, but adorable. *Mon petit* legionnaire! In spite of all your faults, Juan, I think I love you."

"But does your mother?"

"*Papa* thinks you're a real man because you're a legionnaire but *Maman* doesn't care for you at all. She thinks you're just interested in me to get a free bed. I've told her that we're having unprotected sex and she says you must be carrying all sorts of diseases picked up from whores in *l'Afrique*. She wasn't impressed by the way you behaved at lunch last week either. She says you eat as if they're starving you in the Legion."

"They are."

"Then why don't you just say *au revoir* to all that, *chéri*? Tell them that you want out."

"It's a bit more complicated than that."

"But you're a qualified engineer, darling. You're a gentleman, not a criminal. You don't need to be a mercenary. I'm sure we could have a good life together in America."

I was still unsure about deserting but spending time with Marianne helped. She kept my mind off the Legion and motivated me to get out and about to see and do things in the city that I'd never thought about doing since I'd fallen in love with Katarina.

"Tomorrow we'll go to the *Musée du Louvre*," she said one evening. "You're a man of culture, *n'est-ce pas*?"

"Can't we just go somewhere, get drunk, and come back here for sex?"

"Don't be so crude! Frenchwomen are not Germans."

"I know. Frenchwomen are delicate, totally unlike the blonde *Fräuleins*. But actually, I don't know which I prefer, the weak or the strong. Maybe because I'm a bit of both myself."

"So, apart from the fact that I'm French, why do you love me?"

"Quite honestly, because you're bizarre."

Marianne's intellectualism and passion for reading attracted me too. She couldn't pass a bookshop without going inside. "Here," she said, picking up a book, "one of my favorites, *1984* by Orwell. And this one's by my favorite French author, André Maurois."

As the week came to an end, I decided that I had to get myself straightened out. "Marianne," I said, "I've got to tell you things about myself that I've never told you up to now."

"Oh, Juan, what is it?"

"First, my real name's Jaime Roberto Salazar. Juan Sanchez is a name given to me by the Foreign Legion. At this moment, I'm wanted by Interpol, the *gendarmerie,* the *Police Nationale,* and every other French *bureau.* By now, I'm no longer considered just AWOL. I'm a deserter. If I'm caught, I'll be sent to jail and when they let me out, I'll be thrown back into service, with the length of the prison sentence tagged on to my five-year contract."

Marianne whitened. "Oh, Juan, I'm scared."

"But I've thought things through. I'm going back."

"Oh, don't be *un crétin*! Think of what they'll do to you. They'll ship off you to some godforsaken place *en Afrique.* I'll never see you again."

"I simply can't stand the idea of being a deserter for the rest of my life. I have to keep my side of the bargain. I signed a contract. It's like I signed it in my own blood. Marianne, I'm going to give myself up at headquarters in Aubagne. They'll give me two months in jail but then they'll let me out to finish my contract. In Aubagne, instead of wasting my time in Saint-Christol, I'll be able to live a semi-normal life. With a bit of effort, I may even get to play an instrument in the *Musique Principale* and run in the 1er *RE* cross-country team."

She tried to take my hand.

"No, there's no point in arguing, I'm leaving tomorrow. You'd better go back to your parents'. I've things to do. I'll see you in Versailles later on."

That evening, I carried all my belongings out to Marianne's parents' place. She met me outside and led me around to the cellar. "*Maman*'s asleep," she whispered. "She doesn't know you're coming around here."

"*Merci mille fois,* Marianne. If I take anything back with me, they'll just confiscate it. I've got important documents in here," I said, covering my rucksack with a blanket. "A copy of my five-year contract, my driver's license, credit cards, an outdated passport, and fifteen thousand francs in cash."

There was little time for sappy farewells. She gave me a photograph to keep me company during my jail sentence and I sprinted back for the last train into Paris. As I dashed along the cobbled alleyways like a runaway thief, my mind was on the fine *bordel* I'd gotten myself into.

11.

QUARTIER VIÉNOT

As a boy growing up in Marseille, I remember seeing ships leaving port La Joliette for Indochina. My father told me: "Of all those Képis Blancs, most won't make it back to France. Too many are still there, sleeping forever somewhere in Vietnam." He had spent a decade in the Legion, and only wished he could be with them.

Anonymous, Montreal

A chill drizzle was falling as the 07.54 TGV glided out of Paris. I was dressed in *tenue de sortie* and carrying nothing but my ID card, a small amount of cash, and a Stanley knife hidden in the hem of my trouser leg. At 11.19, two minutes late, we arrived in the sweltering heat of Marseille and I marched straight into the *buffet de la gare*. The barman was shuffling chairs around. I slapped my *képi* atop the counter. "*Service!*"

"*Oui, monsieur*. What will *monsieur* have?"

"*Pastis*. What the hell else does anyone drink in this damn town? And make that a double!"

Minutes later, I was ready for another. I was about to ski off down an ice-bound black *piste* and I intended to dull the inevitable pain the only way I knew how. But the more I drank, the more nervous I became. Marianne was right; don't be *un crétin*. What in god's name were they going to do to me?

"Did I say I was finished?" I barked as the barman removed my empty glass. "Another slug of *pastis* piss. Hell no, better still, a Kronenbourg, draft!"

I got the next train to Aubagne, where I took my time, stopping off at the Legion *bistrot* where I'd spoken to the Canadian sergeant so long ago. Everything had come full circle. Now I was the one drinking myself silly. Sitting along the bar was an *REP* man, drinking almost as hard as myself.

When I finally arrived at the barrack gates, I saw a prisoner in filthy fatigues, picking up litter along the inner fence. *"Ca va?"* I shouted. "Be joining you soon!" I presented myself at the guardroom and blurted out my errors with the fervor of a Catholic at confession.

Jail in the Legion is a rite of passage as sacred as earning the *képi blanc*. No one is a true legionnaire until he's done time inside, and the worse the offense, the better. It was going to be tough but not as bad as in Cushny's days. For frowning at a corporal in Sidi-bel-Abbés, he was sentenced to eight days in a 2.5 by 1.0-meter cell with one small air vent and a shit bucket as furniture. Every day he was taken out into the dazzling desert sun and made to march for four hours with a sack of rocks and sand on his shoulder, around and around a clay yard worn smooth by legionnaires' boots. His water ration was one canteen per day, to be drunk while marching, regardless of what was spilled. The modern version, after the reforms of 1983, is an 8 km commando march *au pas gymnastique* carrying a fully loaded rucksack.

"Another deserter for you. Name of Sanchez," said the *PM*, who handed me over to an Asian-looking jail warden. He took away everything I had in my pockets but let me remain in *tenue de sortie*. I was then escorted into a crowded cell. My fellow prisoners were all dressed in Algérian-era fatigues and mismatched *rangers,* without either belt or beret. The *REP* man I'd seen in Augbagne *bistrot* was there as well as a scruffy mutt, the regimental mascot.

There were about ten of us in all, a mixed bag of men and crimes from different regiments. One of them shook my hand. It was Lewinsky, the Pole. He had been sent back from Kosovo for Thai boxing a corporal and leaving him with three broken ribs. His years of service made him the senior prisoner and our unoffical *responsable*.

"You deserted from the 2ᵉ *REG*?" One of them laughed. "How did it take you so long?"

"Other regiments different?"

"There's no way I'd let them transfer me to that *gros bordel de merde*. We've already heard more than enough about it to make anybody want to steer well clear. Forget all that *sketch* they tell you about it being the Legion's future!"

Bertrand, a young Frenchman, had deserted from the 2ᵉ *RÉI*. "I couldn't keep up in the runs. Every day after *sport,* the corporals made the platoon stand in a ring with me in the middle and take turns to kick, punch, and head-butt me. I deserted but my family wouldn't have me back. I had no money and nowhere to go so I had to turn myself in. I'm not going back to the *RÉI*, though." He grinned. "Never! When I get out of here, I'm staying with the 1ᵉ RE in Aubagne."

They told me the warden was an Indian named Bhattacharya. He was easygoing, and everyone was determined that things would remain that way. At the end of the morning he called me back to his office and explained that if I caused no trouble, life in prison would not be too hard. "Legionnaires are deserting every day now. I've known too many good men who left and I can say that I sympathize with your situation."

"How do you feel about the Legion yourself?"

"Morale has plummeted. The politicians in Paris are using us as a peacekeeping force, loaning us out to the UN. That's not what we're for." He ground out his Marlboro under his boot. "I'm approaching the end of my third five-year contract. When that comes up and I start drawing my pension, I'm taking my family to Guyana to open an Indian restaurant."

That evening in the prison courtyard, I overheard him talking to a corporal. "That new man's not going to be with us for long. The *PMs* from the *REG* are picking him up tomorrow."

"They're sending me back to that hellhole in Saint-Christol," I moaned to the others. "But they can't! I'll be damned if they do this to me! Bertrand, is there nothing I can do? I won't go back, the corporals will beat me to pulp."

I was sizing up the walls opposite our cell and trying to work whether they would be able to see me from the guardroom if I climbed on to the roof, when Lewinsky poked my arm. "What's on your mind, *mon ami*?"

"The only thing left for me. I'm getting the hell out of here before lockdown tonight. Where's that roof lead to?"

"Firstly, that's the roof over the *PMs*' quarters. Secondly . . ."

"Are you going to escape?" Bertrand broke in excitedly. "I know how to do it; the *PMs* won't even notice you're missing. Just wait till the warden—"

"Come in here, Sanchez," Lewinsky said, gesturing me back into the cell. "I'm speaking to you as a *camarade*. Don't break out tonight. Bhattacharya's been good to us. He gives us free time and the occasional bottle of *pinard*. If you break out while he's on duty, you'll land him in the shit. And if we allow you to break out, we'll be in the shit, too. The captain will strip him of his rank and our remaining days in here will be liquid hell. I'm not telling you what to do. I'm simply giving you advice. But if you do try, sure as hell, you better hope they don't catch you and throw you back in here with us."

He made me think. How could I justify escaping and leaving the others to suffer for it? I decided that having already compromised my honor with my *REG camarades,* I was not going to do the same with this lot.

Standing in the urinals alongside Bertrand, I asked him, "How was it that you managed to get a permanent transfer to the 1er *RE* after deserting?"

"Simple, when the *PMs* came to take me back to Nîmes, I grabbed a piece of lead piping and took a swing at the captain. I smashed the windows with a chair and screamed that they would never take me alive."

"Were you serious?"

"Oh, no, I just put on a convincing *sketch*. They diagnosed me as having a bipolar disorder and posted me here to Aubagne to serve out my time. It's simple. Once the *PMs* come, go absolutely mad. Throw anything you can get your hands on—chairs, tables, *rangers*. Foam at the mouth if you can."

When we bedded down for the night, they told me this was the cell a Russian had hanged himself in two months before. He had deserted four times but was too *mongol* to get back to his homeland. He was always being picked up by the *PMs* in the rail stations or in the Paris *métro*. On his fourth escape, he got as far as the frontier city of Strasbourg. When the *PMs* came for him, he was standing atop a table, smashing bottles and challenging the entire *bistrot* to a fight.

As we were being marched into breakfast next morning, I could see the waiting *PM* wagon through the bars of the courtyard gate. The *sergent chef* came into the *ordinaire* before I'd had a bite of baguette. "Sanchez, you have five minutes to get your *merde* together!"

I doubled-back to the cell and took down my *képi blanc*. I gazed at its whiteness and ran my fingers gently over the perfect stitching before kicking through the crown with my boot. I took off all my clothes, and stuffed them out through the window bars.

"I said five minutes!" the *PM chef* bellowed, coming into the cell, clutching his nightstick. "Oh, *merde,*" he muttered, when he saw me. I was cowering in a corner, nude and trembling violently, with my face buried in my hands. "Looks like a job for the *capitaine,*" he said into his radio.

Minutes later, the captain strode in and sat on a bed a safe distance away. "Hell there, legionnaire. I see you've got a bit of a problem."

I continued trembling, without acknowledging his presence.

"*Mon enfant,* I'm here to help and listen to what you have to say. I can't assist you if you don't speak."

"Won't go back!" I growled, trying to sound like an angry pit bull.

"So that's what the problem is, is it? Listen, as much as we'd like to keep you here, your regiment needs you more than us."

"I won't go back!"

"There's nothing I can do."

"There's a lot you can do."

"We all make mistakes. No harm will come to you."

"I'm losing my mind! I'm hearing voices telling me to do things!"

"*Jeune* legionnaire, the only thing you suffer from is fear."

"Oh, yeah?" I burst out, waving at him the open Stanley knife from my trouser hem. "See this! This is what I'm going to do!" I held it to the side of my neck.

"Legionnaire put it down. I'll make a deal with you. If you'll just get yourself together and listen, I promise to let you stay here in Aubagne!"

I got to my feet and I tossed the knife on the floor. He picked it up. "I won't be needing your services," he said to the *PM chef*. "As for you, Sanchez, I don't want any more *merde*. If I hear you're acting up again, I'll send you straight back to the *REG*. That clear? And now get yourself changed into prison fatigues, for Christ's sake!"

As soon as he left, I was slapping high-fives with the other prisoners.

"Well-executed *sketch*," *Caporal chef* Bhattacharya said.

I changed into fatigues and tried to find a pair of *rangers* in the stores that fitted me. They were all rock-hard and fossilized into a permanent curl. Even after soaking them in hot water and jumping on them, I couldn't get my feet inside any until I came across a pair five sizes larger than I normally wear. Though they clomped, I didn't think it mattered. I was wrong, as it turned out.

I enjoyed that day's *soupe de midi* like never before. I joked and laughed with the others, even spoke of my career aspirations in Aubagne. The only thing that bothered me was that the *PM* wagon hadn't left.

That afternoon I was summoned to the guardroom and ordered to stand *au garde-à-vous* face to the wall. Considering that in the past deserters were pistol-whipped, this seemed a very mild form of punishment.

"Legion too tough for you?" a *PM* corporal said tauntingly.

"You came to us naked, with one hand covering your balls and the other your ass. We clothed you, fed you, and taught you French. Is this how you pay us back?"

After five hours, the captain came in with four *PMs*.

"About turn!" the *REG chef* ordered "We're going home, Johnny."

"*Mais mon capitaine!* You promised that I could stay, you said—"

"I made no such promises! Take him away."

I acted calm and passive.

"Need help putting him in the wagon?"

"No," said the *chef,* "seems quiet enough."

They locked me in the back and, with a *corporal-chef* at the wheel and the *chef* sitting beside him, we drove off to Saint-Christol. I was checking out every corner of the vehicle. At the front, there was a grille cutting me off from the driver but not from the *chef*. The driver was a squat Tunisian who filled the wagon with his body odor. His *képi* had a ring of sweat around the lower edge. He kept eye-balling me in the surveillance mirror.

When we stopped at a toll station, I thought about kicking out the windows but then I saw *SÉCURITÉ* printed on the glass. Even if I did manage to break through, I wouldn't be outside before the *sergent-chef* came around with his nightstick and beat me back inside. Then I'd be stuck in a confined space with the two *PMs* battering me senseless. We were already over halfway to Saint-Christol and time was running out. Another idea was to knock out the *chef* and get out through his door. If I'd had my Stanley knife, I could have held it to the back of his thick neck and ordered them to stop and give me the keys. But it was all too uncertain; there were too many variables.

"*Oui,* we have him," the *chef* said over the radio. "Should be there by 22.00."

It was dark when we made our unexpected stop at the service station. They fell for my line about needing to piss and came around carrying their nightsticks to open the rear door.

"Hold him here," said the *chef*. "I'll be back in a minute."

"I won't start any *merde*," I said, reaching for the sky as I stepped onto the tarmac. Then I took off in a clomping sprint . . .

I threw off the guards by running across the *autoroute* and clawing my way a couple of hundred meters up the wooded mountainside. The illuminated service area below me was swarming with *PMs* and *gendarmes*. The night was pitch-dark and the temperature had fallen. I looked into the sky to find the North Star and set off south-southwest across the mountains. The Legion's navigation and survival skills served me well. After the first hours I became severely dehydrated and stopped to lick at the dew that had formed under the leaves. I could have made a bed of branches and slept till daylight, but I preferred to struggle on and get out of the region of Provence as soon as possible.

By dawn I'd made it to the outskirts of a village. I prowled around till I found a fountain for a long reviving drink and sat on the wall to work out my next move. Somehow I had to get back to Paris—a daunting task for a penniless fugitive in prison fatigues, without any identity documents and an easily recognizable American accent.

Now that I'd stopped moving, I was getting cold so I poked around in a roadside Dumpster hoping to find a thrown-away jacket or something. I was wrapping an old bit of stair carpeting around my shoulders when I saw a truck pull onto the side of the road and the driver get out for a piss. I ran across to him. "Any chance of a ride?"

"*Pourquoi pas?* I'm going to Marseille. That do you?"

"*Parfait.*"

"We won't get there though till late afternoon. I have a lot of deliveries to make."

"Fine by me." That way I could catch up on some sleep.

We climbed in and drove off.

"American from your accent, *n'est-ce pas?*"

There was no point in denying it.

"Hope you're not the man they're looking for on the radio."

"Oh, no, I'm a junior investment manager in Monaco. We were all up in the mountains playing war-games with the boss. I got lost. They'll be wondering where I am."

When we arrived in Marseille the driver stopped along the street from the Hôtel Mercure in the city center. "There you are, I'll let you off here, *Monsieur Le Gérant de Fortune*." He winked at me. "I don't like *les flics* myself. Anything else I can help you with?"

"Well it's kind of chilly. You wouldn't have something I could wear?"

He rummaged through his dirty-clothes hamper and handed me an oil-stained XXL T-shirt. "You need to ask your boss for a raise. *Bonne chance!*" We shook hands and I got out.

Standing on the sidewalk, I pulled the T-shirt over my prison fatigues. It was an improbable part of town for hitching a ride north to Paris but I had to try. I'd been thumbing unsuccessfully for hours when I heard a police-car siren approaching but I went on waving my arm. With my skinhead hair style and rangers, I reckoned they'd see me as a teenage skateboarder instead of an escaping legionnaire. I was right. They'd just screeched past when I saw an elderly man and his wife out of the hotel and get into their car. I stuck out my thumb and they stopped. They turned out to be Americans and both sounded as if they had had a very good dinner with plenty to drink.

"Can take you as far as Aix-en-Provence."

That wasn't exactly where I wanted to go but I thought it best to put Marseille behind me and got in.

"We're on vacation in Aix and came down here for the day to look around," the driver said.

"I just spent a week here myself. Interesting city, apart from all those Arabs. Had my pockets picked tonight. Two of them bumped into me in the street. They'd disappeared by the time I realized my wallet was gone. It's not so much the money, though; they got away with my passport and all my credit cards."

"Terrible."

"And no point in going to the French police down here, they have this sort of thing all the time. If it's not Arabs, it's gypsies. I just decided I'll have to hitchhike back to Avignon. I've a job there as an engineer."

When the driver let me off in Aix, he handed me a two hundred-franc note. "Sorry about what happened to you. This should get you a rail ticket to where you're going."

I thanked him and hung around until I managed to hitch another ride, which dropped me at a *resto routier* outside Avignon. I was hungry and sat down at a table with a friendly, bearlike truck driver who bought me a beer. After insisting on buying him five more rounds out of the 200-franc bill, I asked whether he was going north to Paris.

"Yes, I am but I'm not what you think I am. I'm not a *routier mais une routière* (not a male truckdriver but a female truckdriver). If you want a ride with me, I want a ride with you."

A Legion deserter had just met up with the fattest woman he could find. My *camarades* would be proud of me.

12.

EARL'S COURT

Rarely do I talk about my time in the Legion. I have found that talking about it makes people uncomfortable. A lot of people experience disquietude in the presence of someone who has stepped beyond the pale.

Evan McGorman

I took the regional train to Versailles. When I got to Marianne's I rang the bell, looking forward to her throwing herself into my arms. The door was opened by her mother. "And what brings you here, pray?"

"We're on maneuvers just north of here. They've given me the day off."

"On a Monday?"

"Er . . . yes, well just part of it. I'm waiting for the results of tests on a knee injury. There's a risk I'm going to invalided out."

"Did you not have time to shave this morning?"

"Ah, we don't shave when we are on field exercises."

"*Eh bien,* Marianne's not here. She's on holiday down in the Basque country. Didn't she tell you?"

"No, that is, not really. I just came by to pick something up."

"*Mais,* Marianne didn't say anything to me about that."

"*Madame* Galleaud, if you would just let me into your cellar, I'll take what I need and be on my way."

After collecting my rucksack, I called Marianne on her cell phone. "Hi, I'm in Paris, darling. I just got out, left the Legion for good."

"*Quoi?*"

"I broke out of jail. Didn't mean to. Just happened to on the spur of the moment and . . . *merde,* here I am."

"But should you still be in France?"

"Well, I'm reasonably safe up here in the north as soon as I can get rid of these prison fatigues. But perhaps I'll sneak across to London, to let things cool down a little. Where exactly are you?"

"The Crowne Plaza in Biarritz, on the Basque coast, near Spain."

"On the beach, huh? Well there's an idea."

"Yes. But. Oh no, hold on! You're not coming down here! *Maman* would kill me."

"Look, there's no way I'm letting you have a vacation all by your lonesome self without me. See you when I get there!"

That evening, just forty-eight hours after getting away from the Legion, I was walking into a four-star hotel overlooking the ocean. I went up to Marianne's second-floor suite. She opened her door and slapped me twice across the face, then kissed me, pressing herself urgently into my groin. "I've had a hard week," I said. "Can we eat?"

After a room-service dinner, I settled myself down for an evening of watching TV. After a couple of French variety programs, I started zapping around to see what else was on offer. "Hey, look at this! You got CNN! Now I can catch up on everything that's been going on in America."

"You've been sitting in front of that TV all evening. Come through here and make love to me," she called from the bedroom.

"Won't be a minute . . ."

I finally dragged myself away and got in under the duvet.

"You're dangerous," she murmured nibbling my ear. "And to make matters worse, you're now a fugitive from criminal justice."

"Yes, and you, too, are committing a crime by harboring and assisting me."

"*Maman* phoned today. I told her I knew nothing about where you are. She says you're a *vaurien,* a good-for-nothing."

"I'm sick to death of *Maman.*"

"She worries about me. . . . Oh, oh," she said fondling my limp penis, "aren't you interested anymore?"

"Look, I don't feel like Superman tonight. I'm tired. Just let me sleep, will you!"

Next afternoon we were having lunch on the *terrasse* of a seafront restaurant.

"I feel so much better after those mud baths I've been taking," said Marianne. "Do you think I'm looking less stressed?"

"Sure, and you really needed a good holiday after all those exhausting fifteen-hour teaching weeks you put in."

"What's wrong with you, *mon petit* legionnaire? You've been acting strangely ever since you arrived. You haven't even made love to me yet!"

"Just tired." I turned away to gaze out at the ocean.

That evening I settled down again in front of the television. I was still at it at four o'clock in the morning when she came storming out of the bedroom. "Don't you know I'm trying to sleep? Turn that blasted thing off! I'm getting fed up with you. When you do come to bed you snore and you left piss dribbles all over the bathroom floor again!"

"Maybe I should leave."

"Oh, *mon petit* legionnaire. Have I upset you? You're so adorable when you're angry."

"I'm not your *petit* boy-toy." I opened another bottle of the ruby-red that I'd smuggled in and started skulling it. "Shouldn't be here in the first place. Perhaps I need to move on."

"*Mon petit* legionnaire, how can you? You've got nowhere to go."

I shot out of my chair. "Shut up. Another word, and I'll smash this bottle against the fucking wall! I need time and I need space!" I began packing my affairs.

"*Cheri*, tell me what's wrong."

I kept my war face on and said nothing, She slapped me, then buried her head in my chest. "Don't do this to me," she sobbed.

I pulled her head back and took hold of her chin. "Life's tough and it's unfair! Get that into your small head and stop the blubbering!" I picked up my bag and stepped out into the corridor. *"Au revoir."*

I'd just destroyed a relationship, but I didn't care. I was already drunk, but before boarding the next TVG north, I stopped at a liquor shop for a bottle to keep me company. I got off in Bordeaux and called Michaud on his cell phone.

"Sanchez, you crazy bastard! You didn't tell me you were leaving. I'm in Normandy with my father. I've got two days' leave left. Why not come up and join me?"

He was waiting for me at Rouen station and greeted me with a Gallic hug. "They'll be looking for you everywhere. Your photograph must be in every *sacré poste de gendarmerie* in France." He punched my shoulder. "I just can't believe that after pulling this *merde* off, you still have the balls to run around in the Legion's Gore-Tex top!"

He took me back to his father's one-bedroom flat in a run-down *quartier* near the river. It was crammed with books, black-and-white photographs, and racks of *pinard*. Old *Monsieur* Michaud, a *pied noir,* had lived and worked most of his life in North Africa. He felt lonely in the overcast, northern dampness of Normandy and was eager to talk to me. He especially enjoyed telling me about his favorite wines. "This one's a Spanish *rioja,*" he said, pouring me a glass of rich red. "It'll give your stomach a warm lining against tonight's chill."

"Lovely bouquet," I said, "but I rather like that French white we just had. Which region is it from?"

"*Le Pays d'Oc,* in the south. Particularly good with a bouilla-baisse."

I drained my glass. "You can tell a lot about a man from the wines he drinks."

Michaud took me out to meet some of his friends in the local *bistrot.* This is my friend Sanchez. Johnny, you can call him. He's just escaped from the Foreign Legion."

No one showed the slightest interest and I was delighted to be able to sit back as a silent observer. *"Garçon!"* Michaud yelled, pounding the table. "Bring me my bottle of Jim Beam." We helped ourselves generously, using red wine for chasers. Then he took me over to introduce me to the bar owner, a portly old Jewish gentleman. "Was in the Legion myself," he said. "Long time and several kilos ago. *Un jour* legionnaire *toujours* legionnaire, as they say. *Ah, oui!* And I hear you've got a bit of a problem, *n'est-ce pas? Eh bien,* the *député* for Rouen is a personal friend of mine. He's well-known in the *Assemblée Nationale* and may be able help in ways no one else can. Here's his card. Mention my name when you see him."

I went back to Michaud and the gang but he got up with a chunk of hashish in his hand. "Excuse me a moment. Just going outside for a word with *Monsieur* Brownstone."

An hour later the group broke up but Michaud had not come back. I went out and found him lying on the sidewalk. "On your feet, legionnaire! Someone's likely to kick your teeth in." I dragged him to his feet and managed to get him home. His father was used to seeing him like that. Without saying a word, he arranged the sofa for his son to lie on. I lay down on the floor next to him and fell asleep.

The following morning, we picked up baguettes and *pains au chocolat* from the baker's and met up with Michaud's friends again for midday breakfast in the *bistrot.* Afterward, we went around to one of the gang's pad and spent the rest of the day smoking hash and listening to the sounds of Manu Chao. I showed Michaud the *depute's* card.

"He won't do anything for you."

"Who knows? Maybe he could pull the right string in Aubagne, perhaps get me an administrative discharge."

"If you set foot in his *bureau,* you'll be leaving in handcuffs."

"Christ! Maybe I should just go back to the Legion and turn myself in."

"Do that, and, best-case scenario, the corporals will rape you. Your time with the Legion has come to an end, Sanchez. Let it go."

His words rattled around the inside of my head like a Famas burst ricocheting from an alpine crag. Hours later, I saw him off at the rail station.

"Listen, " he said over a beer, "I know you need a safe place to crash for the next few weeks. Why not with my father? The old man gets on with you and could use your company."

"A mate till the end," I said, squeezing his arm. "*Au revoir* and give my regards to the *camarades*."

Monsiuer Michaud welcomed me to stay on by opening a bottle and began to reminisce. "I'm no longer the man I used to be long ago," he said, "when North Africa was still French and I was a respected engineer. Look at this pokey place I live in! You'd never guess I used to have servants, a chauffeur, and bodyguards." He pointed to a sepia photograph of a dark-skinned boy playing in the dirt, clad in nothing but a burlap poncho. "As a youngster, that was my best friend, an Arab. We were inseparable. I looked like an Arab myself. I never saw him as a Muslim and he never saw me as a Christian."

"He looks sad. What does he do now?"

"Life in *l'Afrique* is short."

"What was it like back then?"

"A dream. Everyone had good jobs and plenty of money. The Arabs were all very polite and helpful."

"So why didn't you stay?"

"De Gaulle. France's greatest statesman, so-called! He betrayed the *pieds noirs* by pulling out of North Africa. Pro-French Algerians who had fought under the tricolor were left behind to be slaughtered by the FLN, the National Liberation Front. Me, I got out with a niggardly pension and a wife who was having a nervous breakdown."

He pointed at a photograph hanging beside the wine rack. "That's me as a young soldier during military service. I saw a lot of the Legion in Colomb Béchar. Life for them was real hell. I'm glad my son didn't serve in those days." He reached over to refill my glass. "He's still a young man. At his age, listening to what others say is difficult but one day he'll find what he's searching for."

"Even if he doesn't, as a Christian, I believe that if you go on searching you are never lost."

We finished another bottle of *pinard* before turning in.

I spent the next few days thinking over my situation and just wandering about the Old Town, with its medieval architecture and the cross marking the spot where Joan of Arc was slowly burned to death. Then one morning as I was bringing in *Monsieur* Michaud's shopping, I heard a police car with siren wailing screech to a halt outside the flat. Michaud must have let something slip when he got back to the *REG*! I looked out the window to see two policemen run up the next-door staircase. They hadn't come for me but I realized then that I was just postponing the inevitable.

"*Monsieur* Michaud," I said, "I like being here a lot but I've been thinking. I'm going to leave tomorrow. There's someone in Paris I have to speak to."

I checked into my usual Paris-Barbès hostel. "Marianne," I said on the phone, "guess who?"

There was a long pause. "Oh, what are *you* phoning me for?" she wailed.

"Just wanted to know how you're doing."

Her mother must have guessed who she was talking to. There were shrieks and sounds of the two of them fighting for the phone. Suddenly it went dead. I had better luck early next morning, just before Marianne left to begin teaching.

"*Maman* doesn't want me speaking to you. She thinks you're dangerous and so do I."

"Marianne." I chuckled. "I'm harmless. You know me, your *petit* legionnaire who likes playing around with his Famas."

"I've told her everything."

"You haven't told her I've deserted, have you?"

"Yes, I have. I'm a not a good liar and thought I'd never hear from you again. If *Maman* knows where you are, she'll have you arrested."

"*Merde!* Marianne, what in hell were you thinking?"

"*Maman* says I'm never to see you again."

"To hell with *Maman*!" I bawled. Then I calmed down and attempted to charm her. "Marianne, when I think of us two together, I fantasize. You know what about?"

"Oh, go on then, tell me." she giggled.

"You're standing close behind me pressing your hard nipples into my back, and without turning around, slowly, very slowly, I'm using my thumb and middle finger to, to torture your mother. The Legion taught me all kinds of fiendish things to do to her. Then, we kill her, take her money, and run away to Monaco. Headlines in the press: 'Legion Deserter and Lover Kill Mother for Fortune.' "

"Silly boy."

"You know why your mother hates me? Secret lust. She dreams of being screwed by a strong young legionnaire but won't admit it. What think you?"

"I think you're what you say in America, fucked-in-the-head. But that's why I love you."

"Remember you saying we could have a good life, the two of us in the US of A? I've been thinking about it. It's a great idea. When are you coming over with me?"

"Don't be crazy. You don't even have a job."

"That's just a matter of time. I'm an engineer, aren't I? We build shit, right? You said it yourself."

Very well," she said. "First find yourself a job, then phone me."

"But, Marianne, you said you wanted to be with me forever, and that you loved me. I'm your *petit* legionnaire, for God's sake!"

"Sometimes I say more than I should. You'll be better going back to America on your own."

"That hurts, Marianne. And I don't even have a—"

"*Au revoir, mon petit* legionnaire."

*   *   *

Later on the *métro* back to the hostel, I was sitting across from an Algerian teenager. I was drinking hard and he kept eyeing me.

"Here," I said, tossing him a can of syrupy Amsterdam Beer. "10.5 percent alcohol. We call this triple-malt in America." He drank deeply.

"Does the Koran allow you to do that?"

"Arabs have been drinking alcohol since the beginning of time. There's a lot about Islam I don't completely agree with. What the West doesn't seem to realize is that we came to Europe to get away from fundamentalism. I love my homeland but I don't like its politics."

"You think France is better?"

"A bit, but not as good as the United States. I'd much rather live in America, a free land, where no one will hate me for being an Arab, where people of all colors can live together in peace, *n'est-ce pas*?"

"Well . . ."

"There is no justice for the Arabs in this country. The police stop anyone with dark skin, demanding to see our papers. If we try to argue, they beat us with nightsticks and throw us in prison. We live in constant fear."

"I'm from an immigrant family myself," I said and began telling him about Marianne.

"*Mon ami Américain*," he said when we got to Barbès Roche-chouart, "don't let these Frenchwomen get you down. Let me invite you back to my humble home for dinner."

"Yes, you're right." I sighed. "And a meal sounds good. *Action!*"

He lived with his mother and cousin in an immaculate, one-bedroom flat. "This is my cousin," he said, introducing me to a handsome, well-groomed man. "He was a lawyer in Algiers, but now he's here in Paris without a work permit earning money as a construction laborer."

A dish of steaming couscous was pushed in front of me. "In our culture, hospitality is a sacred custom. How often has someone French invited you home to eat?"

"Yeh, you have something there. I came to France *pour voir la vie autrement* but I didn't quite find what I expected."

*   *   *

That night I went to see Katarina, my rock. We were chatting over a glass of Chardonnay. "So I said goodbye to her and walked out. Looks like I blew away my dream."

"But aside from Marianne, is it safe for you to stay in France?"

"Oh, I suppose as long as I don't hang around too long and keep out of trouble. I've got no real reason to stay now anyway, but something keeps making me put off getting that one-way ticket back to the States. And then again, I'm in debt and unemployed. I'm going to have to make up my mind to stop playing soldier and face up to the real world." I downed my wine in one gulp.

"You shouldn't drink so much when you're upset."

"You know the Legion desertion rate in peacetime is ten times greater than in war? I may sound masochistic, but I'd have stayed on if it'd been tougher, if there'd been combat and I was fighting for something I believed in. I never gave up in my life before but this time I have to admit defeat—defeat at the hands of the Legion. Not that I blame them, though. Some men belong; some men don't."

"Are you sure you're going to be happy getting into a suit every day, working nine hours, going home to bed, waking up, and getting back into your suit all over again?"

"Maybe yes, maybe no. What I do know is that I'm more confused now than before I joined in the first place, dammit. I went in to become a man and they broke me. Am I any the better for my experiences? I just don't know."

"You haven't changed a bit since I first met you." Katarina smiled at me softly. "You're never happy unless you're struggling. You can accept any kind of hardship if you think you're on a mission from God, but you don't like it when the going gets too easy."

Back at the hostel, most days I had trouble simply getting out of bed. After hours of lying staring at the ceiling, I'd go down and watch *VIVA* in the lounge. The lyrics of the Europop songs I'd listened to in the *REG* kept haunting me. *"Do you think you're better off alone?"* *"If only I could turn back time, if only I could."*

When I went out I'd see legionnaires in *tenue de combat* and green berets patrolling the *métro* with loaded Famas. I could have been one of them. I'd spend hours in the bars and one night I woke up curled into the fetal position in the doorway of an apartment block. I realized that if I stayed in Paris much longer, I'd be joining the ranks of vagabond *anciens* on the streets. I phoned Mother to say I was coming home.

"What have you been doing?" she demanded.

"What do you mean?"

"The Foreign Legion called. They're searching for you. We're all terrified. Luckily, we were able to track down your credit card expenses to London. Get yourself on the next flight home. Now!"

"But I'm in Paris."

"Have you gone completely insane? What are you still doing in France? You're *asking* to be arrested. I'm going to call the State Department."

"Don't you dare do that! Tell them nothing!" I hung up. My problem with the Foreign Legion was strictly between them and me. I'd gotten into this myself and I was not going to ask my government for help. All I needed to get home was a passport. I would have to go to the Embassy in La Place de le Concorde. I was unsure whether they would know about my time in the Legion but I decided to risk it.

Others had similar difficulties. An American legionnaire went there for help in 1917. He said he wanted to go home but the military attaché was unsympathetic. "You come over here and do all sort of foolish things without consulting us, and then you expect us to get you out of a scrape. Do you know you're likely to be arrested at any moment for not being in uniform? We can't help you. In any case, I'm not sure that you haven't lost your nationality altogether. And in that case, I don't know why you've come here. Of course no American ought to enter the Legion, and no gentleman ought to put himself in the position of a common soldier.

Tom Cushny had to listen to a similar story at the British Embassy. The attaché did, however, ask the French war minister, André Maginot of Maginot Line fame, about the possibility of an official discharge from the Legion, but without success. In a letter to Cushny's father the attaché wrote, "I need hardly say that the war minister was most sympathetic, but he made it very clear that it was impossible for him to grant our request. Service conditions in the Legion, he said to me, are no doubt severe, but necessarily so because of the class of man it attracts. If they made an exception for you, every ambassador in Paris would be asking for the release of his nationals."

When I got to the embassy myself I was stalled at the gate by the French *concierge*. "You can't enter the embassy if you cannot prove you're American."

"That's just the point. My passport's been stolen."

After arguing for a half hour, a U.S. Marine Corps guard came out and escorted me inside.

"Well, hello!" I said to him. "How's the Corps treating you?"

"Good days, bad days."

"Hang in there, and you'll do just fine."

"Prior service yourself?"

"Yes, but none of it in the U.S. military."

The marine took me to an official who asked me a lot of questions. "Well, your background checks out," he finally said, "but you don't have a passport. How can we be sure that you are who you say you are?"

I felt awkward sitting there with a *boule-à-zéro* haircut, wearing a Legion parka, trying to persuade him that I was a tourist. I showed him the out-of-date passport I'd stored in the rucksack I left at Marianne's. That convinced him.

An hour later I walked out with a new passport in my pocket and bought myself a flight to the United States. At Passport Control in the Charles de Gaulle International Airport, I was standing in front of an officer of the *Police Nationale* while he examined my passport. If he did an electronic scan on it, my fugitive status would pop up on the screen. I still wasn't sure that I really wanted to return home. I half wanted to be taken into custody and sent back to the Legion. Then again, if they let me through onto the plane, that would be okay, too. It was up to them to decide what's going to happen. "The Legion," I thought, "is like Jesus Christ. No matter what I do, its arms will be ever open to welcome me back." The policeman looked me up and down, ran a fingernail over my passport photograph and called over his superior who studied it carefully, "*Ça va,* it's a replacement," he said, and waved me through.

"Too bad for them," I said to myself. "They had their chance and they blew it!"

Next day, I was back in Indiana under the protection of the Stars and Stripes. Mother greeted her *enfant terrible* at the airport, ecstatic that I'd made it back alive. On the way home, I sat moodily looking out the car window. I felt bad for Mother. She was so happy but I knew she could see that the Legion had returned to her someone who was not quite the son she used to know. "Thank you" and "Missed you, too" was about all I could say to her.

My BMW 535i was waiting for me exactly where I'd parked it in the drive but everything else felt alien. There were religious ornaments everywhere. "I prayed that the Blessed Virgin would bring you back to me," Mother said, "and have kept candles burning ever since."

She tried to hug me but I pushed her away. "I don't like being touched."

In my room, things in my drawers seemed like a stranger's belongings. On my desk was a card made by my six-year old niece. Inside a heart she'd drawn a stick figure of me and written, "Dear God, please help Uncle Jaime come home. He is in danger and we miss him a lot." Downstairs again, I had barely recovered from the stream of in-flight drinks when I got started on a bottle of California red. *"Du vinaigre!"* I complained. "Pure vinegar."

Father came in from work. "Glad you made it back, but what

did you go for in the first place? You've been wasting time ever since you graduated from Purdue."

"What do you think I was doing? You think I was in France on vacation? I was working as a soldier, an élite one at that!"

"Oh? So what did you learn that's going to be of any use to you now? Just like when you started college, you're now unemployed, and living under your parents' roof."

"Don't ever question my decision to join the Legion" I growled. "Look at my hands. Look at them! This is from months of hard work and suffering. I slept in snow, marched until my feet were bloody, got kicked in the nuts for not polishing my boots properly, and carried a rifle. All to make sure that when you open the fridge, you'll find a Pepsi in it!" With a flick of the wrist, I sent my wine-glass spinning across the room to shatter against the wall.

I'd tried to leave the Legion behind me but it'd followed me across the Atlantic. I began living every day of my life as if I was still in its ranks. The Legion's drinking habits had come with me, too. I spent much of the day listening to my stereo blare out CDs of Axelle Red, Mylene Farmer, and the *Chants de la Légion Étrangère*. Mother often found me singing along. "Son, is it necessary to drink so much? You never drank like this before. Why don't you have a word with the priest?"

"I already had a word with a monk."

Everyone and everything seemed alien. "Why do you keep drinking your coffee out of a bowl?" Mother would ask. In Lafayette, there were no *bistrots* like in Montpelier, no ancient cities with Roman remains like Orange. When I walked out of the front door, I was confronted by a suburban sprawl of split-level ranch homes with lawns and sprinklers.

I forced myself into an intense program of physical exercise to maintain myself at the peak of fitness required by the Legion's *Code d'Honneur* and Mother was delighted that I seemed to be getting my drinking under control. But then Camerone Day came around and brought it all back more strongly than ever. *Anciens* in Warsaw, London, Paris, and even Chicago, would be celebrating but in Lafayette nobody knew anything about it. I wanted to go up to people in the street and tell them the story of the battle. I was alone and drunk, the only person to remember the sacrifice of those heroic legionnaires.

One day I received a letter postmarked London. Amazingly, it was from Gwyneth. Reading it brought back fond memories and just when Mother was beginning to hope that I was settling down, I dropped the bomb. "Mother, I'm just not comfortable in America. I'm going to London to see a friend."

On the plane back to *la belle Europe,* I found a pricey pair of Liz Claiborne sunglasses down the side of my seat cushion and stuffed them into my rucksack. From London Heathrow, I took the tube to Earl's Court, where I checked in to the Patrick House hostel. A week's lodging cost sixty pounds and I wondered how long I was going to be able to survive on my savings.

That evening, I phoned Gwyneth at her beauty salon. "Hey, I'm in London again. Up for going out tonight?"

We met outside the Angel Tube Station. She steered me into an off-license shop, where she paid a small fortune for two bottles of French wine and took me back to her flat. We began with a couple of glasses. "Come over here," I said pulling her to my end of the sofa. I kneaded her breasts and kissed her gently on the lips.

"Give me time to cook something," she gasped, pulling my hand out of her bra.

"*Oui, okay.*" I poured another glass and got up. "Let's see what new CDs you have. Hmmm, not bad at all!" She was opening a kitchen cupboard when I slid my hand up her back, under her blouse, and unhooked her bra. She turned and I handed her the sunglasses.

"Oh, how super! Find them on the tube?"

"Kennedy Airport, duty-free," I said and dragged her back to the sofa.

I unbuttoned her blouse again and buried my nose between her breasts. It was wonderful to feel human affection again after everything I had been through. She got up to take off her skirt and I ran a finger lightly over her pubic mound, noticing that it had recently been trimmed.

"Finished with the Foreign Legion, completely!" Gwyneth whispered after we climaxed. "What are you going to do now?"

"Don't know," I said, tickling the inside of her thigh. "This, I suppose."

We were woken next morning by her screeching alarm. While she bustled about the flat, I sneaked in another half hour of shut-eye. She reawoke me with a cup of tea and led me over to the breakfast table.

"Gwyneth," I said, as I finished a plate of bacon and eggs, "I'm still suffering from jet lag. Can't I stay on here and sleep it off?"

"You're such a child." She reached over to fondle my nuts. "Get your clothes on, darling, and walk me to my salon."

"*Putain!*"

On days when Gwyneth was working, I was happy to stroll around Hyde Park, weather permitting, and spend time back at the hostel with the hooligans there. One afternoon, after a lunchtime piss-up, one of them masturbated into the couch in the TV lounge and minutes later, an Australian sat down on it. While everyone was yelling, I noticed a usable pair of South African Army bush boots in the trashcan. There was a set of broken earphones underneath. I tore off the wires to use as laces and put the boots on before walking around the corner to O'Neil's.

"I see you're wearing a trendy new pair of boots." Gwyneth said when I got back to her place. "My fashion sense seems to have rubbed off on you. You Americans are always so behind the times." She was lying on the sofa wearing nothing but a red bra and panties.

"Yeah, I kind of like them, too. My Adidas were just too ordinary." I went into the bathroom and searched through her cosmetics until I found a small bottle of Clinique body lotion. I went back and inserted it inside her, sliding it gently in and out. Once she became accustomed to it, she took over without my assistance. "I can't believe I'm doing this in front of you," she whispered, too embarrassed to look me in the eye.

"I bet you never thought you'd be sleeping with a mercenary, either. Now, keep it up, darling." As she approached climax, I removed the bottle and mounted her. Legion brutality had done strange things to my sexual habits.

Next morning was Saturday. We had sex again, then while she was frying sausages, I went out in bare feet to stand on the cold tiles of her balcony and admire the view. "People in London must really be into all this functionalist architecture," I said. "And everything else is redbrick or yellow, covered with lichen and moss."

"Don't be so negative," she said. "Now come in and eat up these bangers."

"Yeah, maybe I'm a tad negative these days, but it's only because I don't know where my life is going. Now that I'm out of the Legion, it looks like I'm doomed to wander aimlessly throughout the world. What is there for me to do but have sex with jet-set Londoners like you?"

"What about that book you were writing, those Foreign Legion memoirs I read snippets of? Are you going to have them published?"

"If I can persuade anyone to buy them."

"You won't write about me at the Millennium will you, in Soho Square?"

"You bet, darling, every sordid detail."

"Then you should include the bit about spilling your wine all over my carpet."

"Naw, that'd make me look as if I didn't give a shit."

"Don't be so daft!" She pulled me over to the sofa.

"Today," I said massaging the back of her knee, "I'm going to show you my kind of London."

We started by getting smashed in Shoreditch before taking the Tube to Earl's Court to meet with the Patrick House gang. We were sitting drunkenly on the train with our hands all over each other when she started trying to unzip my fly.

"Gwyneth," I said, "we're on the London Underground! It's going to go all over the place."

"What do you mean? There's nothing to feel squeamish about. After all, I swallow."

I lifted her hand away.

"In case nobody heard me," she shouted, "yes, I swallow!"

We staggered into Patrick House and sat down to drink and smoke hashish with all the Commonwealth nationals. They were surprised when I announced that we had a flesh-and-blood Brit in our midst.

"Hello everybody," Gwyneth said shyly. "I've never been in a place like this before."

"Well, this is your baptism by fire, your formal induction to the life of the London backpacker. We're the hidden people—mysterious Aussies, Kiwis, et cetera. People you see and hear, but never dare to get to know." I pulled out a two-liter bottle of cider.

"Oh dear, that's what we drank in the Third Form at school when we hadn't enough money for proper lager!"

"Not enough money? That's why we drink it, too. And you better not sit down over there. There's a dirty mark on that sofa."

"You mean to tell me that you and your mates actually live and sleep in this place?"

"Yup, and occasionally, we even have sex in here. Let me show you my downstairs mattress that I sleep on when I'm not with you."

We went into the basement dormitory with a couple of glasses and a bottle of Merlot and stood at the window to watch the pedestrians passing overhead. I was refilling my glass when she went down on her knees and unzipped my Levi's. She took me in her mouth, looking up at me as she went up and down. I came and she swallowed, washing it down with a gulp from my glass. "Okay," she said, "now let's go."

*   *   *

Somehow the hectic pace of London life helped me to get things into perspective. I remembered what Mother had said about desertion not putting the soul at risk. The Foreign Legion is a man-made institution, after all. But the important thing, I decided, was to wrap up my unfinished business there and get on with my life.

"Is there a frequent ferry service to Calais from Dover?" I asked one morning, lying in bed with Gwyneth.

"The Eurostar leaves every other hour."

"Can't afford it."

"Why do you ask?"

"Because I going back to France. Today."

"Today?" Her hand slid down between my legs but I caught it.

"Gwyneth. I haven't told you exactly how it was I left the Legion. I broke out of jail. Now I've decided I got to go back and tie up the loose ends. It's not because I have to. Everything's great here with you in London, but that's just it. Somehow happiness is not enough, or perhaps it's too much! I feel I need to be pushing myself more. Gwyneth, do you think I'm doing the right thing?"

She cracked a smile. "Yes."

At Calais, I walked through Passport Control unnoticed and was greeted in the rail station by a Foreign Legion recruitment poster: VOIR LA VIE AUTREMENT. I caught a TGV to Marseille. In the seat beside me was a pretty, blond Française carrying a motorcycle helmet. She told me she was a chef in the Armée de l'Air. Something well could have developed but when we were standing on the platform in Marseille's Gare St Charles, I kissed her on each cheek and turned on my heel. I had things to do. I had a package to bury before going on to Aubagne.

It was late in the evening. I started wandering about the city and soon found myself in the Arab quarter, where Marseille becomes Cairo. Clothes were hanging out to dry on the window rails and men were shouting in Arabic at each other from the balconies. Through gaps in the curtains, I could see veiled women sitting with old men drinking spiced tea. The Arabs on the sidewalks stared at me, sneering or trying to sell me hashish.

I stopped at Hotel Mascara, where I checked into a double room for half the price I'd paid for a dormitory mattress in Earl's Court. That night, I knelt down on the tiled floor to ask God to give me the courage to face whatever the Legion had waiting for me the next day. Then I got into bed, too tired to brush away the pubic hairs on the sheets. I longed to be with Gwyneth again, lying beside her in her cozy Council flat, my head resting on her breasts. I was awoken several times in the night by the sounds of Arabs shouting, glass breaking, and police sirens but the soft air from the Mediterranean billowing in through the open window caused me to drift back to sleep.

My first task in the morning was to find somewhere to stash the belongings that I didn't want the Legion to confiscate. I placed several thousand francs, one hundred British pounds, my passport and American Express platinum card in a Ziploc bag and walked through the city streets out into the open countryside. After tramping along a main road for an hour, I reached a secluded spot where no one could watch what I was doing. To the chirping of cicadas, I scraped a hole in the rocky soil and put in the bag. After pushing back the earth, I placed large rocks atop as markers and had a good shit over it all as a deterrent to man and beast. On the back of a TGV pamphlet I sketched myself a rough map and began the long, sweaty march to Aubagne.

As I passed through the Legion gates, I was apprehensive but delighted to be coming home to my adoptive family—the return of the prodigal son! In the guardroom, I stood *au garde-à-vous* and presented myself. My voice was quavering but I spoke with pride.

"Sit down," the adjudant said. "You English?"

"*Non, mon* adjudant, *Américain.*"

"Bear with me for just one moment." He spoke into his phone

and a corporal came in with a large manila envelope. The adjudant emptied it onto the table. "Right, here we have your passport, your address book, your Elastoplast, several documents about I don't know what, and a copy of your university diploma. I think that should do it for you. Just sign here."

I signed.

"Very well," he said, "you can go now!"

"But, *mon* adjudant," I said, "I don't understand."

"What, is there something we haven't given you back?"

"No, *mon* adjudant, but I mean here I am ready and fit for duty."

"Oh, I'm afraid that's not at all possible. You're no longer under our orders. You're now, for want of a better word, a civilian."

"But *mon* adjudant, this cannot be. I've come all the way back from America to finish my five-year contract. I'm ready to take my punishment. Can't you do something?"

"Unfortunately, no. You no longer exist as Legionnaire SANCHEZ, Juan. Your contract is no longer valid. I wish I could do more, but there it is." He rummaged through his drawers and held out a form headed *Bureau des Anciens de la Légion Étrangère*. "Take this. You are now one of our veterans, an *ancien* of the Foreign Legion."

As I walked back down the stairs, I could hear distant sounds from the *Musique Principale* and legionnaires singing. My eyes misted over. Like Winston Smith in Orwell's *1984*. I loved Big Brother. In the 1920's, another American Legion deserter, Bennett J. Doty, was sentenced to eight years hard labor. He was discharged after little more than twelve months by the *Père de la Légion* himself. General Rollet stared at him with his piercing blue eyes and said, "I know you will write about us one day. When you do, make sure you tell your readers that we're tough, but just."

On my way to the rail station, I stopped to buy two six-packs of Kronenbourg. The only proper way to say farewell to the Legion was to get on the piss train and systematically crush each can after draining it. *"A moi la Légion!"* I shouted drunkenly, as I sat waiting for my train. Nobody came. My life in the Legion flashed before my eyes—marching through the beauty of the French countryside, enjoying the splendors of ancient Roman cities in *tenue de sortie,* laughing with my *camarades* on a bistrot *terrasse.* In an age of computerized warfare, I had chosen to serve in an army where men are men. I was on my way out, but the Legion would carry on without me, ever faithful to its tradition of redeeming the lost.

Five years later, back working as an engineer in the United States, I am still pondering my love-hate relationship with the Foreign Legion. Was it a streak of masochism, some competitive need to be tested to the breaking point that led me to join, to run away, and then twice to return voluntarily to what had been a frequently miserable existence? Or is there something deeply mysterious, even magical about the Legion's pull? Could it be a combination of the two? Have I more in common with at least some of the men I served with than I realized at the time? Perhaps all those who enlist, other than to escape jail or starvation, have essentially the same motivation. We want to go through that hell so that one day we can sit down and share a drink with other *anciens* and say, "Yes, we were there. We did that, and we survived." It's not everything. But it's not nothing either.

All civilizations have their sufferers. In every country in Europe and America also, live men for whom life is a penance . . . For all of those whom Dostoevsky calls the "insulted and injured," the Foreign Legion offers refuge.

André Maurois

AFTERWORD

Still in his early thirties, Sanchez's *chef de section* retired after fifteen years of service.

After spending weeks in the hospital from the broken bones and internal injuries suffered after his beating in Valliore, Rhee deserted.

Lohmann was able to return to his sedate life, and his old job as a banker in Johannesburg, South Africa.

Caporal-chef Green finally retired, taking with him the legend of the old Vietnam veteran. Afterward, he and his American wife of thirty years had plans to live and work in South Africa.

Ellison and his assortment of Irish hooligans deserted from the Legion after living in and out of Legion lockup. They never left France, and secured casual work in Paris. Of all things, they were last providing security at Charles de Gaulle International Airport.

Andropov was transferred to Guyanne and is believed to have spent the rest of his contract there.

Kulzer finished his five-year contract with the Legion and was honorably discharged. He was last known to be providing international corporate security and counterterrorism services in Europe and Japan.

Throughout his Legion career, Beam suffered from physical and psychological problems. The *mafia anglaise* simply considered him "nuts." With an arrest warrant in the UK for deserting the British Army, he simply settled in the Vaucluse region with his obese girlfriend and her two teenage sons, who told Beam, who still hadn't grasped French, to "fuck off" on a daily basis.

Even after years of discipline in the Legion, Calderon's temper was by no means diminished. His increased drinking, in fact, made it worse, and he eventually found himself in and out of jail for consumption and brawling. His last episode was stealing a five-ton truck while in a stupor and driving it around the regiment. He never managed to get it out of first gear, and he was chased down by legionnaires on foot. He stopped only when the truck ran out of fuel and crashed into a tree. He was thrown in lock-up for a minimum of forty days.

After deserting, Weber settled with family in Holland, working menial jobs for the time being. He eventually landed a career in London's lucrative IT sector. He lives in Aldgate. While Sanchez was on a business trip to London, he and Weber reunited. They keep in touch to this day.

None of the *mafia russe* members were known to have deserted. Most reenlisted for another five years. Many who finished their contracts moved in together in dilapidated riotous "House of Russia" in the Paris suburbs.

After being completely demoralized with life in the Legion, Sijfert refused to reenlist. He planned on organizing adventure tours and excursions in coastal South Africa; however, he ended up living with his girlfriend in Montpellier. He has also worked security for South African firms in Iraq.

Yokoyama, due to his difficulty with French, continued to have a difficult time in the Legion. During his heavy vehicles permit course, as he approached a three-way intersection, he couldn't understand whether the instructor was directing left or right, so he went straight. He was severely beaten. After another miserable mountain course in Valloire, he was punished by being left outside holding a block of compacted snow on his head. Hours later, instructors found him on the ground unconscious. He spent several weeks in the hospital being treated for hypothermia. He is believed to have deserted.

Woodman served four impeccable years with the Legion throughout France, Corsica, and East Africa. He deserted just before the end of his contract to rejoin the American army fighting in Iraq. He served two tours and is preparing for a third when his injuries heal. Woodman is now married, lives in Georgia, and has finally obtained a United States driver's license. He contacted Sanchez after running across the hardcover edition of *Legion of the Lost,* and they have kept in touch. Woodman's philosophy on his life, war, and the Legion is *"non, je ne regret rien!"*

Gwyneth eventually sold her salon and, with the proceeds, was last known to be living and backpacking in Southeast Asia.

At the time this book was written, a legionnaire in Castelnaudary was beaten to death by a superior. The scandal within the Legion was not due to a man being killed, but because one of the several dozen witnesses phoned the civil authorities.

At this time, Jaime works as an engineer in the oil and gas sector, and lives in Houston, Texas, with his girlfriend, a German medical researcher, and their newborn. He is contemplating either enrolling in business school or joining the priesthood.